CRIMINOLOGY AND LAW

CRIMINOLOGY AND LAW

Ed Johnston and Sophie Marsh

Hall and Stott Publishing Ltd
27 Witney Close
Saltford
BS31 3DX

British Library Cataloguing in Publication Data

ISBN 978 1 9162431 0 1

Typeset by Style Photosetting Ltd, Mayfield, East Sussex

CONTENTS

TABLE OF CASES

L

R

TABLE OF LEGISLATION

INTRODUCTION

Criminology and Law

To start with, the authors would like to congratulate you on selecting a degree in which you will encounter many stimulating and challenging topics, and which will provide you with a skillset that you can take into many different professional disciplines. Over the course of your programme, you will study many modules that interweave and dissect through the areas of both Criminology and Law – what we have tried to do in this book is to offer you a sample, not only of what you will study, but also of *how* you will study. We have created a book which covers a number of interconnected areas, from the actors and powers contained within the criminal justice system, to what the law says about violent offences and how criminology can assist us in discovering *why* people commit crime. The notion of sexual violence is subjected to the same dual analysis of what the law *says* is a crime and the criminological analysis of why gender-based offending exists. The book finishes with a contemporary look at offences, which may potentially be missing from the criminal law syllabus yet exist in the real world. You will find, as you move through your programme, that the law is often seen to be both slow and reactionary – as such we will briefly introduce you to the law surrounding revenge porn, up-skirting, coercive control and issues encountered with police-issued fines for breaches of the Covid-19 lockdown.

One of the core advantages of a Criminology and Law degree is the fact that both sides of your degree will sit neatly side by side. Effectively, they discuss different sides of the same coin. Your criminology studies will explore the social and personal aspects of crime: what makes an offender commit crime, what can be done to reduce offending, and what punishments ought to be meted out by those with the power to administer punishment. On the law side, you will gain an understanding of what Parliament intends by passing a particular law, and you will develop critical analysis skills to unpick problems with the law. Ultimately, these skills will equip you for almost any career, but studying the law will also provide you with both the discipline and training to enter legal practice.

You will have a challenging yet highly enjoyable task on your hands. You will be taught (and, by time graduation arrives, master) two distinct but interwoven disciplines. In order to achieve this level of mastery, you will have to think both as a criminologist and as a lawyer at different times.

Referencing your work

One of the most important elements of the student journey is learning to use referencing correctly. In order to produce a 'great essay', you will need to use an excellent method of referencing. As a Joint Award student, you are likely to need to learn the law referencing system, OSCOLA, and the criminology system, which is called Harvard. We thought it would be prudent here to introduce these concepts to you.

In short, referencing is basically the practice where every time you mention a quote, case or piece of legislation in your work, you provide evidence as to where you found the original source. Effectively, this safeguards you from being accused of poor academic practice where you might land yourself in front of a plagiarism panel. If you support your work with sources, you are not plagiarising the work of somebody else. You are, in fact, supporting your own contentions and opinions with evidence. As mentioned above, there are two systems that are generally used on any Criminology and Law Programme and we will introduce them to you now.

OSCOLA

In Law, you will use the OSCOLA method of referencing. OSCOLA stands for the Oxford Standard for the Citation of Legal Authorities. This method of referencing is achieved by using footnotes. Once you have made your point or used a case, you will insert a footnote that will then provide a full citation so the reader can easily ascertain where you got your particular point of view or source from. The majority of word processing software will have an 'insert footnote' button, so you do not need to enter the number yourself. You will, of course, need to insert the authority relied on.

If you are citing a quote or passage from a book, you will need to enter: the author(s) initial and surname, the title of the book (in *italics*), the publisher's name, year of publication and page number. In a nutshell, the reader can find exactly where you found the source and can read it for themselves. It would look like this:

E Johnston and T Smith, *Criminal Procedure and Punishment*, 2nd edn (Hall and Stott, 2020) at p 56.

When you are using a case to support your arguments, you will need to cite the case in your footnotes. The name of the case is written in italic font and the footnote will look like this:

R v Turnbull [1977] QB 224.

If you have mentioned the case name in your paragraph, you will only need to put the citation in the footnote (the citation is the law report or judgment reference that comes after the parties' names). For example, if you wrote 'in the case of *R v Turnbull*, it was held that …' you would place a footnote after the case name and then write out the citation as follows:

[1977] QB 244.

Harvard

If OSCOLA is best described as a method of using footnotes, Harvard referencing would be described as based on in-text citations. By that, we mean you write the citations in the narrative of your text. The system is designed so the reader of your work can directly engage with the original source material, without having to look up the relevant footnote. When using Harvard, you need to provide the author(s') name(s) and year of publication in the main body of your work. The full details of the original source can be found in a reference list that you create at the end of

Here are a couple of examples:

> When dealing with issues surrounding arrest, 'the requirement for detention to be necessary is designed to be a due process safeguard' (Johnston and Smith, 2020, p 69).

You will see that a page number is included with this reference – that is because you are using a direct quote. However, if you reinterpret the quote in your own words, there is no need to include the page number. See below:

> The necessary provision is a due process safeguard to ensure the police do not overuse their power (Johnston and Smith, 2020).

Both sentences are effectively claiming the same thing, but one contains a direct quote (and therefore a page number) and one is a reinterpretation, so you only need to provide the source.

Generally, a Law School will expect you to use OSCOLA to support your work and there are benefits to this. Most law schools do not count footnotes as part of your overall word count for an assignment. As such, the case names and citations will be excluded from your word count. When writing your criminology papers, there is no way to separate your in-text citations from your essay and therefore your references will be counted toward your word count. Most schools using Harvard will offer a 10% buffer to compensate students.

This small section is a brief introduction to referencing and acts as a foundational stepping-stone, but do ensure you attend lectures and workshops on this topic in order to meet your institution's policy– there are rules regarding the use of sources such as websites and other media sources, so please check your own institution's guidance before writing an assessment. We cannot stress enough the importance of being able to grasp this often dull but essential requirement. Solid referencing will go a long way to a solid essay.

We hope you enjoy the book and your degree; the book is designed to bridge the gap between both sides of your degree. How and why people commit crime is just as important as the intention Parliament had when passing a particular law. We will try to provide you with the skills and knowledge to identify synergies and comparisons between the two elements of your degree. Much like this book, your Criminology and Law degree should not be seen as two separate topics; by fusing the two together you will have a greater understanding of both component parts.

We wish you the very best of luck with your studies!

Acknowledgements

Writing a book is often fraught with difficulty, and it is a time-consuming labour of love that eats into our free time with our loved ones.

With that in mind, Ed would like to thank his partner, Wolfy, for her constant support, helpful advice and critique of the chapters. He would also like thank his children, Jacob and Erin – you are such sources of inspiration.

Sophie would like to thank her partner, Charlie, for his unconditional support and encouragement. She would like to thank her parents, John and Lesley, for their unwavering belief and support.

The authors would like to thank Duncan McPhee, who contributed the excellent and insightful Chapter 4 on Policing and Criminological Perspectives, and Sue Hall and David Stott for their assistance and understanding when delays occurred owing to the Covid-19 pandemic. David would also like to thank Mark Thomas for his expert help at the editorial stage.

Ed and Sophie
May 2021

Actors and Responsibilities in the Criminal Justice System

1.1 Introduction

In order to understand how a particular justice system works, it is imperative that we understand the roles and responsibilities of the various actors within the process. This chapter will provide you with an introduction to the people and authorities that make the criminal justice process of England and Wales work: the police, the prosecutor, the defence lawyer, magistrates and judges. We will briefly analyse their responsibilities and how they make the system function. The system is not perfect, and there is much room for improvement at every stage and with every actor in the process. This chapter should give you a flavour of why and how each component part exists in England and Wales. By understanding the roles and process, you will be able to further critique the myriad issues involving each actor as you move through your studies.

1.2 The police

The genesis of the police force in England and Wales can be traced back to the early 19th century. Prior to this period, a 'team of justices' was used to enforce the law in rural areas.[1] However, owing to political protests and a rising crime rate, the team of local justices was not sufficient to enforce the law in more urban areas. If we think of an image to describe a police officer in the early part of the 20th century, we may envisage a picture of a 'bobby on the beat'; here, an officer walking around, patrolling an area whilst whistling and occasionally stopping for a chat with local residents. McLaughlin suggests that this 'bobby' has been culturally constituted through a set of popular fictional storylines.[2]

When the Metropolitan Police was created in 1829, its official mandate was crime prevention.[3] However, the role of the police officer was met with scepticism and disorder; at public meetings police officers were called names such as 'robin redbreasts, crushers, bluebottles, bobbies, coppers, raw lobsters and peelers'.[4] The working class took objection to the fact that there would be a greater regulation of public spaces, and the middle class were unhappy that they had to pay for a service which lowered the tone of their neighbourhood.[5] If we fast-forward almost 200 years, people are still protesting against the police, their conduct and their powers.

1. RI Mawby, 'Models of Police' in T Newburn, *Handbook on Policing* (Willan, 2012) 17.
2. E McLaughin, *The New Police* (Sage, 2006) 2.
3. ibid 3.
4. ibid.
5. ibid.

March 2021 saw a spate of public protests against the Policing, Crime and Security Bill which effectively enhances the police power to curtail public demonstrations. Effectively, since their creation, the police have always faced pressure to have their powers curtailed or the institution abolished.

At the outbreak of the Second World War, there were almost 200 separate police forces that were split up across England and Wales. By the mid-1970s, these were reduced to 43.[6] Each of the 43 forces had a clear hierarchical structure of accountability from chief constables, police authorities and central government. Arguably, this relationship with central government means that the role of the police has never been too far from political influence. The 1980s and the miners' strike best emphasise the politicisation of the police, where 'the police were clearly used to enforce government policies, notably in breaking the power of the unions'.[7] In a similar time period, relations between the police and BAME communities were teetering on the brink of destruction. In 1981, the catalyst for the Brixton riots was 'essentially an outburst of anger and resentment by young black people against the police'.[8] Born against this backdrop of racial mistreatment and sub-standard treatment of suspects in the police station, the Police and Criminal Evidence Act (PACE) 1984 came into force. The Act contains a great number of due process safeguards to ensure that the police use their powers correctly. For example, the Act introduced restrictions on the use of stop and search, which now requires a justifiable reason to be carried out (a safeguard not in place at the time of the Brixton riots). There are also time limits on detention at the police station, a suspect can have breaks and free access to a defence representative, and there are prohibitions on the use of oppressive questioning, with the ramification that evidence so obtained should be inadmissible at trial.

So, this short, potted history of the police tells us a number of things. Crime prevention is their primary goal, but arguably the bigger role they had to play was as officers of the peace – looking to defuse situations rather than making an arrest and instigating criminal proceedings. Nowadays, things are different, and the bobby on the beat is no more. Since 2010, the police have lost around 10,000 frontline officers and resources are tight. The approach to defusing situations has been replaced by arresting a suspect once the relevant PACE test has been met (the tests of reasonable suspicion and necessity will be explored in **Chapter 3**). Having a tougher approach to law and order is seen to be vote winner by politicians – look at any political party's manifesto over the last 30 years and you will see something along the lines of 'We will be tough on crime!' This approach is questionable, as it makes the public believe there is a growing crime problem that needs addressing. Crime levels have been relatively stable over the last few years, and the year ending June 2020 saw a 4% reduction in crime (although this might have been influenced

---

6.   Mawby (n 1) 20.
7.   ibid.
8.   Scarman, Lord, *The Brixton Disorders 10-12 April 1981* (Cmnd 8427, 1981).

by the Covid-19 pandemic).[9] Nevertheless, we hear near-constant calls for an increase in police powers so they can protect society from the 'bad guys'. The modern police officer has a vast array of powers to infringe the liberty of a suspect, often with a low threshold to satisfy in order to wield these powers. The conversationalist, walking the streets, whistling his favourite tune is gone. The officer in the 21st century is a law enforcer and protest stopper, with powers often increasing following public disturbances. They have arguably become used as a political tool, deployed so those in power can say, 'We are keeping you safe, so vote for us.'

1.3 The prosecution

The Royal Commission established in 1962[10] recommended that a separate body should be created to separate the investigative and prosecution stage of criminal proceedings. This added layer of independence would ensure that tension between the two stages would not arise. However, this recommendation was not implemented, and many police forces continued to prosecute their own cases in magistrates' courts. For cases that would be heard in the Crown Court, the police instructed solicitors and barristers to prosecute cases on their behalf.[11] As this situation evolved, the police gradually started to employ their own in-house prosecuting solicitors who would act on the instructions of the police.[12] The prosecutor would have little recourse if the police wanted to go ahead and prosecute a weak case or 'overcharge' a suspect.

This arrangement between the police and the prosecution came under attack in the report on the 'Confait affair'.[13] This case raised questions about the procedures followed by the police during the interrogation of three youths, suspected of the murder of a male prostitute. The interrogation led the youths to falsely confess to the murder of Maxwell Confait. In 1977, an inquiry into the investigation was opened and recommended many of the provisions contained within PACE 1984, as well as establishing the Crown Prosecution Service (CPS) under the Prosecution of Offenders Act 1985. Both changes dramatically altered pre-trial investigation. The report revealed that the officer in charge of the investigation was willing to breach the existing Judges' Rules and put severe pressure on the suspects when questioning them. The prosecutor was deemed unable or unwilling to act independently from the police, and the youths were wrongly convicted of

---

9. www.ons.gov.uk/peoplepopulationandcommunity/crimeandjustice/bulletins/crimeinenglandand wales/yearendingjune2020#:~:text=The%20police%20recorded%205.8%20million,July%202019% 20to%20March%202020.&text=Overall%2C%20theft%20offences%20fell%20by,the%20year%20ending %20June%202020 (accessed 28 April 2021).
10. *The Royal Commission on the Police* (Cmnd 1728, 1962).
11. For a further discussion of the police's use of solicitors and barristers in the 1970s, see J Sigler, 'Public Prosecutions in England and Wales' [1974] Crim LR 642.
12. *The Investigation of Criminal Offences in England and Wales: The Law and Procedure* (Cmnd 8092-1, 1981) 49–52.
13. See *Inquiry into the Circumstances leading to the Trial of Three Persons on Charges arising from the Death of Maxwell Confait* (HCP 90, 1977).

murder.[14] The report, chaired by Sir Henry Fisher, proposed a number of recommendations: that the Judges' Rules should be overhauled, and that the safeguards provided to suspects, such as having a right to have a solicitor present during interrogation and the right of young people to have an appropriate adult present, should be made clearer.

Following this case, the Royal Commission on Criminal Procedure (the Phillips Commission), reporting in 1981, proposed that an independent body be created to take over cases that the police decided to prosecute. If the prosecutor did not believe that the case should be taken to court then the prosecutor would have the authority to discontinue the case, have the charges changed or have the police investigate further in order to obtain more evidence. The Government accepted the majority of the recommendations made by the Phillips Commission. As highlighted above, this resulted in the Prosecution of Offenders Act 1985 and established the Crown Prosecution Service (CPS). The head of the CPS would be the Director of Public Prosecutions (DPP). The Director's position was not a new creation; it was initially created in the late 19th century to advise the police on criminal matters and handle serious cases. Despite the CPS having a national identity, prosecutors were based locally, and the CPS was organised into areas that matched police forces, each headed by a Chief Prosecutor.

Generally, in England and Wales, prosecutors are responsible for charging decisions. In order to charge a suspect with a crime, the prosecutor will apply one of two charging tests:

(a)   the Full Code Test; and

(b)   the Threshold Test.

Paragraph 4.1 of the *Code for Crown Prosecutors* (the *Code*)[15] states that in order to start or continue with a prosecution, the Full Code Test needs to be met. If the Full Code Test cannot be met, the prosecutor is permitted to continue with the prosecution by using the Threshold Test. Should any prosecution not satisfy these tests, the charges against the suspect will be dropped.

The Full Code Test

There are two stages to the Full Code Test, and both need to be passed in order to continue with a prosecution. The first stage is the evidential stage. Here, the prosecutor needs to be satisfied that there is sufficient evidence to provide a realistic prospect of conviction. In order to reach this decision, the prosecutor must consider what the defence might be and how that will likely affect the prospect of conviction.[16] Put simply, a realistic prospect of conviction is something that is greater than a 50% chance. You might think that this prospect is quite low. However, this is the most stringent hurdle that the prosecution has to pass through. Once the prosecutor has decided that the evidential stage is met, they can move on to the public interest stage. In every case where there is sufficient

---

14.   ibid.

15.   www.cps.gov.uk/publication/code-crown-prosecutors (accessed 28 April 2021).

16.   ibid para 4.6.

evidence to justify a prosecution (or to offer an out-of-court disposal), the prosecutor needs to consider if a prosecution is in the public interest.[17] Paragraph 4.10 of the *Code* highlights an important safeguard – the prosecutor has some level of discretion in deciding whether to prosecute a suspect. The *Code* states that 'it has never been the rule that a prosecution will automatically take place'. This means that if the prosecutor does not consider that it is in the public interest to prosecute an offence, they are not compelled to do so.

In order to ascertain if something is in the public interest, the prosecutor needs to consider:[18]

- the seriousness of the offence;
- the level of culpability of the suspect;
- what were the circumstances of the offence and level of harm caused to the victim;
- the age and majority of the suspect at the time of the offence; and
- whether a prosecution is proportionate.

The Threshold Test

Should the prosecutor be unable to satisfy the Full Code Test, that does not mean that it is the end of proceedings. There is a safety net built in, which means that if the Full Code Test is not satisfied, the prosecutor can apply the Threshold Test. There are five conditions to the Threshold Test:[19]

(1) The prosecutor must be satisfied that there are reasonable grounds to suspect that the person to be charged has committed the offence in question.

(2) There needs to be a reasonable belief that the continuing investigation will yield further evidence (within a reasonable time period) that will establish a realistic prospect of conviction. The prosecutor must consider:

   (a) the nature of any further evidence and the impact it will have on the case;
   (b) the charges that all evidence will support;
   (c) the reasons why this evidence is not available immediately;
   (d) the time required to obtain the evidence;
   (e) whether the delay in applying the Full Code Test is reasonable.

(3) The seriousness or the circumstances of the case and level of risk posed by granting bail justifies the making of an immediate charging decision.

(4) There are continuing substantial grounds to object to a bail application.

(5) It is in the public interest to charge the suspect.

The evidence used to inform the charging decision must be regularly assessed to ensure that charging the suspect is still appropriate, as is the objection to bail. The Full Code Test must be applied as soon as the anticipated further evidence is generated.

As you can see, in order to charge a suspect, the prosecutor has a great deal of discretion in their decision. Furthermore, and perhaps more concerning, is the fact

---

17. ibid para 4.9
18. ibid para 4.14(a)–(g).
19. These are set out in Section 5 of the *Code*.

the threshold needed to be satisfied in order to charge someone is very low indeed. Ultimately, the prosecutor needs a reasonable belief that the person committed the crime. Effectively, this has already been satisfied because, without this reasonable suspicion, the person would not have been arrested by the police.

1.4 The defence

Defendants have not always benefited from representation at trial. It was only in the mid-18th century that a prohibition on defence representation was lifted. The introduction of defence counsel to the criminal trial disentangled two activities that were previously the sole responsibility of the unrepresented defendant: it was the duty of the defence lawyer to probe whether the prosecution had submitted a tenable case, and the lawyer would offer evidence of a defensive nature to rebut the prosecution's allegations. The defence lawyer was able to insist on asking the judge whether the prosecution had discharged its burden of adducing sufficient evidence to support a verdict in its favour. The defence lawyer would typically move for a verdict of an acquittal at the conclusion of the prosecution's evidence. If a judge overruled this, the defence would then present its evidence.[20] Further, the inclusion of the defence lawyer changed the structure of the trial; it broke up the dual roles of speaking and defending that had previously been the responsibility of the accused. The defence lawyer assumed the role of defender, insisting on prosecutorial burdens of proof and largely shutting down the role of the accused.[21] The trial had evolved, and the new 'lawyer-dominated' trials were no longer the place where the accused merely aired their response to the charge, but it became the forum in which the accused's defence counsel tested the prosecution's case, and adversarialism was born.

The early 20th century saw the continuation of the 'testing the prosecution's case' form of trial. The defence lawyer was firmly established as a key actor in the criminal justice process. In fact, the position and role of the defence lawyer gained further importance as access to legal representation was increased. The Poor Prisoners' Defence Act 1903 established that legal aid would be provided for trials on indictment for serious offences, where this would be in the interests of justice. It was not only the defence lawyer's role at trial that grew in importance during the early part of the 20th century; the defence lawyer was also becoming more active at the pre-trial stage. The Judges' Rules of 1912 stated that suspects should be able to consult with a solicitor, albeit with a caveat that this caused the police no unreasonable hindrance.[22] This reaffirmed the position of the 'testing of the prosecution's case' over the 'accused speaks' trial.

---

20. JH Langbein, *The Origins of the Adversary Criminal Trial* (Oxford University Press, 2005) 258.
21. ibid 307.
22. However, research shows that only 9% of suspects sought legal advice and only 7% received it. See P Softly, *Police Interrogation: An Observational Study in Four Police Stations,* Royal Commission on Procedure, Research Study No 4 (1980).

Whilst the availability of defence representation via legal aid was increased by the 1903 Act, judges were encouraged not to actively advertise that access to legal advice was readily available. However, attempts to keep the right to legal advice under wraps were effectively removed by the advent of the Legal Aid and Advice Act 1949. In theory, the 1949 Act would have a great impact on the defence lawyer's role: it provided for legal representation for all except those who could not by any reasonable view be regarded as appropriate for state assistance at all.

In 1950 the Council of Europe recognised the importance of the defence lawyer's role in the criminal justice process in the European Convention on Human Rights,[23] an international treaty that protects the human rights and fundamental freedoms of citizens of member states of the Council of Europe. Article 6 protects the right to a fair trial, and specifically Article 6(3)(c) allows a defendant to either defend themselves or be defended through legal assistance of their choosing. If they are unable to afford legal assistance, it is to be given free of charge when it is in the interests of justice to do so.

Reporting in the 1960s, the Widgery Committee[24] recommended that legal aid should be granted taking into account:

(a)   the gravity of the charge; whether the accused is in real jeopardy of losing their liberty or livelihood;

(b)   whether the case raises a substantial question of law;

(c)   whether the accused can state their own case and follow proceedings;

(d)   whether legal representation is desirable in the interests of someone other than the accused. For example, in the case of sexual offences against young persons, when it is undesirable that the accused should cross-examine the witness in person.[25]

Following the recommendations of the Committee, the Criminal Justice Act 1967 set out the guidelines governing when the use of legal aid should be authorised. This has been repealed and replaced by a similar test in the Legal Aid, Sentencing and Punishment of Offenders Act 2012, which states that any grant of legal aid must be in 'the interests of justice'[26] as defined in s 17(2):

(2)   In deciding what the interests of justice consist of for the purposes of such a determination, the following factors must be taken into account—

(a)   whether, if any matter arising in the proceedings is decided against the individual, the individual would be likely to lose his or her liberty or livelihood or to suffer serious damage to his or her reputation,

(b)   whether the determination of any matter arising in the proceedings may involve consideration of a substantial question of law,

(c)   whether the individual may be unable to understand the proceedings or to state his or her own case,

---

23.   This is formally known as the Convention for the Protection of Human Rights and Fundamental Freedoms.

24.   Departmental Committee Report: *Legal Aid in Criminal Proceedings* (Cmnd 2934, 1966).

25.   ibid at para 180.

26.   Legal Aid, Sentencing and Punishment of Offenders Act 2012, s 13(2)

(d) whether the proceedings may involve the tracing, interviewing or expert cross-examination of witnesses on behalf of the individual, and

(e) whether it is in the interests of another person that the individual be represented.

Should the above factors be met, a person will qualify for legal representation in court.

However, when considering the role of the defence lawyer, there is a danger of oversimplifying it as one that merely advances the interests of the client. The role of the defence lawyer can be seen to operate on three interwoven levels: first, they are the mouthpiece of their client; secondly, they are an officer of the court; and thirdly, they act as a zealous protector of the rights of their client.[27] Despite being charged with advancing their client's case, however, the defence lawyer's obligation to their client is, at times, tempered by obligations owed to other parties in the criminal justice process. This notion was expressed by Lord Reid in the case of *Rondel v Worsley*:[28]

> Counsel has a duty to fearlessly raise every issue, advance every argument and ask every question, however distasteful, which he thinks will help his client's case. But as an officer of the court concerned with the administration of justice, he has an overriding duty to the court, to the standards of his profession and to the public, which may often lead to a conflict with his client's wishes …[29]

It is clear from this statement that the role of the defence lawyer is not as clear-cut as merely advancing the case of their client and acting in their best interests. At times, they will be charged with actively engaging in ethical decision-making. These ethical obligations will be discussed below, but here we are attempting to construct a theoretical conception of the defence lawyer. It has been claimed that the defence lawyer operates on the horns of a trilemma: they need to accumulate as much knowledge about the case as possible; to hold it in confidence; and yet to never mislead the courts.[30] The adversarial criminal process in England and Wales is rooted in the image of the defence lawyer acting as the accused's shield from the powerful state; this notion has in turn cultivated the ideal of neutral partisanship being a central tenet of the role of the defence lawyer.[31] This duty of neutral partisanship reflects a dual part of the adversarial ethos: the accused is to be adequately protected from the 'oppressive' state, and the truth is best discovered by arguments on both sides of the question.[32] Despite this notion of 'zealous advocacy' being the root of the adversarial process and the best way to discover the truth, very little is said on how ethical implications should underpin the role of the

---

27. M Blake and A Ashworth, 'Ethics and the Criminal Defence Lawyer' (2004) 7 *Legal Ethics* 167–90 at 167.
28. [1969] 1 AC 191.
29. ibid at 227–28.
30. Blake and Ashworth (n 27) 173.
31. *ibid* 169.
32. *Ex parte Lloyd* (1822) Montagu's Reports 70, 72n per Lord Eldon.

defence lawyer. Does the notion of zealous advocacy permit the lawyer to take advantage of any legal point that favours their client? Should the defence lawyer be so aggressive in challenging the prosecution's witnesses that their evidence is rendered weak, muddled or confusing?[33] It is clear that part of the defence lawyer's role is to act as a zealous advocate in advancing their client's best interests, but how is this primary goal tempered by various obligations to other parties? To answer that, the obligations placed on the defence lawyer will be examined to ascertain how they impact the role.

Following Lord Reid's judgement in *Rondel v Worsley,* the obligations of the lawyer's role can be deconstructed into three core duties:

(1)   the duty to the client;
(2)   the duty to the court and the administration of justice;
(3)   the duty to the public.

Ultimately, the role of the defence lawyer is one that involves juggling a number of conflicting and difficult obligations. The role is greater than merely advancing the case of the client. Whilst the duty to the client involves acting in a partisan manner, the notion of partisanship is heavily impinged by duties to the court and the administration of justice, as well as a duty to the public. The duty to the court and the administration of justice frowns upon certain acts that may be beneficial to the client, such as ambush defences, which despite being legitimate are discouraged by the court for fear that they distort the search for the truth. The duty to the public ensures that the behaviour of the lawyer is ethically and morally correct.

1.5   The judge

As the role of defence lawyers has evolved with the development of the justice system over time, the same can be said for the role of the judge. Prior to the defence lawyer becoming a central cog in the trial process, it was the judge who was responsible for calling and questioning witnesses; essentially, they were the prober of truth who painted a story of facts for the jury to consider and then return their verdict. However, as the trial process became more dominant, the responsibility of the judge dwindled and they became more of a passive umpire. By the mid-20th century, the notion of passivity fully encapsulated the role of the judge. In 1944, Lord Greene (then Master of the Rolls) stated that it is outside the parameters of the judge's role to conduct cross-examination. For if he 'descends into the area [of trial combat he] is liable to have his vision clouded by the dust of conflict'[34] and would no longer be a neutral umpire. This stance continued into the late 1950s when Lord Justice Denning arguably expressed the classic conception of a judge:

> The judge's part in all this is to hearken to the evidence, only himself asking questions of witnesses when it is necessary to clear up any point that has been

---

33.   See D Napley, *The Technique of Persuasion,* 4th edn (Sweet and Maxwell, 1991) 57.
34.   Per Green MR, in *Yuill v Yuill* [1945] 1 All ER 183 at 189.

overlooked or left obscure; to see that the advocates behave themselves seemly and keep to the rules laid down by law; to exclude irrelevancies and discourage repetition; to make sure by wise intervention that he follows the points that the advocates are making and can assess their worth; and at the end to make up his mind where the truth lies. If he goes beyond this, he drops the mantle of a judge and assumes the robe of an advocate.[35]

Ultimately, the judge ought to sit and listen, and intervene only where necessary, so that the advocates would not be unduly hampered by judicial intervention.[36]

This cloak of passivity was worn until the early part of the new millennium. In 2001, Lord Justice Auld's *Review of the Criminal Courts of England and Wales* created a seismic shift in judicial demeanour. Auld LJ suggested that 'the criminal trial is not a game under which a guilty defendant should be provided with a sporting chance. It is a search for the truth.'[37] This reminder served as a catalyst for a judicial sea-change, where judges became more actively involved in cases in order to search for the truth.

The courts were very quick to reclaim control of the trial process and embrace this change. In *R v Chabaan*,[38] the defendant appealed against his conviction on the basis that the judge would not allow an application to hear expert evidence. He expected the case to dealt with in a swift and efficient manner. On appeal, Judge LJ stated that a trial judge was 'always responsible for managing the trial ... that is one of his most important functions'.[39] As such, the judge was well within his right to refuse the application as 'the entitlement of a fair trial is not inconsistent with proper judicial control over the use of time ... every trial that takes longer than necessary is wasteful of limited resources.'[40]

This approach was codified in 2003 by the introduction of the Criminal Procedure Rules, which included the overriding objective to deal with cases justly.[41] The Rules have been revised a number of times over the last 17 years, but the overriding objective has remained the same. This objective is achieved by what is called 'active case management'. Here the role of the judge has been transformed from passive observer to active case manager, which completely shifts the responsibilities of the judge. The Rules define active case management (r 3.2(2)) as:

(a) the early identification of the real issues;

(b) the early identification of the needs of witnesses;

(c) achieving certainty as to what must be done, by whom, and when, in particular by the early setting of a timetable for the progress of the case;

(d) monitoring the progress of the case and compliance with directions;

---

35. Denning LJ in *Jones v National Coal Board* [1957] 2 QB 55 at 64.
36. See further E Johnston, 'All Rise for the Interventionist: The Judiciary in the 21st Century' (2016) 80(3) *Journal of Criminal Law* 201–13.
37. Auld LJ, *Review of the Criminal Courts of England and Wales* (2001) 154.
38. [2003] EWCA Crim 1012.
39. ibid at [35].
40. ibid at [36].
41. Criminal Procedure Rules 2020, r 1.1.

(e) ensuring that evidence, whether disputed or not, is presented in the shortest and clearest way;

(f) discouraging delay, dealing with as many aspects of the case as possible on the same occasion, and avoiding unnecessary hearings;

(g) encouraging the participants to co-operate in the progression of the case; and

(h) making use of technology.

This mantra of case management was further reiterated in *R v Jisl*,[42] where Judge LJ re-emphasised the approach to case management:

> Justice must be done. The defendant is entitled to a fair trial: and, which is sometimes overlooked, the prosecution is equally entitled to a reasonable opportunity to present the evidence against the defendant. It is not however a concomitant of the entitlement to a fair trial that either or both sides are further entitled to take as much time as they like … Resources are limited … It follows that the sensible use of time requires judicial management and control.[43]

It is clear that the role of the judiciary has changed. Judges have shed the cloak of passivity and are no longer the neutral umpire. They are viewed as a case manager, with a responsibility to preserve resources and lead the trial to a timely conclusion.

1.6 The jury and the magistracy

When we think about a criminal trial in England and Wales (or any other common law jurisdiction for that matter), we think about a jury trial where the defence and prosecution lawyers battle it out in the arena of the courtroom with the goal of convicting or acquitting the defendant. Arguably, this premise has been entrenched in common law, where the right to be tried by one's peers has been a cornerstone in the process of ascertaining justice.[44] The core functions of juries, the composition and selection of the 12 jurors and the purpose that they serve is primarily governed by the Juries Act 1974.

It is essential to understand how often jury trials are used in England and Wales. Statistics tell us that juries are rarely used in England and Wales, despite them being viewed as a quintessential foundation of criminal procedure. The vast majority of defendants who would be eligible for a jury trial (ie charged with an indictable-only or either-way offence) avoided this by entering a plea of guilty in 79% of cases in the third quarter (Q3) of 2020. This was an increase of 10% on the same quarter in 2019 (69%).[45] Moreover, in Q3 2020, only 8% of all defendants

---

42. [2004] EWCA Crim 969.

43. ibid per Judge LJ at [114].

44. C Davies and C Edwards, '"A Jury of Peers": A Comparative Analysis' (2004) 68 *Journal of Criminal Law* 150.

45. Ministry of Justice, *Criminal Court Statistics quarterly, England and Wales, July to September 2020* (December 2020): https://assets.publishing.service.gov.uk/government/uploads/system/uploads/attachment_data/file/944734/ccsq_bulletin_jul_sep_2020.pdf (accessed 28 April 2021).

dealt with at the Crown Court entered a plea of not guilty. This is representative of an 11% point fall on Q3 2019.[46] This demonstrates that jury trial is infrequently used due to high guilty plea rates. To put this into context, in March 2020, there were roughly 245,000 individuals dealt with for indictable-only offences.[47] Therefore, if roughly 8% of defendants plead not guilty, then this would amount to around 19,600 individuals choosing trial by jury. Again, this is a significantly low number compared to those pleading guilty prior to trial.

Over the course of recent years, there has been a steady call in the media to abolish jury trials,[48] as they lack the efficiency of the magistrates' court. This problem has been exacerbated by the Covid-19 pandemic. At the end of Q3 2020, there were 50,918 outstanding cases in the Crown Court, an increase of 44% on Q3 2019 (35,478 cases). This is the highest level of outstanding cases seen since the end of 2015 and continues the consistent increases seen since Q1 2019.[49] Furthermore, in Q1 2019, the mean number of days from first listing in the magistrates' court to completion in the Crown Court was 178 days.[50] This is just over five months, which emphasises the protracted nature of this process.

In order to increase the efficiency of the court process, the Single Justice Procedure (SJP) was created in 2015.[51] This allows for cases involving adults charged with summary offences to be dealt with by a single magistrate, sitting without a prosecutor or defendant being present. The number of SJP cases has increased each year since its introduction, accounting for 57% of all completions at the magistrates' court in Q1 2019.[52] Therefore, since its introduction, 87% of SJP cases are listed and completed at the magistrates' courts on the same day.[53] The speed and efficiency of this process is extremely attractive to policy makers, and it has been estimated that the removal of jury trials could save the criminal justice system around £30 million per year.[54]

Nevertheless, despite the costs, it is clear that jury trial can hold advantages for the defendant over trial in the magistrates' court. 'Jury equity', arguably the biggest advantage, means that regardless of the evidence advanced at court, the jury do not have to return a verdict that follows the evidence. That may sound bizarre, but it is correct – if the evidence points to the guilt of the defendant, the jury are well

---

46. ibid.
47. Ministry of Justice, *Criminal Justice Statistics quarterly: March 2020* (August, 2020): www.gov.uk/government/statistics/criminal-justice-system-statistics-quarterly-march-2020/criminal-justice-statistics-quarterly-march-2020 (accessed 28 April 2021).
48. See www.theguardian.com/commentisfree/2021/jan/22/justice-system-crisis-abolish-jury-trials-covid; www.thetimes.co.uk/article/call-for-trials-without-juries-amid-fear-that-crisis-will-put-criminals-on-streets-qk93vdttf (accessed 28 April 2021).
49. Ministry of Justice (n 47).
50. Ministry of Justice, *Criminal court statistics quarterly, England and Wales, January to March 2019* (June 2019): https://assets.publishing.service.gov.uk/government/uploads/system/uploads/attachment_data/file/812556/ccsq-bulletin-q1-2019.pdf (accessed 28 April 2021).
51. Criminal Justice and Courts Act 2015.
52. Ministry of Justice (n 50).
53. ibid.
54. BBC News, 'Cut jury trials, says victims' champion Louise Casey' (November 2010): www.bbc.co.uk/news/uk-11680382 (accessed 1 July 2021).

within their rights to return a 'not guilty' verdict because they believe that is the correct thing to. In *R v Ponting*,[55] a civil servant leaked documents concerning circumstances surrounding the sinking of the Argentinian cruiser, the *General Belgrano*, by a British submarine during the 1982 Falklands War. The defendant was prosecuted under the Official Secrets Act 1911 but appealed to the jury that his actions were in the public interest. Notwithstanding the judge's direction that he had no defence in law, the jury returned a not guilty verdict. Evidently, this case demonstrates that juries cannot be trusted to deliver procedural justice. However, it could be argued that the jury took an ethical approach and, debatably, did the 'right' thing. Furthermore, the case of *R v Biezanek*[56] reinforces this concept of jury equity, where the jury refused to convict a defendant of supplying cannabis for medical reasons. The defendant's daughter had an incurable illness, and the defendant sought to rely on the defence of duress of circumstances. The jury acquitted her after 40 minutes of deliberation. Again, it could be argued that, morally, the jury came to the right decision. However, the defendant was factually guilty and was acquitted notwithstanding the evidence against her.

These two cases pose an interesting argument – is it more important for juries to return a legally sound verdict, or should they rely on their conscience and ethics when reaching their verdict?

But what if we simply cannot trust juries to reach a sound verdict? This was illustrated in the case of *R v Young*,[57] which saw four jurors consult an ouija board outside of the deliberation room to determine their decision on the defendant's guilt. A unanimous guilty verdict was reached, but this was later quashed and a retrial ordered. However, it nevertheless illustrates the silliness and lack of responsibility with which some jurors may act.

A core responsibility of the juror is to shut out all irrelevant considerations and only pass a verdict based upon the evidence which has been advanced at trial. However, in high-profile cases, which have garnered much media attention, is this really possible? In 2010, a Ministry of Justice report found that in a sample of jurors, 70% serving on 'longer, high-profile cases' recalled media coverage of the case.[58] A further 35% recalled pre-trial media coverage, and 20% found it difficult to disregard these reports.[59] This has frequently raised concerns about jury fairness and created a lack of trust within the system.[60] Therefore, both external influence and latterly the effects of the Covid-19 pandemic have suggested a public desire to make jury trials redundant.[61] Conversely, the Bar Council and Law

---

55. [1985] Crim LR 318.
56. (1993, unreported).
57. [1994] 11 WLUK 246.
58. Houses of Parliament, *POSTNOTE: Unintentional Bias in Court* (Cm 512, 2015).
59. Bar Council, 'Guest blog: How will restricting jury trial and reducing jury numbers effect the delivery of justice' (2020): www.barcouncil.org.uk/resource/guest-blog-how-will-restricting-jury-trial-and-reducing-jury-numbers-affect-the-delivery-of-justice.html#_ftn25 (accessed 28 April 2021).
60. C Thomas, 'Are juries fair?' (2010) *Ministry of Justice Research Series 1/10*, 40.
61. BBC News (n 54).

Society Survey in 2002 found that over 84% of the public trusted a jury to come to the right decision and felt that trial by jury was fairer than being tried by a judge.[62]

However, if all cases were heard by either a single judge or a bench of magistrates, there could be a higher number of miscarriages of justice. Yes, the magistrates' court deals with cases in a far more efficient manner, but it is in Crown Court jury trials where the most serious cases are heard and the most severe sentences handed down. The magistrates' court can impose a sentence of an unlimited financial penalty or six months' imprisonment (or 12 months for two or more either-way cases).

If we were to have more cases heard in the magistrates' court, we might want to increase the training offered. Magistrates are lay people, and it is not a prerequisite to have any formal legal education; anyone can be a magistrate so long as they embody the six key qualities of the role:

(1) good character
(2) commitment and reliability
(3) social awareness
(4) sound judgement
(5) understanding and communication
(6) maturity and sound temperament.

Once the required threshold to be a magistrate has been met, basic training is given to ensure candidates can carry out their duties. Whilst we may be critical of magistrates as an alternative to judge and jury, they carry out an important function of dealing with low-level crime, something that the criminal justice system is inundated with, and generally in serving the community.

This section has shown that there is a clear desire to keep cases away from juries. Whilst in some circumstances, juries can be seen as irresponsible and lacking accountability, they provide a fundamental cornerstone to our criminal justice system – even if they are rarely used. Decisions about modifying the criminal process should not be informed by efficiency drivers alone. Economic savings for the justice system cannot and should not trump the fair trial rights of defendants. Trial by jury 'is the lamp that shows that freedom lives',[63] and this lamp should be upheld and protected in modern society.

1.7 Conclusion

This chapter has outlined the myriad conflicting goals that are entrenched within the criminal justice system of England and Wales. In a suspect's first encounter with the system, they will be met with the police, who are looking to arrest the person they suspect has committed the offence. In high-profile cases, the police are under an inordinate amount of pressure to catch the culprit. At times, the police

---

62. Law Society Gazette, 'Public opposes curb on jury trials, survey says' (2002): www.lawgazette.co.uk/news/public-opposes-curb-on-jury-trials-survey-says/35989.article (accessed 28 April 2021).

63. P Darbyshire, 'The lamp that shows that freedom lives – is it worth the candle? [1991] *Criminal Law Review* 740.

face a great deal of public scrutiny and opposition, merely for doing the job the government has tasked them to do, often at a great threat to their lives and safety.

Once the police have arrested a suspect, it is for the prosecution to charge the suspect and prepare the case for trial. The defendant might have a defence lawyer who will look to zealously defend their client from the charge and seek to establish doubt in the prosecution's case in order to secure an acquittal. This acquittal might be given by a jury, but statistically it is more likely that the case will be heard in the magistrates' court by a bench of lay people. All of these actors have conflicting goals and objectives, and they are all important cogs in the wheel of criminal justice.

2 Actors and Responsibilities: A Criminological Outlook

2.1 Introduction

This chapter will critically analyse the key actors within the criminal justice system, such as the police, magistrates, juries, offenders and victims. It will consider their responsibilities and representation from a criminological perspective – a comparison of the legal outlook in **Chapter 1**. It will consequently discuss:

- the need for social control;
- diversity, representation and accountability in the criminal justice system;
- victims and victimology; and
- the representation of offenders within the criminal justice system.

2.2 The need for social control

2.2.1 Introduction to social control

Why do we have legislation? Why do we have the police and a criminal justice system that can impose punishment on a citizen? What is the need for social control? These questions are raised when considering the purpose of our criminal justice system. Subsequently, this section will attempt to examine the need for social control, both historically and in modern society.

2.2.2 Control Theory

Control Theory was developed by an American sociologist named Travis Hirschi in the 1960s.[1] Control Theory is informed by a particular understanding of human nature. There is an understanding that, by nature, human beings are both rational and egoistic. Humans are therefore motivated by an egoistic desire to satisfy their pleasures (also known as self-interested hedonism). However, unlike other animals, human beings are rational and thus can pursue efficient goal satisfaction. Two consequences follow as a result of our pleasure-seeking: rule-breaking if the rules obstruct our goals (egoism); and rule-breaking if the benefits outweigh the penalties (rationality). Subsequently, Control Theory argues that such rational and egoistical thinking results in a breakdown of social control, contributing to the explanation of criminal activity. Moreover, such rule-breaking may also be opportunistic (an influence of a consumer society). Thus, crime control has become a major issue following the 1960s as a result of the increase in consuming goods.[2]

---

1. T Hirschi, *Causes of Delinquency* (University of California Press, 1969) 1.
2. ibid 10.

In his book, *Causes of Delinquency*,[3] Hirschi argues that conformity within society is a result of being subordinate to existing social controls.[4] In order to ensure that citizens conform with social control, social order is based on regulation (social bonds) and not integration (value-commitments). Social bonds refer to people or institutions that we interact with on a daily basis, such as family and schools. Consequently, these external (social) controls keep members of society from breaking rules by controlling the egoistic deviant. Hirschi therefore identifies four different types of bonds that contribute to social conformity.

Attachment

The first of these social bonds is attachment, which refers to an emotional bond that links society and social institutions together. There are two types of attachments: close emotional bonds, and superficial bonds with institutions. Hirschi argues that humans conform when they develop close and personal attachments with those who are deemed good role models. In particular, these role models may be parents or teachers. Moreover, Hirschi argues that such attachments can be superficial and can amount to attachments to institutions, such as school or the workplace.[5] However, these attachments to social institutions are only formed if they are deemed as benefiting own interests. Such attachments can only be maintained by regular social interactions between those in the institutions. For example, children may only attach to teachers and the school if the role model and institution meet their needs, such as status and reward.[6] Children who are denied status and reward may engage in deviant behaviour, such as messing around in class and refusing to do homework.[7] Hirschi argues that children who fail to attach to the institution of the school are therefore less likely to form attachments to other social institutions, as school is the first instance in which children will learn the rules and expectations of society. Deviant children are likely to become deviant adults as a result of poor education and limited access to goods and therefore may engage in criminal activity in order to possess such goods.[8]

Commitment

The second social bond amounts to commitment. Hirschi argues that this is a superficial commitment (a sense of dedication) to other people, social groups, institutions and social rules. The strength of this commitment will reflect the time and energy put into the person, people or institution. Thus, deviant behaviour occurs when the commitment is weakened. For example, a student who has conformed to the expectations of teachers has committed to the school and has been rewarded with the high regard of teachers and peers. On the other hand,

---

3.   Hirschi (n1).
4.   ibid 109.
5.   ibid.
6.   B Costello and P Vowell, 'Testing Control Theory and Differential Association: A Reanalysis of the Richmond Youth Project Data' (1999) 37 *Criminology* 815, 816.
7.   B Costello and J Laub, 'Social Control Theory: The Legacy of Travis Hirschi's Causes of Delinquency' (2020) 3 *Annual Review of Criminology* 21, 30.
8.   Hirschi (n 1) 120.

children who have not been rewarded will have a weak commitment to the school. Subsequently, this student is more likely to engage in deviant behaviour as a result of a weak social bond of commitment.[9]

Involvement

The third social bond surrounds involvement. Hirschi maintains that this involvement refers to participation, such as in the activities of an institution or a social group. In order to participate, humans must conform to the rules of the institution or social group which consequently reduces opportunities to deviate.[10] For example, encouraging children to participate in a sports team, keeping the child busy, will reduce the opportunity to engage in deviant behaviour. Lack of participation in institutions or social groups therefore influences deviant behaviour as a result of pleasure-seeking.

Belief

The final bond refers to belief. Hirschi believes that this belief indicates humans' strength and intensity to their moral commitments and societal values. Whilst this bond may not be a deep and passionate belief, such as religion, this belief surrounds a conventional habitual belief in the rules and values in a culture.[11] For example, humans conform to beliefs about society because those beliefs are held and approved by the rest of their culture. In addition, there is a societal expectation to endorse such beliefs, amounting to a social pressure. Consequently, if a person's belief in societal values is not deep, the belief can easily be undermined. Thus, if these rules and values pose a barrier to pleasure-seeking, this person may engage in deviant behaviour in order to benefit their self-interest.

2.2.3 The need for the criminal justice system

When each or any of these social bonds are weakened, a person may engage in deviant behaviour in order to pleasure-seek. This may amount to deviant behaviour, such as taking something that does not belong to you, graffitiing the property of another or driving too fast. For Wilson and Kelling, allowing one window to be broken in a neighbourhood would lead to all windows being broken.[12] Respectable people would therefore leave the neighbourhood, leaving the delinquents to run riot. As a result of society condemning such behaviour, there is a need for social control.

Consequently, over a number of centuries, this has arguably resulted in the introduction of legislation, policy and the police in order to sanction those who deviate from social norms. Examples include criminalising the act of theft or speeding. Thus, for Control Theorists, a tough criminal justice system is necessary to ensure that the risks of crime outweigh the benefits (the egoistic pleasure-seeking). Moreover, Wilson and Kelling argue that the role of the police is not

---

9.   ibid 125.
10. ibid 31.
11. ibid 132.
12. J Wilson and G Kelling, 'Broken Windows' (1982) *Atlantic Monthly* 249, 29 (at 30).

simply to respond to crime but to 'sweep the streets clean of all disorderly or anti-social behaviour'. Examples include moving on beggars, limiting the public consumption of alcohol, criminalising the use of illicit drugs and restricting the commission of sex work. In addition, such behaviour may result in sanctions being imposed, such as a custodial sentence, a fine or a community order. However, it is important to note that Control Theory fails to account for the commission of violent behaviour, as such behaviour is not always the result of pleasure-seeking. This will be explored in **Chapter 6** – 'Understanding Violent Crimes: Criminology'.

2.2.4 Conclusion

Hirschi's Social Control Theory is able to provide a criminological explanation for the need for the maintenance of order. When social bonds are broken, such as attachment, commitment, involvement and belief, the risk of deviant behaviour is increased. Such deviant behaviour may escalate into criminal activity, leaving neighbourhoods exposed to a 'criminal invasion'.[13] Subsequently, the criminal justice system has allowed for such deviant behaviour to be criminalised and therefore punished by the state. Whilst control perspectives are by no means the only criminological frameworks relevant to understanding the operation of the criminal justice system (you will be exposed to many others over the course of your studies), they are a useful starting point when considering the broader role of the criminal justice system in responding to crime and deviance.

2.3 Diversity, representation and accountability in the criminal justice system

2.3.1 Introduction

This section attempts to analyse the diversity, representation and accountability of a number of different actors in the criminal justice system in England and Wales. It will consider the police, the jury and the magistracy, and whether such elements of the criminal justice system adequately represent the diverse population of modern England and Wales.

2.3.2 The police

There are currently 43 police forces across England and Wales.[14] However, the Commissioner of the Metropolitan Police stated that crime could not be controlled by police alone and that significant levels of public cooperation were needed. Subsequently, there was a momentous movement away from the role of the police as primary law enforcers or as a crime control agency,[15] for example with the implementation of Police Community Support Officers in 2002 in order

---

13. ibid.
14. Home Office, *Police Workforce, England and Wales, 31 March 2020* (2020) 2.
15. T Newburn, *Criminology*, 3rd edn (Routledge, 2017) 641.

to address lower-level crime and to build relationships with the public.[16] This highlights a more community-orientated, service-orientated aspect of police work with an emphasis on improving relationships with local communities. Nonetheless, despite these efforts, the police have been heavily criticised for not being representative of the community due to a distinctive lack of diversity.

The notable *Stephen Lawrence Inquiry Report*[17] labelled the Metropolitan Police as 'institutionally racist' in 1999. Macpherson's report declared that challenging such racism was the responsibility of the police. Thus, former Home Secretary, Jack Straw, drafted an *Action Plan* which sought to implement a number of Macpherson's recommendations in order to overcome the racist nature of the police force.[18] Such recommendations included increasing the representation of ethnic minority groups at each rank within the police force, which placed an emphasis on recruitment targets and the retention of minority ethnic staff.[19] Despite Macpherson's attempt to overcome racist attitudes within the police force, the early 2000s saw an increase in disproportionate misconduct proceedings against black, Asian and minority ethnic (BAME) officers.[20] Subsequently, police forces have attempted to increase the recruitment of BAME groups in order to increase diversity in the police.

Such attempts to increase the representation of ethnic minority groups has seen a slight improvement. In the year ending March 2018/19, there was a total of 103,347 police officers in England and Wales. However, just 7% of those officers were from BAME groups[21] despite these groups accounting for 14% of the total population.[22] This was a 6% increase on the year earlier, following a consistent increase each year since 2010. Despite this slight increase in diversity, such statistics clearly suggest a significant under-representation of BAME groups within the English and Welsh police force.

Moreover, BAME groups are not the only demographic to have faced discrimination in the 43 police forces across England and Wales. The masculine identity of the police force has been recognised throughout its history. The first female chief constable was not appointed until 1995, 166 years after the establishment of the police. Today, a staggering number of female police officers have reported experiencing harassment in the workplace,[23] notwithstanding their under-representation throughout police ranks. In the year ending March 2018/19,

---

16. C Paskell, '"Plastic Police" or "Community Support"? The Role of Police Community Support Officers Within Low-Income Neighbourhoods' (2007) 14 *European Urban and Regional Studies* 349, 349.
17. W Macpherson, *The Stephen Lawrence Inquiry* (Cm 4262, 1999) para 2.19.
18. G Smith, H Johnson and C Roberts, 'Ethnic Minority Police Officers and Disproportionality in Misconduct Proceedings' (2015) 25 *Policing and Society* 561, 561.
19. Macpherson (n 17) recommendation 64.
20. Smith (n 18) 561.
21. Home Office, *Police Workforce, England and Wales, 31 March 2019*, 2nd edn (2019) 7.
22. Office for National Statistics, *Ethnicity and National Identity in England and Wales* (2011).
23. J Brown, J Fleming, M Silverstri, K Linton and I Gouseti, 'Implications of Police Occupational Culture in Discriminatory Experiences of Senior Women in Police Forces in England and Wales' (2019) 29 *Policing and Society* 121, 121.

just 30% of all police officers were female,[24] despite accounting for 52% of the population.[25]

2.3.3 The jury

Juries bear the responsibility of deciding whether, based on evidence presented to them in court and the direction of a judge, a defendant is guilty or not guilty of the offence with which they have been charged. Juries are comprised of 12 untrained lay persons, the ordinary citizen, with the intention to reasonably reflect the composition of society. The involvement of such lay people should reflect a representation of the public voice within the criminal justice system.[26] Whilst misconceptions assume that jury trials are common, they account for just 1% of all criminal case proceedings in England and Wales. Jury members will be summonsed to court but may not necessarily sit on a case. In the year ending 2019, just 58% of juries summonsed actually heard a case.[27]

There has been much debate over the last few decades regarding the retention or abolition of the jury.[28] The contempt of court offence restricts jury members from disclosing any information about their deliberation. Whilst this acts as a means of security, it removes any accountability as jury members can essentially ignore the evidence and the law, basing their verdict on their own opinion. This is demonstrated in the case of *R v Ponting*,[29] where the defendant was acquitted by the jury due to matters of public interest despite compelling evidence that the defendant had committed the offence. Thus, there exists debate on whether to reform or completely abolish the jury secrecy rule as jurors lack any accountability in making adverse and life-changing decisions.[30]

Furthermore, the element of jury secrecy has come under much scrutiny due to the inability to explain jury decision-making. In fact, Rose and Ogloff argue that jury comprehension of judicial directions is 'abysmally low'.[31] Whilst there remains impetus to remove the role of juries in sexual offences trials,[32] Thomas found little evidence to suggest that juries are not fair.[33] Her Ministry of Justice Report 2010 discovered that only 31% of 797 jurors at three courts who sat on the same simulated trial and heard exactly the same judicial directions were able to understand the directions fully in the legal terms used by the judge – yet over half

24. Home Office (n 21) 7.
25. Office for National Statistics (n 22).
26. GOV.UK, Jury Service (2021), available at: www.gov.uk/jury-service (accessed 28 April 2021).
27. Ministry of Justice, *Criminal Court Statistics Quarterly: January to March* 2020 (2020) 5.
28. T Brooks, 'The Right to Trial by Jury' (2004) 21 *Journal of Applied Philosophy* 197, 197.
29. [1985] Crim LR 318.
30. Brooks (n 28) 197.
31. V Rose and J Ogloff, 'Evaluating the Comprehensibility of Jury Instructions: A Method and an Example' (2001) 25 *Law & Human Behavior* 409, 411.
32. A Coffey, 'Juries May Need to Be Scrapped Because They Believe Rape Myths' (*The Times*, 2018): www.thetimes.co.uk/article/juries-may-need-to-be-scrapped-because-they-believe-rape-myths-cfl3l9qv (accessed 28 April).
33. C Thomas, 'Are juries fair?' (2010) *Ministry of Justice Research Series 1/10*, (i).

perceived them as easy to understand.[34] This suggests that judicial directions are too complex for lay people to comprehend, indicating that the use of legal jargon should be lessened. This could help achieve a better interpretation from members of the jury, limiting the room for errors of interpretation which may lead to injustice.

Moreover, juries remain non-representative of the wider society.[35] Despite this, there is a lack of research in England and Wales to show how often BAME defendants or racially motivated crimes are tried before all-white juries. Nonetheless, Thomas found that 68% of BAME jurors reported that the courts treated BAME defendants more harshly than white defendants.[36] Her study also suggested that juries in Nottingham had much more difficulty reaching a verdict when the case involved a BAME defendant or victim compared to a white defendant or victim. When both parties were white, they always reached a verdict.[37] Subsequently, once more, jury secrecy poses a barrier to the understanding of jury decision-making and whether racial characteristics may impact justice.

2.3.4   The magistracy

Magistrates are volunteers, lay people, that decide cases within the magistrates' court. They sit in benches of three, and whilst they do not need legal qualifications, they will receive extensive training before commencing their role. All cases begin in the magistrates' court but do not necessarily end there, depending on the type of case.[38] Magistrates' sentencing powers are somewhat limited compared to those of a judge, but nonetheless they hear over 90% of all cases in the criminal justice system.[39]

The role of magistrates has sparked much debate within the criminology discipline. Whilst there is no gender discrepancy, unlike in the police – with around 55% of magistrates being female[40] – there is certainly a lack of diversity with regards to age, ethnicity and class. In 2018, 85% of magistrates were over the age of 50, and 55% were over the age of 60. Just 3.4% of magistrates were under the age of 40.[41] This suggests a middle-aged characteristic of the magistracy, which is therefore not representative of the general population, nor is it beneficial to comprehension levels as older age has been correlated with a lack of comprehension of the law.[42]

---

34. ibid (vi).
35. ibid (i).
36. ibid 53.
37. ibid 16.
38. GOV.UK, Criminal Courts (2021), available at: www.gov.uk/courts (accessed 28 April 2021).
39. House of Commons, Justice Committee, *The Role of the Magistracy: Follow-Up. Eighteenth Report of Session 2017-19* (2019) 3.
40. Courts and Tribunals Judiciary, *Judicial Diversity Statistics 2018* (2018) 1.
41. House of Commons (n 39) 14.
42. Thomas (n 33) (vi).

Moreover, just 11% of magistrates in England and Wales identify as BAME, leaving almost 90% of magistrates as white. In fact, research suggests that BAME defendants are more likely to opt for a trial by jury for an either-way offence as they do not believe that they will receive a fair hearing from magistrates, despite harsher sentencing in the Crown Court.[43] This is supported by literature, which suggests that BAME women are more likely to be convicted than their white counterparts in the magistrates' court.[44]

In 2017, David Lammy MP was invited by the House of Commons to examine the progress of increasing ethnic diversity within the magistracy. Lammy commented, 'it feels like the same old people',[45] suggesting no development in improving race equality issues within the magistrates' court. Moreover, in this report, one magistrate from a BAME background claimed he felt 'that the magistracy did not represent him'.[46] Consequently, Lammy recommended that the government should 'set a clear, national target to achieve a representative judiciary and magistracy by 2025'.[47]

2.3.5 Conclusion

To conclude, this section of the chapter has demonstrated a number of challenges to diversity, representation and accountability in the criminal justice system. The police force in England and Wales is significantly lacking in diversity and representation of minority groups, with just 7% of officers from BAME groups[48] and just 30% of all police officers identifying as female.[49] It is necessary to address such lack of diversity and representation in order for the police to reflect the composition of society, maximising its values and attitudes. Moreover, it is apparent that a number of different influences may affect jury decision-making, including race and education, which may impact criminal justice. Ultimately, this results in poor accountability of the justice system, leaving room for wrongful convictions or acquittal of the guilty. Finally, the low representation of BAME groups within the magistracy may have a negative impact on criminal justice as BAME defendants may feel discriminated against. In addition, the aging composition of the magistracy has potential to hinder criminal justice due to the possibility of older age contributing to a lack of comprehension.

---

43. D Lammy, *The Lammy Review: An Independent Review into the Treatment of, and Outcomes for, Black, Asian and Minority Ethnic Individuals in the Criminal Justice System* (2017) 27.
44. ibid 32.
45. House of Commons, Justice Committee, *Oral Evidence: Progress in the Implementation of the Lammy Review's Recommendations* (HC 2086, 2017).
46. House of Commons (n 39) 46.
47. Lammy (n 43) 8.
48. Home Office (n 21) 7.
49. ibid.

2.4 Victims and victimology

2.4.1 Introduction to victimology

Victimology is a relatively modern field of study, emerging in the 1970s, which encompasses theory, research, policy and practice.[50] There has been much debate within criminology regarding what 'victimology' refers to. Thus, there is no accepted definition of 'victimology', nor who a 'victim' is. Some will argue that victimology is a sub-discipline of criminology which focuses on victims of crime alone, whilst others will consider it as victims' state of oppression.[51] Moreover, other academics suggest that victimology does not account for victims of human trafficking, disasters, and other reasons why a person may become a victim.[52]

Meanwhile, some regard victimology as an academic, theoretical discipline which has been manipulated by practitioners to create their own narrative of victimology.[53] Subsequently, O'Connell argues that 'victimologists differ about what victimology should or should not include, about what should be the focus and about what research methods are best'.[54] Ultimately, this has led to differing disciplines of victimology – criminal and non-criminal.[55] Nonetheless, Sarkin defines 'victimology' as 'the study of victims and issues concerning process and patterns of victimization'.[56] Despite the relationship between victimology, psychological trauma and therapy, these fields are typically approached separately with regards to victimisation, which Spalek considers 'strange' given the overlap.[57]

2.4.2 What is victimisation?

Victimisation refers to the process of becoming victimised – to be treated unfairly.[58] Thus, victimisation can be a result of both criminal and non-criminal behaviour. The United Nations defines 'victims of crime' as 'persons who, individually or collectively, have suffered harm, including physical or mental injury, emotional suffering, economic loss or substantial impairment of their fundamental rights, through acts or omissions that are in violation of criminal laws operative within Member States'.[59] Ultimately, anyone can become a victim,

---

50. J Van Dijk, 'Introducing Victimology' in J Van Dijk, R Van Kaam and K Wemmers (eds), *Caring for Crime Victims: Selected Proceedings of the Ninth International Symposium on Victimology* (Criminal Justice Press, 1999) 1.
51. M O'Connell, 'Victimology: A Social Science in Waiting?' (2008) 15 *International Review of Victimology* 91, 91.
52. J Sarkin, 'Why Victimology Should Focus on All Victims, Including All Missing and Disappeared Persons' (2019) 25 *International Review of Victimology* 249, 250.
53. ibid.
54. O'Connell (n 51) 91.
55. B Spalek, *Crime Victims: Theory, Policy and Practice* (Palgrave, 2017) 3.
56. Sarkin (n 52) 251.
57. Spalek (n 55) 1.
58. Cambridge Dictionary, The Meaning of Victimization (2021). Available at: https://dictionary.cambridge.org/dictionary/english/victimization (accessed 18 April 2021).
59. United Nations, *Declaration of Basic Principles of Justice for Victims of Crime and Abuse of Power* (1985). Available at: www.ohchr.org/en/professionalinterest/pages/victimsofcrimeandabuseofpower.aspx (accessed 18 April 2021).

though not all incidences of victimisation are a result of activities that are *necessarily* criminal acts.

2.4.3 Penal criminology

The field of victimology is divided into two parts: penal victimology and general victimology. General victimology focuses on the victims themselves, paying less attention to the causes of victimisation, including people injured in accidents or disasters, whilst penal victimology encompasses a focus on the injuries and damages caused by the commission of offences.[60] Subsequently, penal victimology examines the dynamic interplay between both the victim and the offender in order to explain how people become victims of criminal activity. It therefore considers victimology as a branch of criminology, with the intention of remaining objective and limiting political views by narrowing the scope of victimology.[61] However, this approach has been heavily criticised for creating a connotation of blame, responsibility and accountability for victims of crime.[62]

2.4.4 The issue of victim-blaming

As aforementioned, victims of crime often find themselves being subjected to some level of blame for the crime committed against them. This is particularly common in cases of sexual violence. For example, Dame Alison Saunders argues that a victim of burglary would not be asked, 'what have you done to deserve that?',[63] unlike victims of rape, who may be asked what they were wearing or whether they were walking alone at night.[64] The endorsement of such victim-blaming has created barriers to criminal justice over the last 40 years as complainants may feel that they are to blame for the assault.[65] This has left those subjected to sexual violence being reluctant to report to police through fear of being disbelieved, contributing to a low reporting rate, estimated at 30%.[66] Subsequently, such victim-blaming behaviour, and attitudes within the criminal justice system, have been implicated in many criticisms of the criminal justice system's response to rape that sees low conviction rates (6%, of all reports), high levels of victim withdrawal and low levels of trust in the system.[67]

---

60. Sarkin (n 52) 251.

61. JA Wemmers, 'A Short History of Victimology' in O Hagemann, P Schafer and S Schmidt (eds), *Victimology, Victim Assistance and Criminal Justice: Perspectives Shared by International Experts at the Inter-University Centre of Dubrovnik* (Mönchengladbach Niederrhein Univ of Applied Sciences, 2010) 7.

62. Van Dijk (n 50) 4.

63. A Saunders, 'Sexual Consent is Simple. We Should All Be Clear What Constitutes Rape' (2015): www.theguardian.com/commentisfree/2015/sep/23/sexual-consent-rape-prosecution-myth-consentis (accessed 28 April 2021).

64. D Abrams, G Viki, B Masser and G Bohner, 'Perceptions of Stranger and Acquaintance Rape: The Role of Benevolent and Hostile Sexism in Victim Blame and Rape Proclivity' (2003) 84 *Journal of Personality and Social Psychology* 111, 111.

65. J Temkin, *Rape and the Legal Process* (Sweet and Maxwell, 1987) 10.

66. J Temkin, '"And Always Keep A-hold of Nurse, For Fear of Finding Something Worse": Challenging Rape Myths in the Courtroom' (2010) 13 *NCLR* 710, 710.

67. Office for National Statistics, *Crime in England and Wales: Year Ending March 2020* (2020) 8.

2.4.5 *Crime Survey for England and Wales*

Previous named the *British Crime Survey*, the *Crime Survey for England and Wales* was introduced in order to collect true data on the frequency of crime outside of police reports due to the nature of a lack of disclosing crime to authorities. It encompasses interviewing and surveying the public about their experiences of crime, amounting to one of the largest social research surveys conducted in England and Wales.[68] In the year ending June 2020, the Office for National Statistics suggested that there were 5.8 million police recorded crimes.[69] However, the *Crime Survey for England and Wales* estimated that there were 11.5 million offences conducted in the previous 12 months, highlighting the lack of reporting and detection of criminal activity.[70] However, this method of research has been heavily criticised due to its inability to collect data on every member of the public, thus limiting the validity of these statistics. Moreover, through reluctance of being reminded of their victimisation, some participants may not fully disclose their experiences as victims of crime. Furthermore, the *Crime Survey for England and Wales* does not collect data on all children, thus not accounting for the overall 'dark figure' of crime.[71]

2.4.6 The fear of crime

Despite evidence that the commission of crime is decreasing each year, with a decrease of 4% in 2019/20 (approximately 232,000 offences),[72] there is an ever-growing fear of crime within the British public. Direct victimisation is able to explain the fear of crime for those who have been subjected to criminal offences. It suggests that those who have been directly affected by the actions of an offender may have an increased sensitivity to the risk of crime. Thus, victims of crime are more likely to fear becoming a victim of crime again. Moreover, indirect victimisation is able to offer an explanation of the fear of crime for those who have not been directly affected by crime by suggesting that vicarious experiences of crime may influence a fear of crime as a result of others' experiences. They do not want to be subjected to similar behaviour and consequently fear criminal activity.[73] Both forms of victimisation therefore contribute to a disproportionate fear of crime, ignoring evidence which suggests that crime is in fact decreasing. Politicians may use this fear of crime to their advantage in their manifestos by offering punitive and draconian criminal justice measures to gain public

---

68. A Tseloni and N Tilley, 'Choosing and Using Statistical Sources in Criminology: What Can the Crime Survey for England and Wales Tell Us?' (2016) 16 *Legal Information Management* 78, 82.

69. Office for National Statistics, *Crime in England and Wales: Year Ending June 2020* (2020). Available at: www.ons.gov.uk/peoplepopulationandcommunity/crimeandjustice/bulletins/crimeinenglandandwales/yearendingjune2020#main-points (accessed 28 April 2021).

70. ibid.

71. Tseloni (n 68) 83.

72. Office for National Statistics (n 69).

73. B Doran and M Burgess, *Putting Fear of Crime on the Map: Investigating Perceptions of Crime Using Geographic Information Systems* (Springer, 2012) 26–29.

confidence.[74] Ultimately, this further exacerbates the fear of crime amongst the public, creating a vicious cycle of scaremongering and punitivity.

2.4.7 Conclusion

Victimology is an integral element of criminology. Whilst there are differing angles to exploring victimology, it helps us to understand the impact that crime has on its victims. It is apparent that the fear of crime is greater than the frequency of crime. Nonetheless, victims may be subjected to self-blame and blame from others, resulting in inaccurate recording of crime (especially in cases of rape, sexual abuse and domestic violence) as blame discourages reporting. It is evident that this requires tackling in order to achieve justice for the victims of crime, which may increase conviction rates, therefore restoring public faith in the criminal justice system.

2.5 Offenders

2.5.1 Introduction

This section examines both defendants and offenders at multiple stages within the criminal justice process. It will attempt to analyse the racial disparity in such stages, exploring the over-representation of BAME offenders in England and Wales. Finally, it will consider the impact that incarceration has on the prisoner's family.

2.5.2 Charging decisions by the Crown Prosecution Service

The Crown Prosecution Service (CPS) is responsible for reviewing cases presented to it by the police which ultimately results in a decision of whether or not to charge a suspect. The CPS subsequently prosecutes criminal cases in England and Wales in addition to deciding which charges are most appropriate.[75] David Lammy uncovered a significant over-representation of BAME suspects whose cases are passed on to the CPS for a charging decision. Black boys are 10 times more likely to be arrested for drug offences than white boys. Thus, Lammy argues that such over-representation of BAME suspects is the result of the disproportionate arrest rates of BAME groups by the police.[76] Such disparity will be further explored in **Chapter 4** – 'Policing and Criminological Perspectives'.

2.5.3 Defendants in courts

In 2017, 20% of defendants in the court system of England and Wales were from BAME groups.[77] In 2020, the Ministry of Justice claimed that 'people from a Black,

---

74. Tseloni (n 68) 83.

75. CPS, *About CPS* (2020). Available at: www.cps.gov.uk/about-cps (accessed 28 April 2021).

76. B Shepherd, 'The Lammy Review: Treatment of and Outcomes for BAME Adults and Young People in the CJS' (2017) 64 *Probation Journal* 422, 422.

77. Ministry of Justice, *Criminal Justice System Statistics Quarterly: December 2016, Prosecution and Convictions Tool* (2017) 2.

Asian, "Mixed" or "Chinese and other" background were over-represented as defendants in the criminal justice system in 2019'.[78] They agree with Lammy's argument from 2017 – that this is a result of a disproportionate amount of BAME groups arrested, prosecuted, convicted and imprisoned. Thus, this suggests that Lammy's recommendations had ceased to be implemented between 2017 and 2019, contributing to a racial disparity amongst defendants in the England and Wales criminal justice system. Magistrates are more likely to convict BAME women despite a lack of evidence which suggests that BAME women are more likely to commit crime than white women. Thus, Lammy has suggested greater scrutiny in the magistrates' court when verdicts are being reached.[79] However, as previously discussed, there is a lack of research in England and Wales to analyse whether racial characteristics may impact jury decision-making.

2.5.4 Offenders in prisons and the impact on prisoners' families

Currently, there are approximately 80,000 people incarcerated in prisons across England and Wales, a 60% increase since 1990.[80] The modern prison system was introduced in 1816, but what accounts for the sudden increase in custodial sentences in the last 30 years (an insignificant amount of time in the history of prisons)? The reason for this is unclear. However, Millie, Jacobson and Hough conclude that such an increase is the 'result of an increasingly punitive climate of opinion about crime and punishment … sentencing guidance and guideline judgments'. This suggests that punitive public attitudes are having an impact on the increasing prison population.

Furthermore, statistics suggest that around 27% of the prison population are from BAME groups[81] despite accounting for just 14% of the general population.[82] Again, this highlights the disparity in the representation of the BAME population in the prison system compared to their representation in the general population of England and Wales.

Subsequently, with the ever-growing prison population[83] comes the increasing need to understand the psychological impact on children of having a parent incarcerated.[84] Witnessing the parent's arrest, the loss of family income, caregiving changes and stigma associated with criminal activity are just a few of the emotional difficulties that children experience when their parents receive a custodial sentence.[85]

---

78. G Sturge and B Yasin, House of Commons, *Ethnicity and the Criminal Justice System: What Does Recent Data Say on Over-Representation?* (2020) 1.

79. Shepherd (n 76) 423.

80. G Sturge, House of Commons, *UK Prison Population Statistics* (2020) 3–4.

81. Office for National Statistics, *Ethnicity and National Identity in England and Wales* (2011).

82. Ministry of Justice, *NOMS Annual Offender Equalities Report: 2015 to 2016* (2016) 9.

83. J Murray, D Farrington and I Sekol, 'Children's Antisocial Behaviour, Mental Health, Drug Use, and Educational Performance After Parental Incarceration: A Systematic Review and Meta-Analysis' (2012) 138 *Psychological Bulletin* 175, 175.

84. L Davis and R Shlafer, 'Mental Health of Adolescents with Currently and Formerly Incarcerated Parents' [2016] 54 *Journal of Adolescence* 120, 120

85. Murray (n 83) 175.

Research conducted in England has established that children who experienced parental incarceration within their first 10 years of life were twice as likely to engage in anti-social behaviour up to the age of 48.[86] Anti-social behaviour does not refer to criminal behaviour alone, but accounts for acts such as persistent lying and deceit, as well as later arrests and convictions against the child.[87] This suggests that incarcerating an offender who is a parent has a negative impact on criminal justice by increasing the likelihood of the child engaging in criminal activity.

Whilst there is limited research surrounding potential support services for children whose parents are incarcerated, one study offered insight into the coping strategies that young people employ when a parent is incarcerated. Often struggling to manage the emotional burden carried with having a parent incarcerated, Johnson and Easterling's (2015) research suggested that children use three coping strategies: deidentification from the parent, desensitization from the incarceration, and maintaining strength through control.[88] Through deidentification, adolescents appeared to distance themselves from their parent, limiting their relationship, as an avoidant strategy. Moreover, Campbell et al's study established that a number of adolescents became desensitized from the incarceration.

On the other hand, by minimising the gravity of their circumstances and the negative emotions that surrounds them (referring to it as 'not a big deal'), others found a way to cope with their parental separation. Maintaining some level of control over their lives was a fundamental coping strategy for some adolescents.[89] Examples include using their education to better themselves, and utilising therapy as a way to control their thoughts about their incarcerated parent.[90] These examples of coping strategies suggest that more action is required from social services in order to avoid children carrying the emotional burden of having an incarcerated parent on their own.[91]

2.5.5 Conclusion

It is apparent that BAME groups are disproportionately represented throughout the criminal justice process, from suspect, to defendant, to offender. Such processes include charging decisions by the CPS, decision-making in the courts and incarceration in the prison system. Moreover, with the ever-growing prison population, it is evident that imprisonment affects more people than those incarcerated – it more broadly affects the offender's child.[92] Primary values of the

---

86. J Murray and D Farrington, 'Parental Imprisonment: Long-lasting Effects on Boys' Internalizing Problems Through the Life Course' (2008) 20 *Development and Psychopathology* 273, 273.
87. Murray (n 83) 177.
88. E Johnson and A Easterling, 'Coping with Confinement: Adolescents' Experiences With Parental Incarceration' (2015) 30 *Journal of Adolescent Research* 244, 244.
89. ibid 257.
90. ibid.
91. P Allard, 'When the Cost is Too Great: The Emotional and Psychological Impact on Children of Incarcerating their Parents for Drug Offences' (2012) 50 *Family Court Review* 48, 48.
92. H Codd, *In the Shadow of Prison: Families, Imprisonment and Criminal Justice* (Willan, 2008) 4

criminal justice system to prevent crime are contradicted by increasing the likelihood of later criminal behaviour when a child suffers from parental incarceration.[93]

2.6 Chapter conclusion

Hirschi's Social Control Theory is able to provide a criminological explanation for the need for social control that allows us to place the operation of the criminal justice system in context. However, it is not a 'complete' theory or one without its critics or detractors (for instance, it neglects the commission of violent crimes, such as assault, grievous bodily harm and sexual offences), and whilst undoubtedly influential, it has been subject to revisions and updating since its inception.[94] Whilst victimology helps us to understand how we become victims of crime, it is evident that the fear of crime is much greater than the commission of crime itself. Further, low comprehension of members of the jury and the element of jury secrecy suggest that key actors within the justice system lack accountability for their decision-making. Finally, it is apparent that BAME groups remain over-represented as offenders yet under-represented as members of the jury, the police force and the magistracy. Subsequently, the criminal justice system in England and Wales lacks diversity.

KEY POINTS AND SUMMARY

- Theories of Social Control are able to provide a useful theoretical tool that allows us to place the operation of the criminal justice system in context, and helps us understand some of its aims, goals and practices.
- BAME groups are over-represented as offenders but are under-represented as key actors within the criminal justice system, such as the police, the magistracy and the jury.
- Though victimology may help us to understand how people become victims of crime, victimologists may disagree about what victimology should include. Moreover, penal criminology has been criticised for encouraging victim-blaming.

STUDY QUESTIONS

- Why do we need the police? Would society operate safely without the police?
- Is the police force in England and Wales representative of its population? How may this impact policing?
- How does penal victimology contribute to criminology? What is its impact on criminal justice?
- What impact do custodial sentences have on the offender's family?

---

93. S Phillips and J Dettlaff, 'More than Parents in Prison: The Broader Overlap Between the Criminal Justice and Child Welfare Systems' (2009) 3 *Journal of Public Child Welfare* 3, 4.
94. See, eg, MR Gottfredson and T Hirschi, *A General Theory of Crime* (Stanford University Press, 1990).

The Powers of the Police: The Law

3.1 Introduction

Chapters 3 and **4** are concerned with the powers of the police to investigate crime in the community – on the street, as it were. The subject could feasibly cover a range of matters, including powers of entry, search and seizure, and possibly the ability of the police to ask citizens to 'stop and account'. These chapters will, however, focus on two of the most visible and, arguably, significant powers available to the police: stop and search, and arrest. Both involve substantial invasions of privacy and (temporary) restrictions on liberty, which therefore affect the fundamental human rights of citizens. These interferences with civil liberties can be justified if they are conducted with the aim of investigating and controlling crime, thereby protecting wider society from such behaviour. The right to be protected from crime and to have it investigated by the authorities is an equally important right for all citizens. However, these powers must be used both legitimately and proportionately. One must always question the balance between the competing interests of individual citizens and wider society. Stop and search and arrest have significant scope for upsetting this balance.

These chapters will explore the scope of these two powers and how they operate in theory and practice, and they will examine some of the issues relating to their operation as crime-fighting tools. The chapters will also consider some of the protections afforded to suspects, which were designed to counter any misuse of power that might occur. We analyse how the safeguards should work in theory, alongside a brief analysis of how they do (or do not) work in practice and whether or not they provide the protection they were designed to give.

3.2 Stop and search: the law

Stop and search is a power conferred on the police 'to stop a person or vehicle and to search for certain items or articles which they suspect are connected to criminal behaviour'.[1] The primary power is governed by the Police and Criminal Evidence Act (PACE) 1984.[2] Section 1(2) permits a police officer to search any person or vehicle for the following:

- stolen or prohibited articles;

---

1. See further E Johnston and T Smith, *Criminal Procedure and Punishment,* 2nd edn (Hall and Stott Publishing, 2020) 19.
2. ss 1–3.

- any article in relation to offences under ss 139 and 139AA of the Criminal Justice Act 1988 (this includes having a bladed or pointed article or threatening someone with those items);
- certain prohibited fireworks.

At face value, this provides an extensive list of reasons why a person can be stopped. The use of the word 'prohibited article' is somewhat opaque. Section 1(7) states that this refers to an offensive weapon or an article that is made or adapted for use in the course of or in connection with an offence,[3] or is intended by the person having it with him for such use by him or some other person.[4]

As you can see, what the police can search an individual for is actually rather wide; it will cover many things. Over the last 20 years, the use of the power has received considerable criticism from human rights groups, academics and the courts as a wide police power, and it has been subject to reforms. These reforms include the issuing of guidelines such as PACE Code of Practice A[5] and the Best Use of Stop and Search scheme (BUSS).[6] The aim of these reforms was to define what a lawful search is and to provide officers with more guidance on how to perform such a search. Some limits to how a search can take place are set out in PACE 1984, ss 1, 2 and 3. Section 1 allows the police to search someone, in a public place, if they have reasonable suspicion that the individual may be carrying stolen items, offensive weapons (or items adapted to be used as weapons) or fireworks. Section 2 provides a safeguard against a misuse of this power by setting out what information must be given to the individual, and it states that the search must be for a length of time that is reasonable. This was confirmed to be mandatory in the case of *R v Bristol*,[7] and a search can be deemed unlawful should these provisions not be followed. This is highlighted in the case of *Sobczak v Director of Public Prosecutions*,[8] where an officer failed to provide the individual with the correct information set out in s 2. Finally, s 3 states that an officer must record the search, and this record should be given to the individual straight away unless it is impractical.

The main due process protection in stop and search is the requirement of reasonable suspicion, as stated in s 1 of PACE 1984. There is no statutory definition of what is deemed 'reasonable suspicion', although it is expanded upon in Code of Practice A. The Code provides a two part test, as well as examples of what is not reasonable suspicion. The test is set out as follows: the officer must have formed a genuine suspicion in their own mind, and they must have an

---

3.   s 1(7)(b)(i).
4.   s 1(7)(b)(ii).
5.   Home Office, Revised code of practice for the exercise by: Police Officers of Statutory Powers of stop and search, Police and Criminal Evidence Act 1984 – Code A, December 2014: https://assets.publishing.service.gov.uk/government/uploads/system/uploads/attachment_data/file/903810/pace-code-a-2015.pdf (accessed 4 May 2021).
6.   College of Policing and Home Office, 'Best Use of Stop and Search Scheme', August 2014: https://assets.publishing.service.gov.uk/government/uploads/system/uploads/attachment_data/file/346922/Best_Use_of_Stop_and_Search_Scheme_v3.0_v2.pdf (accessed 4 May 2021).
7.   [2007] EWCA Crim 3214.
8.   [2012] EWHC 1319 (Admin).

objective basis for that suspicion.[9] An objective basis means one based on facts or intelligence, and the officer must be able to explain this suspicion.[10] An example of what would not meet this test are personal characteristics, such as age, race, gender, or an individual's previous convictions. The only time this would be accepted is if the officer has been provided with a description of someone by a witness, and the individual in question meets that description.[11] The obligation to record information is also a due process safeguard, as it opens the police up to public scrutiny and accountability; it is a form of 'administrative accountability'.[12] This was one of the recommendations made by the BUSS scheme[13] that emphasised the importance of recording.

Some of the extended guidance provided to police officers on stop and search is not contained in the legislation but must still be followed. The BUSS scheme also provides guidance on how to conduct a lawful stop and search and emphasises the importance of public confidence and trust in the police. However, the Equality and Human Rights Commission, in 2010, critically reviewed the use of this power and found that it was still being disproportionately used against ethnic minority communities. The Commission concluded that the police were still acting in unlawful and discriminatory ways.[14]

Whilst case law on the lawfulness of stop and search is scant, there are a couple of key cases which hold great importance for the administration of this power. The main issues in the cases centre on the effect a search has on one's liberty, the wide discretionary use of the power and issues concerning what constitutes reasonable suspicion.

In *R (Gillan) v Commissioner of Police for the Metropolis*, Bingham LJ stated that temporary restriction of movement 'could not sensibly be called a deprivation of liberty'[15] and doubted that an 'ordinary superficial search' of the person could show a lack of respect for private life. On appeal, the European Court of Human Rights (*Gillan and Quinton v United Kingdom*)[16] took a wider view and found that the unlawful use of stop and search breached the right to privacy (ECHR, Article 8) and potentially violated the right to liberty (Article 5). Regarding Article 5, the Court observed that the applicants were entirely deprived of any freedom of movement for the duration of the search (20–30 minutes). They were obliged to remain where they were and submit to the search or face sanctions. This element of coercion was 'indicative of a deprivation of liberty'. The Court also expressed concern about the discriminatory use of the power against black and Asian

---

9.   Code A (n 5) para 2.2(i) and (ii).
10.   ibid.
11.   Code A (n 5) para 2.2B.
12.   B Bradford and I Loader, 'Police, Crime and Order: The Case of Stop and Search' in Bradford et al (eds), *SAGE Handbook of Global Policing* (SAGE, 2016).
13.   BUSS scheme (n 6) para 1.4.
14.   Equality and Human Rights Commission, *Stop and think: A critical review of the use of stop and search powers in England and Wales* (2010) 68.
15.   [2006] UKHL 12 at [22].
16.   (2010) 50 EHRR 45.

persons. In *Howarth v Commissioner of Police for the Metropolis*,[17] McCombe J stated that the rights of expression and of assembly protected by the ECHR are indeed precious in a democratic society. However, there was a significant danger of the law becoming 'over precious' about minimal intrusions into privacy.

The issues surrounding what constitutes 'reasonable suspicion' were addressed in *Hussien v Chong Fook Kam*,[18] prior to the enactment of PACE 1984. Lord Devlin stated that a lower standard is required for reasonable suspicion than would be required as prima facie proof. This means that officers can consider evidence that would not be admissible in court.[19] In the more recent case of *Howarth* (above), the court stated that 'it is well recognised that the threshold for the existence of reasonable grounds for suspicion is low'.[20]

The cases relating to the right to liberty suggest that it is important that officers act lawfully to avoid a breach of human rights. However, the wide discretion and low standard of reasonable suspicion suggest that, in practice, constraints on the police are limited, arguably allowing them to stop and search whomever they wish.

It could be argued that a wide-ranging power such as stop and search could have a side benefit to its use. One could hold the view that the power deters people from committing crime, therefore reflecting the idea of the police as 'peace officers', with the goal of keeping the peace in society. One could suggest that there is a deterrent effect to stop and search; the individual searched will be less likely to carry prohibited items, but also, indirectly, any bystanders who witness the search will also be less likely to carry prohibited items. It has also been suggested that this makes it an effective method of repressing crime.[21] Bradford also acknowledges that it is an investigative power but suggests in practice that it is more of a crime control method, although we can see the failures attached with that approach. Furthermore, it is arguable that the use of the power creates social marginality, as it is directed and used disproportionally against black, Asian and minority ethnic (BAME) groups.[22] In 2019/20, only 13% of all PACE 1984 stop and searches resulted in arrest.[23] Tiratelli et al provide an explanation for such low arrest rates. They state that the use of stop and search is not targeted at crime hotspots most of the time, where it would have a more significant impact on crime. Without a different approach, stop and search is likely to have only a marginal effect on criminal activity.[24]

Hough emphasises the importance of the lawful use of stop and search as the public's trust in the police is more important in a wider societal context.[25] This

---

17. [2011] EWHC 2818 (QB).
18. [1970] AC 942.
19. ibid 943.
20. [2011] EWHC 2818 (QB) at [31].
21. M Tiratelli, P Quinton and B Bradford, 'Does Stop and Search Deter Crime? Evidence from Ten Years of London-Wide Data' (2018) 58 *British Journal of Criminology* 1212.
22. Bradford (n 12).
23. J Brown, 'Police powers: stop and search', House of Commons Library (2020), 26: https://commonslibrary.parliament.uk/research-briefings/sn03878/ (accessed 4 May 2021).
24. Tiratelli (n 21).
25. M Hough, 'Procedural Justice and Professional Policing in Times of Austerity' (2013) 13 *Criminology and Criminal Justice* 181.

means that the due process protections such as reasonable suspicion are necessary to limit the 'significant discretion'[26] that officers have; they should be a 'proactive restraint' on police powers.[27]

These are contentious issues and have been subject to several government reviews. The HMICFRS report in 2013 made recommendations on what police forces could improve on,[28] but the follow-up report published in 2015 found that insufficient progress had been made.[29] It concluded that there was little understanding of what an effective and lawful search was, and that there should be a codified universal definition created that all officers, nationally, could use and understand. This lack of understanding meant that 27% of searches did not include sufficient grounds to search and therefore ought to have been illegal.[30] The report also found that the recording of searches needed to improve. In response to this, the College of Policing outlined a definition of a lawful and effective search.[31] It suggested that a stop and search is most likely to be fair and effective when:

- the search is justified, lawful and stands up to public scrutiny;
- the officer has genuine and objective reasonable suspicion that they will find a prohibited article or an item for use in crime;
- the person understands why they have been searched and feels that they have been treated with respect; and
- the search is necessary and the most appropriate method the police officer can use to establish whether the person has such an item.

The House of Commons also conducted research into the effectiveness of the stop and search power and concluded that reforms from previous reports and Code of Practice A[32] had led to a substantial reduction in its use and improved police practice, but that its disproportionate use against BAME groups continued.[33]

It is important to note that there is other legislation that conveys the power of stop and search on the police. Section 60 of the Criminal Justice and Public Order Act 1994 and s 47A of the Terrorism Act 2000 allow the police to use the power without the need for 'reasonable suspicion'.[34] However, this book is designed to give you a flavour of the issues you will cover in your studies and, as such, we do not go into more detail here.

---

26. Bradford and Loader (n 12).
27. ibid.
28. HMICFRS, 'Stop and search powers: are the police using them effectively and fairly?' (July 2013).
29. HMICFRS, 'Stop and search powers 2: are the police using them effectively and fairly? (March 2015).
30. ibid.
31. College of Policing, 'Definition of Fair and Effective Stop and Search': www.app.college.police.uk/app-content/stop-and-search/ (accessed 4 May 2021).
32. Code A (n 5).
33. Brown (n 23) 28.
34. See further Johnston (n 1) 26–28.

3.3 Arrest: the law

As with stop and search, there are sometimes difficulties in identifying when the power of arrest should be used. The statutory power of arrest is contained in s 24 of PACE 1984 and is one of the most visible forms of policing,[35] but it also holds stark ramifications for those arrested. It has long been recognised that arrest 'represents a major disruption to a suspect's life',[36] often rendering suspects 'powerless, humiliated and terrified'.[37] The obvious fragility of situations involving arrest places much emphasis on the importance of police officers exercising their powers not only correctly and fairly, but legally. While in most instances it will be apparent that an arrest has been carried out, this is not always the case. In short, the courts have adopted two 'distinct and arguably different approaches to the concept'.[38]

The first approach states that arrest is a factual state of affairs, dependent entirely on 'whether [an individual] has been deprived of his liberty to go where he pleases', per Viscount Dilhorne in the case of *Spicer v Holt*.[39] The second approach, in contrast, is dependent on the context and intention of the arresting officer. As suggested by Johnston and Smith, these two approaches blur the line between what are two entirely 'separate concepts: the fact an arrest has occurred … and the lawfulness of an arrest'.[40] These interpretations have the potential to confuse officers as it needs to be clear when an arrest has taken place in order to ensure that the appropriate procedure and safeguards are being adhered to and, more importantly, to ensure that the arrest is lawful.

Undoubtedly, arrest interferes with a person's human rights, in particular Article 5 of the ECHR (the right to liberty). As such, it is of paramount importance that practices and safeguards are adhered to in order to ensure that an arrest is carried out legally, and that an individual's rights are protected accordingly. Section 24 of PACE 1984 (as substituted by s 110 of the Serious Organised Crime and Police Act 2005) provides police with the widely applicable power to arrest without a warrant any individual for any offence. Before the amendment, there was a limit on what offence a person could be arrested for: offences were arrestable and non-arrestable.[41] However, the current legislation means that there is no distinction between offences, and the police are now able to arrest for any offence, no matter how minor or trivial.[42] As a safeguard to this wide power, a further due process protection was introduced. An arrest always needed to be based on a

---

35. ibid 41.
36. Royal Commission on Criminal Procedure, *Investigation and Prosecution of Criminal Offences in England and Wales: Law and Procedure* (Cmnd 8092, 1981).
37. A Sanders, R Young and M Burton, *Criminal Justice* (OUP, 2010).
38. ibid 3.
39. [1977] AC 987, HL.
40. Johnston (n 1) 43–44.
41. G Pearson, L Turner and M Rowe, 'Policy, Practicalities, and PACE s 24: The Subsuming of the Necessity Criteria in Arrest Decision Making by Frontline Police Officers' (2018) 45(2) *Journal of Law and Society* 282.
42. ibid 282.

reasonable suspicion,[43] but the arresting officer now has to ensure that the arrest is 'necessary'.[44]

Reasonable suspicion

The threshold of reasonable suspicion is akin to the threshold required to conduct a stop and search, and we briefly re-cap the issues here. At face value, one could argue that reasonable suspicion is a high threshold that protects the public from the misuse of police power. However, when scratching beneath the surface, we can see that the level required to satisfy the threshold is, in fact, very low. In *Hussien v Chong Fook Kam*,[45] the court said that 'suspicion can take into account matters that cannot be put into evidence at all [and] also matters which, though admissible, could not form part of a *prima facie* case', which demonstrates the low threshold. This is further shown in the leading case of *Castorina v Chief Constable of Surrey*,[46] which involved a burglary at a small office premises. When the police interviewed the business owner, they asked if the owner had any issues with staff or former staff, as they suspected that the burglary was an 'inside job' and committed by someone familiar with the firm and the office layout. The owner claimed that he did not have any concerns, but that he had recently dismissed an employee in her 50s; he did state, however, that he did not believe she would have done it. The police interviewed the suspect regardless, and although she had no previous convictions, she could not provide an alibi for the time in question and was therefore arrested. She was later released without charge, sued the police for false imprisonment and was subsequently award a sum of £4,500. The police appealed against this decision which was allowed by the Court of Appeal. The Court decided that it was appropriate for the suspect to be linked to the burglary (despite the business owner suggesting otherwise) and that the arresting officer's conduct was reasonable. Woolf LJ suggested that an officer must pass a three limbed test to decide whether or not an arrest is 'reasonable':

(1) Does the arresting officer suspect the person they have arrested to be guilty of the offence in question – this is a subjective requirement.

(2) If the officer has this suspicion, is there reasonable cause for this suspicion – this is also a subjective requirement.

If the two subjective limbs are satisfied, the officer can move on to the third and final limb of the test, which is objective in nature:

(3) Is the use of arrest '*Wednesbury* reasonable',[47] ie would an ordinary reasonable person believe that the action taken was reasonable? Ultimately, the decision to arrest could not be viewed as bizarre or irrational.

If this test is satisfied then a person can be lawfully arrested. However, when looking at the facts of the *Castorina* case, it could be argued that the threshold is

---

43. PACE 1984, s 24(1).
44. PACE 1984, s 24(4).
45. [1970] AC 942.
46. *Castorina v Chief Constable of Surrey* (CA, 10 June 1988).
47. Lord Greene in *Associated Provincial Picture Houses Ltd v Wednesbury Corporation* [1948] 1 KB 223.

very low. Here we have a middle-aged woman, of previous good character, arrested on the basis that she had the opportunity to commit the alleged offence – despite the fact that the business owner did not suspect or believe she had committed it. Arguably, the law provides little protection for those arrested as it appears that people can be arrested on little more than a whim or a 'hunch'.

That being said, reasonable suspicion is not the only threshold the police have to pass. The arrest also needs to be necessary.

Necessity

Section 24(5) of PACE 1984 outlines the reasons that would constitute a necessary arrest:

(a) to enable the name of the person in question to be ascertained …;

(b) correspondingly as regards to the person's address;

(c) to prevent the person in question—

    (i) causing physical injury to himself or any other person;

    (ii) suffering physical injury;

    (iii) causing loss of or damage to property;

    (iv) committing an offence against public decency …;

    (v) causing an unlawful obstruction of a highway;

(d) to protect a child or other vulnerable person from the person in question;

(e) to allow the prompt and effective investigation of the offence or the conduct of the person in question;

(f) to prevent any prosecution from the offence being hindered by the disappearance of the person in question.

Aside from s 24(5)(e), all the other justifications of necessity are rather narrow in focus. However, s 24(5)(e) is extremely wide, and the police could fit almost any justification within this particular test.

The *Oxford English Dictionary* defines 'necessary' as 'indispensable, vital, essential or requisite'. But have the courts defined the power in this manner? In *R v Richardson*, the court said that the meaning of necessity was 'the ordinary English word'.[48] In *Graham v West Mercia Constabulary*,[49] the court outlined a test to satisfy the provision: 'did the arresting officer actually believe it was necessary to arrest the person in question for reasons set out in s 24(5), and if so, did [they] have reasonable grounds for that belief?'[50] The court is effectively saying that it needs to be necessary to arrest someone, and therefore the officer should have given some consideration to the alternatives to arrest. The level of consideration needed is low, as illustrated in *Re Alexander*[51] where the court said, '[I]t is necessary that [the officer] make some evaluation of the feasibility of achieving the object of the arrest by some alternative means.'[52] The level of evaluation is not very

---

48. [2011] 2 Cr App R1 at 62.
49. [2011] EWHC 4 (QB).
50. *ibid* at [56].
51. [2009] NIQB 20.
52. ibid 16.

high, and the court went on to say that if the officer believed that arrest was both 'practical and sensible', that would satisfy the necessity provision.[53]

This suggests that 'necessity', using its English meaning of 'indispensable or vital', has been diluted by the courts. The level to reach 'indispensable or vital' is a world away from 'practical and sensible'. Thus, in terms of the power of arrest, we are left with due process protections that effectively exist only in theory. In practice, the police have a wide power of arrest which they can use with little regard to the due process protections afforded by PACE 1984.

3.4 Custody: police powers and suspects' rights

The Custody Officer (CO) has the responsibility of deciding upon a suspect's arrival at the police station whether detention is necessary[54] to secure evidence or to obtain evidence by questioning. It was made clear in *Al Fayed v Commissioner of Police of the Metropolis (No 3)*[55] that this must be more than merely '*desirable or convenient*'. The CO is a senior officer, independent of the investigation and as such possesses what has been described as a quasi-judicial role. The CO can only be overruled by an officer of the rank of superintendent or above.

However, evidence suggests that the CO's role is not the quasi-independent, due process check and balance on police power that is intended in the legislation, and that the PACE provisions are now largely presentational.[56] As Kemp points out, the custody suite is police territory and is therefore subject to police priorities as well as the 'collegial ties' between COs and other officers[57] and the fear of being overruled by more senior officers. McKenzie[58] observed that the 'necessary' test was not a working rule, and that the CO was simply rubber-stamping approval for detention in almost all cases. McConville et al[59] similarly highlight the vast gap between regulation and practice. This could be attributed to increasingly dominant managerial influences within the police which have led to increased pressure on the CO to authorise detention.[60] Recently, Dehaghani[61] found that this problem is still persisting, with authorisation of detention routinely given and, in some cases, assisting the arresting officer in establishing grounds for detention. There also appears to have been some endorsement of this approach in

---

53. ibid 40.
54. PACE 1984, s 37(3).
55. [2004] EWCA Civ 1579.
56. R Dehaghani, 'Automatic authorisation: an exploration of the decision to detain in police custody' [2017] Crim LR 3, 187–202.
57. V Kemp, 'Authorising and reviewing detention: PACE safeguards in a digital age' [2020] Crim LR 7, 572–87.
58. I McKenzie, 'Helping the police with their enquiries: the necessity principle and voluntary attendance at the police station' [1990] Crim LR 22.
59. M McConville, A Sanders and R Leng, *The Case for the Prosecution* (Routledge, 1991).
60. Kemp (n 57).
61. Dehaghani (n 56).

the courts.[62] This general acceptance that suspects will be detained in the police station is nothing new and has plagued this area of law for over 30 years. In 1990, McKenzie concluded that the authorisation of detention was effectively a rubber-stamping exercise.[63] Ultimately, this due process safeguard is diluted by the working realities of police work that afford little attention to the safeguards provided by PACE 1984. This was emphasised by McConville et al who asked a CO if he would ever refuse detention. He said:

> No, probably not ... often the bloke is remonstrating saying it wasn't me, I haven't done it ... but I have to take into account the policeman's word, so I accept him [into custody] on what the policeman tells me.[64]

This highlights the fact that the CO does not have enough independence from the police. Johnston and Smith suggest there are three core issues that dilute the effectiveness of an 'independent' CO:[65]

(1) The arresting officer can influence the custody decision, despite the intention of the PACE framework to introduce independence and separation from the investigation.

(2) A lack of weight is given to the suspect's perspective.

(3) There is pressure on the CO to routinely authorise detention.

Much like the protections afforded to suspects regarding stop and search and arrest, protections regarding detention at the police station look good on paper, but the reality is that they are either (at best) diluted or at times ignored. The rules are presentational, rather than working rules. Simply put, the CO is not sufficiently independent from those officers who arrest and request detention at the police station.

The right to a defence lawyer

The suspect has a number of safeguards provided by PACE 1984 whilst in police detention. Arguably, none are more important than access to free and independent legal advice. Under s 58(1) of PACE 1984, 'a person arrested and held in custody in a police station or other premises shall be entitled, if he so requests, to consult with a solicitor privately at any time'. This is a major protection for those arrested, but the uptake of this free service is surprisingly low. Kemp[66] found that in 2018 only 48% of people requested legal advice, meaning that over half of suspects do not exercise this vital right. Skinns [67] suggested a number of reasons why this might be, including the age and ethnicity of the suspect, a distrust in lawyers and a belief that

---

62. *DPP v L* [1999] Crim LR 752; *Al Fayed v Commissioner of Police of the Metropolis (No 3)* [2004] EWCA Civ 1579; *Richardson v Chief Constable of West Midlands Police* [2011] EWHC 733 (QB); *Hayes v Chief Constable of Merseyside* [2011] EWCA Civ 911; *Hanningfield v Chief Constable of Essex* [2013] EWHC 243 (QB).

63. B Irving and I McKenzie, *Police Interrogation: The Effects of the Police and Criminal Evidence Act 1984* (The Police Foundation, 1989).

64. M McConville, J Hodgson, L Bridges and A Pavlovic, *Standing Accused* (Oxford: Clarendon, 1994) 44.

65. Johnston (n 1) 71.

66. Kemp (n 57).

67. L Skinns, 'The Right to Legal Advice in the Police Station: Past, Present and Future' [2011] Crim LR 19.

legal advice will slow down the process. There are also arguably some questions about the quality of advice. Cape[68] suggested that 15% of advice was by telephone only, and there remain high profile cases such as the 'Cardiff Three' case[69] where, despite having a lawyer present, the suspects were effectively bullied into a confession, with the protection of a lawyer making little practical difference to the outcome of the interview. McConville[70] also stated that due to low status and low pay, law firms encouraged a 'routinized' approach which potentially does little to protect the suspect in the police station.

3.5 The decision to charge and out-of-court disposals

3.5.1 Charging

In **Chapter 1**, we outlined that one of the prosecution's duties is to charge suspects, once the police believe they have enough evidence against the suspect. However, the working practices of the police meant that they effectively assumed the decision to charge in all but the most serious cases. In his *Review of the Criminal Courts*, Auld LJ made a recommendation that this decision ought to be transferred back to the CPS.[71] This recommendation was accepted, and the Criminal Justice Act 2003 introduced a practice of 'statutory charging'. This meant that the prosecution would be responsible for the decision to charge a suspect in all but the most minor of cases.[72] Again, this meant that there was a layer of independence between the police investigation and the charging stages of the criminal justice process. However, this was not to last long. In 2010, the Coalition Government believed that some charging decisions ought to be given back to the police in order to increase the efficiency of the system and reduce delays. As such, in 2013, the Director of Public Prosecutions released guidance on what types of offences the police would now be responsible for charging. The current position is outlined in the 6th edition of the guidance and states:[73]

> The police may charge:
> - Any summary only offence, irrespective of plea;
> - Any offence of retail theft (shoplifting) or attempted retail theft, irrespective of plea, provided it is suitable for sentence in the magistrates' court; and
> - Any either way offence anticipated as a guilty plea and suitable for sentencing in the magistrates' court.

---

68. L Bridges and E Cape, 'CDS Direct: Flying in the Face of the Evidence' (Centre for Crime and Justice Studies, 2008).
69. *R v Miller, Paris & Abdullahi* (1993) 97 Cr App R 99.
70. M McConville and J Hodgson, 'Custodial Legal Advice and the Right to Silence, the Royal Commission on Criminal Justice', Research Study No 10 (1993) 20.
71. Lord Justice Auld, *Review of the Criminal Courts of England and Wales* (The Auld Review) (Ministry of Justice, September 2001).
72. Criminal Justice Act 2003, s 28 and Sch 2.
73. See *Charging (The Director's Guidance)*, 6th edn, December 2020, Annex 1: www.cps.gov.uk/legal-guidance/charging-directors-guidance-sixth-edition-december-2020 (accessed 4 May 2021).

Provided that this is not:

- a case requiring the consent to prosecute of the DPP or a Law Officer;
- a case involving a death;
- connected with terrorist activities or official secrets;
- classified as a Hate Crime or Domestic Abuse;
- a case of harassment or stalking;
- an offence of Violent Disorder or Affray;
- causing Grievous Bodily Harm or Wounding, or Actual Bodily Harm;
- a Sexual Offences Act offence committed by or upon a person under 18;
- an offence under the Licensing Act 2003.

So, the police have a wide array of offences for which they can charge a suspect. However, it is important to note the reason why the prosecution, instead of the police, started charging suspects – to create a layer of independence between the differing stages of the criminal justice process. Is it possible that such independence exists if the police are responsible for the investigation and charging of the offence? We have highlighted above that the Custody Officer routinely follows police representations when officers seek authorisation to detain suspects in the police station. It is not unreasonable to question if the Custody Officer will take the same approach when making a decision to charge.

3.5.2 Out-of-court disposals

Government national statistics suggest that in the 12 months ending December 2019, 1.52 million individuals had been dealt with by the criminal justice system in England and Wales (excluding being cautioned).[74] Of that figure, 1.37 million people were prosecuted. What these figures tell us is that not everyone who has committed an offence will be prosecuted and tried at court. So how do we deal with those offenders?

The police have the power to dispose of a case in two different ways. They can offer a caution to the offender or give a penalty notice for disorder. Both of these resolutions are called 'out-of-court disposals'. They offer the police wide powers to end an incident with a punishment, but, as we will see, they are subject to few protections to guard against misuse.

Cautions

There are two types of caution that are available for the police to use: the simple caution and the conditional caution.

The simple caution

This is a disposal the police can use as a response to low-level offending. It would be unrealistic to think that every single criminal offence should be prosecuted, as this would be an inefficient use of resources that would undoubtedly clog up the

---

74. https://www.gov.uk/government/statistics/criminal-justice-system-statistics-quarterly-december-2019/criminal-justice-statistics-quarterly-december-2019-html#:~:text=.gov.uk.-,Main%20Points,latest%20year%20when%20excluding%20cautions (accessed 4 May 2021).

(already stretched) court system even further. As such, this efficient response applies to the least serious levels of offending. However, it is important to note that in order to give a caution, the officer needs to be satisfied that if the case went to trial, the Full Code Test would be satisfied. However, this poses quite a problem. As this is a low-level offence, it is highly unlikely that a full investigation would be carried out, so the officer would not have the full picture of facts to ensure the Full Code Test would be adequately satisfied. This is an example of a safeguard existing on paper, yet in reality being almost worthless. Furthermore, a caution would not be appropriate if the offender had been cautioned or convicted for the same offence within the previous two years.

When offering a caution, the officer needs to consider a number of different factors. The police can offer a caution for any summary only or triable either way offence. It would be rare for a caution to be given for an indictable-only offence.[75] Section 17 of the Criminal Justice and Courts Act 2015 governs the use of cautions and suggests that any cautioning decision will be impacted by the following factors:

- There must be an admission of guilt. Where there is not an admission of guilt from the offender, the caution cannot be offered as an inducement for the offender to admit their guilt.
- The seriousness of the offence. The more serious the offence, the more unlikely that a caution would be a suitable punishment.
- The age, mental well-being and previous criminal history of the offender.
- The impact on the victim.

Once these stages have been considered by the officer, they are free to issue a caution if it is a suitable response. Should the offender accept the caution, it is important to remember that this is not a criminal conviction, although there are a number of ramifications for those that accept a caution:

- Whilst it is not a conviction, the acceptance of a caution will be recorded on the offender's record. Therefore, should future offending take place, this could influence how the police deal with the person, in terms of the response to their offending.
- It could harm one's employment prospects. The caution is likely to show up on a Disclosure and Barring Service (DBS) check. Therefore, it may hinder an opportunity to gain employment.
- In the unlikely, although not unforeseeable, event that a caution is issued in relation to a sexual offence, the offender might be subject to registration on the Sex Offenders Register.
- Should the person ever go through the civil justice system, for example, the Family Court, the caution may be submitted in evidence against the person.
- Finally, the caution may have an impact on the person's travel. For example, certain countries might bar entry to a person with a caution.

---

75. Criminal Justice and Courts Act 2015, s 17(2) prohibits the police from offering a caution unless the CPS agrees that this is an appropriate response in the circumstances.

When being offered a caution, the person does not have to accept it. Should the person refuse the caution, it is likely they will be charged with the criminal offence and face trial – remember, in order to give a caution, the Full Code Test needs to be satisfied (in theory), so there will already be a realistic prospect of conviction.

The conditional caution

Should a simple caution not be suitable, the police can offer the offender a conditional caution. The criteria for issuing the conditional caution are the same as for issuing a simple caution. Again, the conditional caution is not a criminal conviction, although, as highlighted above, there are ramifications for acceptance. The Code of Practice for Adult Conditional Cautions[76] suggests that conditional cautions provide an opportunity:

- to offer a proportionate response to low-level offending;
- to make amends to the victims/local community;
- for offenders to engage with rehabilitative services;
- to punish the offender.

The conditional caution is essentially a caution with conditions attached. Should the conditions be adhered to, the offender will not face prosecution for their offending. The conditions applied to the caution can serve myriad purposes. These include the rehabilitation of the offender,[77] to make reparation for the offence[78] or to punish the offender.[79]

As we have seen, there is a wide range of offences that could result in an offender receiving a caution. However, these two responses are not the only form of out-of-court disposal. We will now look at penalty notices for disorder.

Penalty notices for disorder

In short, a penalty notice for disorder (PND) is a fine that is given to an offender by the police. This is often issued on the street by the police and is subjected to almost no oversight or scrutiny. These fines were introduced as a way to keep low-level offending out of both the police station and the court. The fines were introduced by the Criminal Justice and Police Act 2001 and came with two levels of fine. The lowest level of PND is £60 and can be given for trespassing on the railway, throwing stones at a train and littering, among other offences. The upper tier fine is £90 and can be issued for a wide range of offences, which raises questions about police accountability and how the police use their powers. However, in general, the majority of PNDs issued were for:

- being drunk and disorderly;
- possession of cannabis;
- retail theft under £100; and
- behaviour likely to cause harassment, alarm or distress.

---

76. Ministry of Justice, 2013.
77. Criminal Justice Act 2003, s 22(3)(a).
78. ibid, s 22(3)(b).
79. ibid, s 22(3)(c).

These offences made up 92% of all PNDs issued in 2019.[80] Johnston and Smith suggest that the use of PNDs allows the police to 'draw' people into the criminal justice system[81] and catch more 'criminals'. Perhaps a better way forward would be giving those who offend a warning, which would keep them out of the criminal justice system, rather than issuing a low-level fine that arguably provides no deterrence at all.

3.6 Conclusion

This chapter has analysed the law of both stop and search and arrest. It has illustrated that the level of suspicion to stop and search or arrest someone is relatively low and open to wide interpretation. Further, due process safeguards, which look adequate on paper, afford the suspect very little protection when transferred to the working practices of the police.

The little weight attached to due process safeguards is mirrored when considering detention at the police station. We saw that the Custody Officer routinely rubber-stamps detention, with little regard for the relevant test. Whilst the suspect has access to free and independent legal advice, we have seen that take-up of this vital safeguard is low.

Finally, we have seen that the police have a vast range of powers they can use to punish an offender without bringing the matter to the police station or the court. They can offer a caution (either simple or conditional) or issue a PND. Whichever route the police take, there is little scrutiny or oversight regarding the use of these powers. This leaves the police open to claims of misuse of power or being able to use their powers in a discriminatory manner. More oversight of decisions is required to ensure that the powers of the police are discharged both fairly and appropriately.

---

80. At the time of writing, the 2020 statistics have not been published. They were due to be published in Summer 2021. However, owing to the Covid-19 pandemic, there would be little value in analysing the statistics as the UK was in a state of national lockdown.
81. Johnston (n 1) 259.

4 Policing and Criminological Perspectives

4.1 Introduction

The police service stands out as a highly conspicuous part of the broader criminal justice system of England and Wales. The ever-present debate surrounding its form, function and deficiencies, combined with the newsworthiness of crime and crime control, and the popularity of 'police drama' as a centerpiece of mainstream entertainment, has kept policing 'front and centre' of much academic, political and public discussion. Following on from the previous chapter which explored police powers and the law, this chapter will explore some key criminological perspectives and critiques of policing that have featured prominently in this field. However, as a note of caution, it should be remembered that the breadth and volume of policing studies, as exemplified by the ever-evolving nature of the police service itself, cannot be captured succinctly. What follows here is a selective overview of the central features of the criminological terrain in this area; essential reading for those seeking to place the discussion of police powers in a broader, criminological context.

In thinking about both the *police*, and *policing*, it is important to remember that there is much diversity in its practice, organisation and in its people. Modern policing comprises a range of duties and priorities, is reliant upon its relationships with a vast range of services and stakeholders and is beset by many challenges and complexities.

4.2 Policing and social control

As has been outlined previously in this book (see **Chapter 2** – 'Actors and Responsibilities'), the police can, in very broad terms, be described as an institution or 'agent' of *social control*. In a basic sense, we can think of control perspectives as those in criminology which make particular assumptions about human nature (ie that, intrinsically, human beings are self-interested, impulsive and prone to disagreement) and as concerned with all processes through which order and stability is brought about. Social control, according to Cohen, refers to *'organised ways in which society responds to behaviour and people it regards as undesirable in one way or another'*,[1] and on this basis, it is easy to see why control perspectives are commonly associated with policing. Indeed, as Innes (2003) suggests, *'the concern of the state with social control is perhaps most visibly and dramatically embodied in the figure of the police officer'*.[2]

---

1. S Cohen, *Visions of Social Control: Crime, Punishment and Classification* (Polity, 1985) 1.
2. M Innes, *Understanding Social Control* (OUP, 2003) 63.

Control perspectives have made a significant contribution to criminological thinking and are firmly established as a prerequisite area for any student of the discipline.[3] Although there are many variations and interpretations of social control, many reorientate the central criminological question of 'why do people commit crime' and instead look to understand the reasons for which motivations, propensities and proclivities to crime and deviant behaviour are either suppressed or responded to. In effect, understanding those reasons why people *don't* commit crime commits one to an analysis of all processes which seek to produce conformity, or *social order*.[4] Of course, this can be achieved in many different ways, and it is not just an arrest (or threat of) or subsequent further action by the police that can be said to serve these ends.

Clearly, the task of maintaining or reproducing 'order' is not something that is the preserve of the police or other agents of the criminal justice system, and understanding how other institutions of social control (for example the family unit, religious structures or the education system) are also engaged in this endeavour helps us distinguish between 'the police' and '*policing*'. For instance, Jones and Newburn refer to policing as '*organised forms of order-maintenance, peace keeping, rule or law enforcement, crime investigation and prevention and other forms of investigation and information brokering*'.[5] While acknowledging the formal dimensions of the policing role (ie law enforcement, investigation), this definition also invites us to consider how a lot of what we understand to be 'policing' is in fact not performed by the police but by a range of other institutions. For example, through providing incentives and rewards for good behaviour, and sanctions and consequences for undesirable behaviour, it can be said that an extended family unit has particularly powerful tools for *policing* the conduct of its membership. Similarly, if certain standards or obligations are not met, many different forms of community are able to draw on the power of shame to regulate the activities of the broader group.[6] Those scholars that have sought to refine the concept of social control have suggested that distinctions can be drawn between either '*formal*' or '*informal*' social control, for instance suggesting that the former is based upon codified law.[7] Though, as Innes[8] suggests, this distinction seems unambiguous at first, a binary division of social control into 'either/or' denies the nuanced realities of criminal justice. For policing specifically, a vital element of police work relies upon the idea of *discretion*.

Discretion refers to the idea of using subjective judgement to apply one course of action to a situation from a list of possibilities. Of course, this is a feature of

---

3. Many criminological theory textbooks will summarise the work of influential theorists such as Walter Reckless, David Matza, Michael Gottfredson and Travis Hirschi amongst others. See for example T Newburn, *Criminology*, 3rd edn (Routledge, 2017) or D Downes and P Rock, *Understanding Deviance*, 6th edn (OUP, 2011).
4. Innes (n 2) 5.
5. T Jones and T Newburn, *Private Security and Public Policing* (OUP, 1998) 18.
6. J Braithwaite, *Crime, Shame and Reintegration* (Cambridge University Press, 1989).
7. D Black, *The Behaviour of Law* (Academic Press, 1976).
8. Innes (n 2).

everyday life in all professions, and police officers in undertaking their duties are no different. Police officers have lots of choices and decisions to make, including *where* and *how* to conduct their activities. Indeed, prioritising which of their immediate tasks are most pressing and important is a critical feature of the role. Quite simply, the police are unable to arrest and prosecute every criminal act that comes to their attention, and so making decisions about which acts are investigated, who is arrested, cautioned or charged with an offence and who is simply 'given advice' are inevitably linked to calls of judgement. Police discretion, defined by Walker and Katz as '*an official action based on that individual's judgement about the best course of action*',[9] is seen as an inevitable risk, yet a necessary and even desirable feature of police work.[10] Law requires interpretation (bad law even more so), and the exercise of discretion in policing allows for an element of 'common sense' to be built into police interactions, as a counterweight to a rigid and inflexible written framework. However, there are risks in making the application of law more 'human' as that carries with it human fallibilities and traits, bias and stereotyping.

Though the role of discretion is often best illustrated in 'everyday' policing scenarios, or incidents that may occur whilst on patrol (notoriously, the practice of stop and search, discussed later), these issues also impact the investigation of serious offences. Let us consider for instance the role of an investigator in the context of a rape investigation. As an area of law governed by the Sexual Offences Act 2003,[11] the investigation and prosecution of rape has attracted a significant amount of attention amidst concerns about low conviction rates,[12] victim care[13] and investigative standards.[14] As a notoriously complex offence, officers investigating rape and other sexual offences will undertake their work as directed by policy approaches and their training, though there are inevitably many points where decisions (eg about the sequencing of an investigation, evidence gathering, or the questioning of the parties involved) require officers to use their judgement.[15] Many scholars have argued that rape investigations continue to be impacted by the application of 'rape myths' by those conducting investigations.[16] 'Rape myths', defined by Lonsway and Fitzgerald as '*attitudes and beliefs that are generally false but are widely and persistently held …*',[17] have the propensity to

9.   S Walker and C Katz, *The Police in America*, 4th edn (McGraw-Hill, 2002) 246.
10. T Newburn and R Reiner, 'Policing and the Police' in M Maguire, R Morgan and R Reiner (eds), *The Oxford Handbook of Criminology*, 5th edn (OUP, 2012).
11. Sexual Offences Act 2003, s 1.
12. Victims Commissioner Annual Report 2019-20: https://s3-eu-west-2.amazonaws.com/victcomm2-prod-storage-119w3o4kq2z48/uploads/2020/07/Victims-Commissioners-Annual-Report-2019-20-with-hyperlinks.pdf (accessed 22 June 2021).
13. L Kelly, J Lovett and L Regan, 'A gap or a chasm? Attrition in reported rape cases' (Home Office Research Study 293, 2005).
14. Independent Police Complaints Commission, 'IPCC independent investigation into the Metropolitan police service's inquiry into allegations against John Worboys' (IPCC, 2010).
15. MK Dhami, S Lundrigan and S Thomas, 'Police Discretion in Rape Cases' (2020) 35(2) *Journal of police and criminal psychology* 157–69.
16. K Hohl and E Stanko, 'Complaints of rape and the criminal justice system: fresh evidence on the attrition problem in England and Wales' (2015) 12(3) *Eur J Criminol* 324–41.
17. KA Lonsway and LF Fitzgerald, 'Rape myths: In review' (1994) *Psychology of Women Quarterly* 134.

affect officers in their decision making,[18] which is illustrative of the fact that even in the most serious of cases, the application of the law is undertaken by police officers who are drawing on their experiences (both professional and personal) in addition to 'formal' legal processes and bequeathed powers.

It is important to consider the broader relationship between the police and society and recognise that there are many different approaches that can be taken. Here, it is important to highlight the difference between policing 'with' people and 'against' people.[19] The former can be associated with the principles of *community policing* and the notion of 'policing by consent', which can be traced back to the instructions issued to every new police officer upon the establishment of the Metropolitan Police in 1829. Amongst other things, the principles sought:

- 'To recognise always that the power of the police to fulfil their functions and duties is dependent on public approval of their existence, actions and behaviour and on their ability to secure and maintain public respect.' (Principle 2)
- 'To recognise always that to secure and maintain the respect and approval of the public means also the securing of the willing co-operation of the public in the task of securing observance of laws.' (Principle 3)
- 'To maintain at all times a relationship with the public that gives reality to the historic tradition that the police are the public and that the public are the police, the police being only members of the public who are paid to give full time attention to duties which are incumbent on every citizen in the interests of community welfare and existence.' (Principle 7)[20]

One common discussion question that is often posed as part of introductory classes on policing is to invite students to consider what they think would happen in the absence of a formalised 'Police Service'. While the discussion is always interesting, and guaranteed to produce a range of views, the outcome is usually a consensus view that that society would naturally find ways to regulate behaviour and respond to transgressions. This should not be surprising when considering that the establishment of organised policing is a relatively recent development, both in the context of England and Wales and elsewhere.[21] In their summary, Bowling and Foster suggest that, in the recent past, the police themselves have 'failed to understand that it is "policing" rather than "police" that is vital to social order'[22] and that over-emphasising the role of the police may create unrealistic expectations of them, as well as sidelining other mechanisms of social control (eg

---

18. B Hine and A Murphy, 'The influence of "High" vs. "Low" rape myth acceptance on police officers' judgements of victim and perpetrator responsibility, and rape authenticity' (2019) 60 *Journal of criminal justice* 100–107.
19. B Bowling and J Foster, 'Policing and the Police' in M Maguire, R Morgan and R Reiner (eds), *The Oxford Handbook of Criminology*, 3rd edn (OUP, 2002).
20. https://www.gov.uk/government/publications/policing-by-consent/definition-of-policing-by-consent (accessed 22 June 2021).
21. C Robinson and R Scaglion, 'The Origin and Evolution of the Police Function in Society' (1987) 21(1) *Law and Society Review* 35–49.
22. Bowling (n 19).

community-based approaches) that reside outside of the criminal justice system. Combined with the public and political appetite for 'control' and 'order',[23] the idea that the Police Service (and other criminal justice institutions) are given ever greater powers in pursuit of solving all our social problems is a central feature explored by David Garland in his influential work, 'The Culture of Control'.[24]

Nonetheless, the police are often seen by the public as an institution whose essential function is to exercise and deliver particular forms of social control. In recent research carried out by the Police Foundation,[25] when asked to rank policing priorities, the public tend to reaffirm the idea that it is crime fighting, public safety and the apprehension of criminals that should lie at the heart of the role, with items such as *'tackling sexual violence, abuse and rape'*, *'tackling knife crime and serious violence'* and *'responding quickly to public calls for urgent assistance'* ranking far higher than other responsibilities such as supporting victims, keeping those in custody safe or facilitating and participating in restorative justice schemes. It is understandable perhaps why the public perception of the role would seem to be fixed on the more exciting or 'crime-related' elements of the job, rather than the mundane or everyday elements such as administration, resolving neighbourhood disputes or taking part in uneventful patrols. On the latest evidence, it seems that public perceptions of the police as 'crime fighters' in the first instance continue to be influential. Whatever the form, Bittner's view of the police as an institution that is called upon fundamentally to provide the maintenance of social order remains a compelling vision: expected to intervene where *'something that should not be happening is happening and someone must do something about it now!'*.[26]

4.3 Models of policing

Of course, there are many ways of doing police work, and prevailing models are dependent on political and culturally relative factors; policing a democracy will take a different form to that exercised in a military dictatorship or totalitarian state. In the United Kingdom, it is possible to delineate between a number of specific approaches or 'models' of policing practice:

- *Community policing* refers to a philosophical approach to policing that sees the practice and policies of policing conducted in partnership with the community in which it operates. These approaches involve frequent opportunities for contact between officers and stakeholders and is based on the idea that

---

23. See the discussion around issues such as 'penal populism' in A Bottoms, 'The Politics of Sentencing Reform' in C Clarkson and R Morgan (eds), *The Philosophy and Politics of Punishment and Sentencing* (OUP, 1995).

24. D Garland, *The culture of control: crime and social order in contemporary society* (OUP, 2002).

25. A Higgins, 'Policing and the Public: Understanding Public Priorities, Attitudes and Expectations' (Police Foundation, 2019).

26. E Bittner, 'Florence Nightingale in Pursuit of Willie Sutton: A Theory of the Police' in H Jacobs (ed), *The Potential for Reform of Criminal Justice* (Sage, 1974), vol 3; now in E Bittner, *Aspects of Police Work* (Northeastern University Press, 1990) 249.

policing is embedded within communities, and that communities are active participants in policing.[27] Such an approach is synonymous with the Peelian principle of 'policing by consent'. Community policing carries an intrinsic appeal but has a mixed history of successful implementation.[28]

- *Problem-orientated* policing is considered a corollary of community approaches associated with the work of Herman Goldstein.[29] This approach involves the police taking a broader, more strategic approach to crime within communities and organising the response around *patterns and recurring themes*, rather than simply responding to discrete incidents of crime. Examples include focusing on 'hot spots' of crime (where multiple incidents happen in the same area) and work around patterns of offending and victimisation.

- *Intelligence-led* policing refers to a strategy of policing interventions that is precipitated by 'intelligence' – ie, information and data that allows for the effective deployment of resource. It strives to maximise performance and efficiency of resource. This approach is heavily invested in the new technologies of policing and how those technologies can be deployed for risk management and proactive security.[30]

Though not considered a model in the same sense as those listed above, recent years have seen an emphasis placed upon 'evidence-based policing', which sees the police working closely with academic and research partners to *'create, review and use the best available evidence to inform and challenge policing policies, practices and decisions'*.[31]

4.4 Police culture

Some of the most high-profile research that sits within the broad footprint of policing research is focused around the issue of police or 'cop' culture. The phrase 'cop culture' itself transcends the academic material and is perhaps familiar to a broader audience, even if, in its more general application, its usage is strained or misappropriated. As many others writing on this topic will set out, cultural accounts of policing are some of the earliest, and still most influential, in the field,

---

27. R Trojanowitz and B Bucqueroux, *Community Policing* (Anderson, 1998); N Tilley, 'Modern Approaches to Policing: Community, Problem Orientated and Intelligence-led Policing' in T Newburn (ed), *Handbook of Policing* (Willan, 2008).

28. J Skolnick and DB Bayley, *Community Policing: Issues and Practices around the World* (National Institute of Justice, 1988); JR Topping 2008, 'Community policing in Northern Ireland: a resistance narrative' (2008) 18(4) *Policing & Society* 377–96.

29. H Goldstein, *Problem-Orientated Policing* (McGraw-Hill, 1990).

30. P Manning, *The Technology of Policing: Crime Mapping, Information Technology, and the Rationality of Crime Control* (New York University Press, 2008); CB Sanders and S Hannem, 'Policing the "Risky": Technology and Surveillance in Everyday Patrol Work' (2012) 49 *Canadian Review of Sociology* 389–410.

31. UK College of Policing, 'What is evidence-based policing?': https://whatworks.college.police.uk/About/Pages/What-is-EBP.aspx (accessed 22 June 2021).

with the work of Banton,[32] Skolnick,[33] Van Maanen,[34] Cain,[35] Holdaway[36] and Reiner[37] (to recount just a few from a wide field) proving enduringly influential, and setting the context for many other studies which continue to apply some of the core principles of the early work to diverse and contemporary themes. These early works referred to were largely dependent on *ethnography*,[38] itself an extremely valuable approach to research that allows for a sustained immersion of the researcher into particular settings and for the observation of *'cultural groups in their natural settings over long periods of time'*.[39] In policing settings, generally inaccessible to outsiders, this often involved these early works being performed from the inside, sometimes covertly,[40] or under the auspices of undertaking training courses allowing a researcher a form of temporary, yet privileged access.

The understanding that all workplaces are defined and shaped by occupational culture(s) is a broadly accepted principle relevant to the sociology of all work.[41] For police officers, who are bound together in uniform, and set a collection of complex and sometimes daunting tasks, the development of an environment which offers both support and, potentially, solutions to the unique challenges collectively faced by its members, may lead to the development of a pervasive and particularly well-fortified form of occupational culture. Skolnick, in addressing some of the core characteristics of cop culture, emphasised three main elements: suspiciousness, internal solidarity/social isolation, and conservatism,[42] all of which were suggested as consequences and products of the challenges of the policing role.

Although, given the breadth of policing roles and contexts, there are clearly risks in generalising about police culture, it is still useful to consider it in broad terms. For Chan,[43] police culture is outlined as *'a layer of informal occupational norms and values operating under the rigid hierarchical structure of police organisations'*, whereas Reiner[44] suggests *'a patterned set of understandings that help officers cope with and adjust to the pressures and tensions confronting the police'*. Police/cop culture is an essential component of understanding the context in which officers make decisions and interpret the formal 'rules based' structures that define their

---

32. M Banton, *The policeman in the community* (Tavistock, 1964).

33. JH Skolnick, *Justice without trial: law enforcement in democratic society* (Macmillan, 1966).

34. J Van Maanen, *Observations on the Making of Policemen* (1973).

35. M Cain, *Society and the policeman's role* (Routledge, 1973)

36. S Holdaway, *Inside the British police: a force at work* (Blackwell, 1983).

37. R Reiner, *The politics of the police*, 3rd edn (OUP, 2000).

38. For an excellent discussion of the role of ethnography as applied to police culture, see F Cosgrove and P Francis, 'Ethnographic Research in the Context of Policing' in P Davies, P Francis and V Jupp (eds), *Doing Criminological Research* (Sage, 2011).

39. J Creswell, *Research design: Qualitative, quantitative and mixed methods approaches*, 2nd edn (Sage, 2003) 14.

40. S Holdaway, *The British Police* (Edwin Arnold, 1979).

41. TJ Watson, *Sociology, work and organisation*, 7th edn (Routledge, 2017).

42. Skolnick (n 33).

43. J Chan, *Changing Police Culture: Policing in a Multicultural Society* (Cambridge University Press, 1997) 43.

44. Reiner (n 37).

role, and essentially as a framework for considering what they are *really* doing as opposed to what outsiders may *think* they are doing.

In her analysis, Westmarland[45] points out that there are several reasons for studying police culture, with much of the focus revolving around the use of discretion. Whilst in an ideal world, officers would make decisions objectively and without bias, they will inevitably draw upon personal experiences and the practices embedded within their cultural environment and see those things as providing some parameters around which to base important decisions. It suggests of course that human (police officer) decisions are not made in a vacuum, and that the cultural environment of policing is therefore just as critical an element in understanding the application of policing as personally held opinions and bias; effectively how 'on the job socialisation'[46] explains officer behaviour. In the past, the prevalence of police culture has also been considered as a sizeable barrier to reform and change within the service itself.[47]

In joining the ranks of those whose works he described as 'ritualistically footnoted',[48] Robert Reiner's[49] work on police/cop culture provides seven distinctive features of the thesis:

(1) *Mission.* That police work goes beyond simply being 'a job' and that those tasked with it see it as having a more profound purpose for the good of society.

(2) *Suspicion.* A distinctive and defining facet of the policing role.

(3) *Isolation/Solidarity.* A sense of separation from the rest of society as an inevitable consequence of their role as *policing* others. Officers will develop close relationships with other officers as a result of shared experiences and occupational challenges, supporting and 'having each other's backs', sometimes in the face of public hostility.

(4) *Conservatism.* Seeing 'keeping order' as equivalent to 'keeping things the same'.

(5) *Machismo.* That traditional policing roles are synonymous with masculine values. The work is dangerous, exciting, and it requires brave and physically strong (male) officers. This element of the culture has potential consequences for women both inside the police (ie, officers themselves) and the *policing of* women.

(6) *Pragmatism.* Associated with a realistic and 'matter of fact' attitude.

(7) *Racial Prejudice.* That the evidence of racial prejudice within policing practice is compelling enough to include this as part of the culture itself.

---

45. L Westmarland, 'Police Cultures' in T Newburn (ed), *Handbook of Policing* (Willan, 2008).
46. H Campeau, 'Police Culture at Work: Making Sense of Police Oversight' (2015) 55(4) *British Journal of Criminology* 669–87.
47. Reiner (n 37).
48. R Reiner, 'Revisiting the Classics: Three Seminal Founders of the Study of Policing: Michael Banton, Jerome Skolnick and Egon Bittner' (2015) 25(3) *Policing & Society* 308–27.
49. Reiner (n 37).

For Reiner[50] and others,[51] storytelling and canteen culture serve as powerful mechanisms through which the culture is maintained and the process by which many new officers become familiar with the values and work-arounds embedded within. A glance at the composite elements offered by Reiner provides some clear causes for concern (notably around machismo/sexism and racial prejudice) and, accordingly, it is easy to see why the framework of police culture has been used as a lens through which to explore many problematic elements of policing. That said, it is also important to acknowledge that a tight-knit and supportive culture may bring some benefits, such as enabling police officers to cope with the pressures of the role. For instance, Waddington suggests that rather than seeing police culture as unambiguously malign, researchers need to exercise caution in interpreting 'canteen culture', suggesting that *what occurs is expressive talk designed to give purpose and meaning to inherently problematic occupational experience*.[52]

Much has been made of the 'macho' elements of the police role and its effects on those inside the culture as well as those to which policing is applied. A gendered analysis of police culture has been fixed on exploring the impact of masculinity, and indeed the specific experiences of women as police officers and as a social group *in receipt of policing*.[53] Reflecting broader patterns in society, the history of policing is certainly one which has seen women at the margins. As Martin put it:

> The incursion of women into traditionally 'male' occupations has been opposed, resisted and undermined wherever it has occurred. In few other occupations, however, has their entry been more vigorously fought – on legal, organisational, informal, and interpersonal levels – than in policing.[54]

Though policing has become more representative in recent years thanks to a raft of equality initiatives, the latest evidence showing that women make up 31% of police officers in England and Wales[55] demonstrates that policing can still be viewed as a predominantly male occupation. For women working within this environment, studies have revealed experiences of discrimination and harassment,[56] which have seen female officers adopt a range of coping strategies.[57] Similarly, the police culture thesis has provided a lens through which the

50. R Reiner, *The politics of the police*, 4th edn (OUP, 2010).

51. C Shearing and R Ericson, 'Culture as figurative action' (1991) 42(4) *British Journal of Sociology* 481–506; see also MJ van Hulst, 'Storytelling at the Police Station: The Canteen Culture Revisited' (2013) 53(4) *British Journal of Criminology* 624–42.

52. P Waddington, 'Police (canteen) sub-culture. An appreciation' (1999) 39(2) *British Journal of Criminology*, 287–309 at 287.

53. F Heidensohn, *Women in control?: The role of women in law enforcement* (OUP, 1992).

54. SE Martin, *Breaking and Entering: Policewomen on Patrol* (University of California, 1980) 79.

55. Home Office, 'Police Workforce': https://assets.publishing.service.gov.uk/government/uploads/system/uploads/attachment_data/file/955182/police-workforce-mar20-hosb2020.pdf (accessed 22 June 2021).

56. E Cunningham and P Ramshaw, 'Twenty-three women officers' experiences of policing in England: The same old story or a different story?' (2020) 22(1) *International Journal of Police Science & Management* 26–37.

57. J Brown and F Heidensohn, *Gender and Policing* (Palgrave Macmillan, 2000).

experiences of LGBT[58] officers, and officers from minority backgrounds, may be studied.[59] [60]

Although it is clear that cultural accounts remain hugely influential, some other caveats also need to be noted. It must be recognised that many of the classic studies fail to capture the range of different roles and specialist environments that define modern policing. Speaking of one homogenous culture in a world of different policing styles and models, specialisms, jurisdictions and political contexts has its obvious shortcomings, and accordingly the field of cop culture has been criticised in the past for its lack of development and failure to acknowledge the nuances of policing.[61] However, Reiner and others have pointed out that the police culture thesis was not meant to be 'monolithic' or universal even if presented as such by others. It follows that variations within forces have been discerned, with differences being observed between managers and street level officers,[62] between different police forces,[63] and naturally between individuals whose experiences will be shaped by social and demographic factors. With contemporary studies of police culture now examining it across an even broader range of policing contexts, there is an interesting debate to be had about whether the old thesis (or at least elements of it) present an enduring truth about policing,[64] or whether indeed things are changing.[65]

As the above discussion illustrates, the field of police culture is broad and encompasses a wide range of themes and subtexts. Of all the notable features of the police culture thesis, it is worth exploring one element in more detail here – racial prejudice.

4.5 Ethnicity, race and racism

In England and Wales, as is the case in many jurisdictions around the world, the relationship between the police and black, Asian and minority communities has been historically complex and fraught with difficulties. Characterised by mistrust and punctuated by a series of notorious failings, the nature of this relationship remains a focal concern. As has been outlined, the police role involves the discharge of some significant responsibilities, whether this is through providing

58. M Jones and ML Williams, 'Twenty years on: lesbian, gay and bisexual police officers' experiences of workplace discrimination in England and Wales' (2015) 25(2) *Policing & Society* 188–211.

59. ME Hollis, 'Accessing the experiences of female and minority police officers: Observations from an ethnographic researcher' in K Lumsden and A Winter (eds), *Reflexivity in Criminological Research* (Palgrave Macmillan, 2014) 150–61.

60. S Holdaway, 'Responding to racialized divisions within the workforce – the experience of black and Asian police officers in England' (1997) 20(1) *Ethnic and racial studies* 69–90.

61. J Chan, 'Changing police culture' (1996) 36 *British Journal of Criminology* 100–34.

62. ER Ianni and F Ianni, 'Street Cops and Management Cops: The Two Cultures of Policing' in M Punch (ed), *Control in the Police Organization* (MIT Press, 1983).

63. B Loftus, *Police Culture in a Changing World* (OUP, 2009).

64. B Loftus, 'Police occupational culture: classic themes, altered times' (2010) 20(1) *Policing & Society* 1–20.

65. N Caveney, P Scott, S Williams and L Howe-Walsh, 'Police reform, austerity and "cop culture": time to change the record?' (2020) 30(10) *Policing & Society* 1210–25.

robust responses to public order issues, the effective investigating of criminal behaviour, providing victim care or engaging communities more broadly in issues of public safety. Whatever model of policing is deployed, most rely on public trust and can only be carried out effectively if considered as a legitimate action. Whilst levels of trust and confidence in the police can vary across society and in all groups, it is in minority communities where these deficits have been most prominently explored. In a recent poll, it was found that two thirds of those from a minority background believed the police are biased against them, with that proportion rising to 80% of black British respondents.[66] Set against a backdrop where the general risk of becoming a victim of crime is higher for those from the non-white population,[67] and where research on homicide rates evidence that the rate of victimisation is as much as 5.6 times higher for black people than their white counterparts in England and Wales (and with Asian rates twice as high as White rates[68]), issues of unequal treatment, bias and (institutional) racism continue to present themselves as critical challenges.

Though a complete analysis of the history of relations between the police and minority communities is beyond the scope of what can be covered here, there are notable developments that help frame the issue over the past decades. Following the economic policies that encouraged extensive immigration from the former colonies and the subsequent establishment of sizeable black communities in the UK, tensions emerged in the 1970s that saw black people more readily linked with crime in public and media discourse. For writers such as Stuart Hall, fear of crime and the disproportionate framing of black criminality (specifically the 'black mugger') amounted to a 'moral panic' that further contributed to a deterioration of community relations between black communities and the police.[69] In reflecting on the development of this relationship, Smith suggests that *'bias against black people specifically in law enforcement and criminal justice process seems like the counterpart to a growing tendency from the late 1970s onwards for young black people to define their identity in opposition to the central structures of authority in British society, most notably the police'.*[70]

The 1981 Brixton riots resulted in the *Scarman Report*,[71] which drew attention to the excessive use of stop and search strategies responsible for exacerbating

66. Hope not Hate, 'Minority Communities in the Time of Covid and Protest: A Study of BAME Opinion' (2020): https://www.hopenothate.org.uk/wp-content/uploads/2020/08/BAME-report-2020-08-v3-00000003.pdf (accessed 22 June 2021).
67. Office for National Statistics (ONS), 'Crime in England and Wales: Annual Trend and Demographic Tables': https://www.ons.gov.uk/peoplepopulationandcommunity/crimeandjustice/datasets/crimeinenglandandwalesannualtrendanddemographictables (accessed 22 June 2021).
68. S Kumar, LW Sherman and H Strang, 'Racial Disparities in Homicide Victimisation Rates: How to Improve Transparency by the Office of National Statistics in England and Wales' (2020) 4 *Camb Journal of Evidence Based Policy* 178–86.
69. S Hall, C Critcher and T Jefferson, *Policing the crisis: mugging, the state and law and order* (Macmillan-Winthrop, 1978).
70. DJ Smith, 'Ethnic Origins, Crime, Criminal Justice' in M Maguire, R Morgan and R Reiner (eds), *The Oxford Handbook of Criminology* (OUP, 1997) 753.
71. Lord Scarman, *The Scarman report: the Brixton disorders 10–12 April 1981* (Penguin, 1982).

tension, and, years later, the racist murder of Stephen Lawrence in 1993 led to a Judicial Inquiry and the publication on 24 February 1999 of the *Macpherson Report*.[72] The police investigation into the murder of Stephen Lawrence, who was stabbed to death in a racially motivated attack at a bus-stop by a group of young white men, was found to be grossly deficient, professionally incompetent and marred by institutional racism, a concept which has taken centre stage in conversations about race and justice ever since:

> 'Institutional Racism' consists of the collective failure of an organisation to provide an appropriate and professional service to people because of their colour, culture or ethnic origin. It can be seen or detected in processes, attitudes and behaviour which amount to discrimination through unwitting prejudice, ignorance, thoughtlessness, and racist stereotyping which disadvantage minority ethnic people.[73]

Notably, the definition of institutional racism offered by Macpherson sought to distinguish itself from the more general concept of racism that relates to the actions, thoughts and behaviours of individual officers towards individuals from minority backgrounds and sought to focus on more subtle and collective practices. In his report, Macpherson found institutional racism to be apparent in several areas of police practice: failures of police training in issues relating to diversity, failures to address the lack of confidence minority communities have in the police leading to the under-reporting of 'racial incidents', and the disparity in stop and search figures between black people and white people. Resultantly, and with 'Institutional Racism' featuring as a 'potent mobilising concept,'[74] the *Macpherson Report* (featuring no less than 70 recommendations) was a catalyst for a comprehensive programme of reform that sought to address issues of trust and confidence between the police and minority communities in the years ahead. More than 20 years later, and following the publication of the *Lammy Review*[75] and the *Report of the Commission on Race and Ethnic Disparities*,[76] the issues of over-representation and disproportionality in the criminal justice system continue to present themselves as significant challenges giving rise to new recommendations. Today, as was the case 20 years ago, stop and search practices are identified as particularly contentious for a black community described as 'over-policed and under-protected'.[77]

---

72. W Macpherson, 'The Stephen Lawrence Inquiry, Report of an Inquiry by Sir William Macpherson of Cluny' (Cm 4262-I, 1999).

73. ibid para 6.34.

74. A Souhami, 'Institutional racism and police reform: an empirical critique' (2014) 24(1) *Policing & Society* 1.

75. D Lammy, 'The Lammy Review: An independent review into the treatment of, and outcomes for, Black, Asian and Minority Ethnic individuals in the Criminal Justice System' (2017).

76. Commission on Race and Ethnic Disparities, 'The Report' (2021) https://assets.publishing.service.gov.uk/government/uploads/system/uploads/attachment_data/file/974507/20210331_-_CRED_Report_-_FINAL_-_Web_Accessible.pdf (accessed 22 June 2021).

77. Macpherson (n 72) para 45.7.

4.6 Stop and search

In England and Wales, the law relating to stop and search, as enacted in the Police and Criminal Evidence Act 1984 (PACE),[78] has been covered in **Chapter 3**. Though the majority of stops and searches are conducted in accordance with PACE, which requires the element of reasonable suspicion on the part of the officer, other police powers (albeit less commonly exercised), such as those contained in the Criminal Justice and Public Order Act 1994,[79] allow for conditions in which a stop and search may be performed without this requirement.[80] Whether the reasonable suspicion requirement, important for preventing a theoretical abuse of police power, is applied or not, it is difficult to completely disentangle the decision of an officer to perform a stop and search from discretionary decision making. Stop and search has been appropriately described as '*one of the most common forms of adversarial contact between the police and public*',[81] an adversarialism that is perhaps definitive of the experience of many people from minority backgrounds as a glance at the most recent data for England and Wales evidences. Between April 2019 and March 2020:

- there were 6 stops and searches per 1,000 White people, compared with 54 per 1,000 Black people;[82]
- there were 16 stops and searches per 1,000 people with Mixed ethnicity, and 15 per 1,000 Asian people;[83]
- the three Black ethnic groups had the highest rates of stop and search out of all 18 individual ethnic groups;[84]
- the 'Black Other' group had the highest rate overall with 157 stops and searches per 1,000 people – this group includes people who did not identify as Black African or Black Caribbean, or were not recorded as such;[85]
- there were 71 stops and searches per 1,000 Black people in London, compared with 28 per 1,000 Black people in the rest of England and Wales.[86]

This latest evidence of disproportionality is a continuation of the narrative that has persisted in every data release for the last 30 years, though it should also be stated that rates of stop and search have been falling since 2009 for every ethnic group. Of course, there are some limitations to assessing the official figures on stop and search, for the data itself cannot tell you *why* these differences are observed. As

---

78. Police and Criminal Evidence Act 1984, ss 1–3.
79. Criminal Justice and Public Order Act 1994, s 60.
80. Section 60 of the Criminal Justice and Public Order Act 1994, for instance, allows for a stop and search of any pedestrian without the requirement of reasonable suspicion, though for a limited duration and within a limited geographical area.
81. R Delsol and M Shiner, 'Introduction' in R Delsol and M Shiner (eds), *Stop and search: the anatomy of a police power* (Palgrave Macmillan, 2015) 1.
82. 'Stop and Search': https://www.ethnicity-facts-figures.service.gov.uk/crime-justice-and-the-law/policing/stop-and-search/latest (accessed 22 June 2021).
83. ibid.
84. ibid.
85. ibid.
86. ibid.

Quinton and others have emphasised,[87] the data *can* be explained by racism and discrimination, though that involves certain *assumptions* being made about police decision making. Nonetheless, the statistical disparities are still problematic in that they do provide clear evidence of a greater degree of police contact with those from minority backgrounds. This is important when considering issues such as community relations and also because stop and search can be a precursor to arrest and other sanctions which see people travelling further into the criminal justice system.

Research on stop and search has found that several factors can be implicated in disproportionality. One such perspective relates to the notion of 'availability' and suggests that a young, black demographic is more susceptible to stop and search because this group is more likely to be present in the urban street environment where typically most stops are conducted.[88] Therefore, the social economic structures which see a concentration of ethnic minority communities in high density urban environments (for Reiner, a source of *situational discrimination*[89]) may contribute to an understanding of the figures. However, choices about how locations are chosen and where stop and search is targeted may themselves be driven by discrimination or bias.

British Asians are also impacted by disproportionality and are stopped and searched at higher rates than to be expected for their representation in the broader population. The now defunct s 44 of the Terrorism Act 2000 which allowed for stop and search to be conducted without the requirement of reasonable suspicion was implicated in the criminalisation of Asian-Muslim men,[90] and as part of a broader umbrella of police practices linked to counter-terrorism that established British Muslims as a 'suspect community'.[91] Whilst s 44 can no longer be used in this way, its legacy is illustrative of the way in which the practice of stop and search can feature as part of a constellation of discriminatory practices that define the relationship between the police and minority communities as one lacking in trust. With the clear potential for stop and search practices to '*drain trust in the CJS as a whole*',[92] it will be essential for the police to assess their use and impact on minority communities in the future. This is especially so, perhaps, when the criminological research has called into question the usefulness of stop and search as an effective tactic to control and deter crime.[93]

---

87. P Quinton, 'Race Disproportionality and Officer Decision Making' in R Delsol and M Shiner (eds), *Stop and search: the anatomy of a police power* (Palgrave Macmillan, 2015).
88. MVA Consultancy and J Miller, 'Profiling Populations Available for Stops and Searches' (Home Office, 2000); PAJ Waddington, K Stenson and D Don, 'In Proportion: Race and Police Stop and Search' (2004) 44(6) *British Journal of Criminology* 889–914.
89. Reiner (n 50).
90. A Parmar, 'Stop and search in London: counter-terrorist or counter-productive?' (2011) 21(4) *Policing & Society* 369–82.
91. C Pantazis and S Pemberton, 'From the "Old" to the "New" Suspect Community: Examining the Impacts of Recent UK Counter-Terrorist Legislation' (2009) 49(5) *British Journal of Criminology* 646–66.
92. Lammy (n 75) 18.
93. M Tiratelli, P Quinton and B Bradford, 'Does Stop and Search Deter Crime? Evidence From Ten Years of London-wide Data' (2018) 58(5) *British Journal of Criminology* 1212–31.

4.7 Conclusion

This chapter has offered an overview of the main themes commonly explored in criminological assessments of policing, highlighting the role of the police in providing a form of *social control*, and the models through which this can be delivered. It is clear that a range of complex challenges are implicated in police work, with the resultant pressure helping create a particular *police culture* which can in turn be used as a lens to explore many elements of practice.

STUDY QUESTIONS

- What do you understand to be the difference between 'police' and 'policing'?
- What are 'models of policing'? Can you think of strengths and weaknesses for those models discussed in this chapter?
- Why is discretion an important concept in policing?
- What do you understand by the term 'police culture'? What are its core elements?
- How would you describe the relationship between the police and ethnic minority communities in the United Kingdom?

5 Understanding Violent Crimes: The Law

5.1 Introduction

Criminal Law is likely to be one of the fundamental modules you will study on your Criminology and Law course. In this chapter, we will touch upon some of the guiding principles needed to convict a defendant of a crime and look at a number of offences. The offences covered in this chapter fall under the umbrella of 'offences against the person'. This generally means that an act will have been carried out by one person against another.

We have shown (in **Chapter 1**) that in order to successfully convict a defendant, the prosecution must discharge the burden of proof. In short, this means that the prosecution must prove that the defendant committed the alleged offence, and disprove any defences raised by the defendant, 'beyond reasonable doubt'. This is known as the 'Golden Rule' or 'golden thread' of criminal prosecution. It is best summarised by Viscount Sankey LC in *Woolmington v DPP*,[1] where he said: 'Throughout the web of the English Criminal Law one golden thread is always to be seen, that it is the duty of the prosecution to prove the prisoner's guilt.' This is an important rule; it ensures that the defendant is 'innocent until proven guilty' – a right which is a fundamental human right.[2] Generally speaking, it will always be for the prosecution to prove the guilt of the defendant beyond a reasonable doubt. 'Beyond reasonable doubt' is the 'standard' of proof in criminal law – that is the standard the prosecution has to satisfy before someone can be convicted. This is rather a high burden – if a judge, jury or magistrate was satisfied only that it was 'highly likely' that the defendant committed the alleged offence, the standard of proof would not be satisfied and the defendant would be acquitted.

In certain circumstances, a defendant might wish to run a particular defence. The defendant will bear an evidential burden to provide evidence to make an issue live, but they are not required to prove the defence. It remains for the prosecution to disprove a defence. However, a reverse burden exists in respect of certain defences, eg diminished responsibility (see **5.8.3**). In that instance, the standard of proof for the reverse burden is 'on the balance of probabilities'. In real terms, this means a greater than 50% chance of being true – so a far less onerous burden than 'beyond reasonable doubt'.

---

1.   [1935] AC 462.
2.   European Convention on Human Rights, Article 6(2).

5.2 Elements of an offence

Before we look at the specific violent offences, we need to discuss how a defendant can be found guilty of a crime. In order to be convicted, the prosecution has to establish three core elements to an offence:

(1) the *actus reus*
(2) the *mens rea*
(3) the absence of a defence.

5.2.1 *Actus reus*

In *Haughton v Smith*[3] it was held that a man cannot be guilty of a crime unless he has a guilty mind. In a nutshell, this means that it is not merely enough to do a guilty act; there must be a guilty state of mind behind it. When establishing the *actus reus*, the prosecution is effectively establishing that the defendant committed the physical element of the crime. However, not all crimes require a physical act, and Thomas provides a useful summary as to what might amount to the *actus reus* of a particular crime:[4]

* acts
* conduct
* omissions
* consequences
* surrounding circumstances
* state of affairs.

5.2.2 *Mens rea*

This is often referred to as the guilty mind, for example, the intention of the defendant. Much like the *actus reus*, it would be far too narrow to simply suggest that the defendant needs to intend to carry out the act. There are a number of ways in which a defendant may satisfy the *mens rea* of an offence, including:

* intention
* foreseeability
* recklessness
* negligence.

The elements of an offence will dictate which form of *mens rea* is capable of satisfying the definition of the offence, and thus discharge the prosecution's burden of proof

5.2.3 Defences

In order for a defendant to be convicted of a crime, there needs to be the absence of a defence. In general, if the defendant can raise sufficient evidence of a defence, such that the prosecution is unable to disprove that defence, the defendant's

---

3.   [1975] AC 476.
4.   M Thomas, *Criminal Law*, 2nd edn (Hall and Stott, 2020) 23.

liability may either be absolved entirely, or reduced to a lesser crime. There are three types of defences that a defendant can run:

(1) *Complete defence* – this is a full and complete defence. An example of this would be that the defendant acted in self-defence, which would mean that their conduct was not unlawful and the court would return a 'not guilty' verdict.

(2) *Partial defence* – the defendant is still culpable for an offence but the charge will be reduced. An example of this would be loss of self-control, which if successfully pleaded would allow the defendant to be convicted of manslaughter rather than murder.

(3) *Special defence* – these are defences applying only to certain offences. Diminished responsibility is a good example of such a defence, which applies only to murder. Here, the defendant has a recognised medical condition that impairs their ability to form a rational judgement.

So, these are the issues that the prosecution has to overcome in order to successfully convict a defendant at trial. Now, we will examine offences against the person in more detail

5.3 Offences against the person – introduction

Whilst we cannot cover every criminal law offence that you will encounter on your criminal law module, we have decided to look at offences against the person by way of introduction. The following sections will explain the legal principles of each offence, what elements of the offence the prosecution is required to prove beyond reasonable doubt, and leading case authorities so you can support your arguments. As discussed in the introduction, every point or argument you make requires a supporting authority. This means you will need to reference, *inter alia* ('among other things'), a case, statute, academic article, book or government study to support your answer. This section will outline the elements of a particular offence and consider some of the leading cases in that particular area.

5.4 Common assault

Common assault is the collective term to describe the two separate offences of assault and battery – the lowest level of violent offences a person can commit against another. These offences are charged under s 39 of the Criminal Justice Act 1988 and carry a maximum sentence of six months in prison. This means that such cases will be heard in the magistrates' court as the maximum sentence is within the sentencing powers of the magistrate. Whilst we say that these offences are of the 'lowest level', they can have a huge impact on the victim. Goff LJ made a distinction between the offences when he defined them as follows: 'An assault is an act which causes another person to apprehend the infliction of immediate, unlawful force on his person; a battery is the actual infliction of unlawful force on another person.'[5]

---

5. *Collins v Wilcock* [1984] 3 All ER 374.

When we think of common assault, we will generally assume that it is one person hitting another in some form of altercation. That would clearly meet Goff LJ's definition of the offence as the victim will apprehend the infliction of immediate, unlawful force (assault – for example when you see the punch coming) and the battery will be the actual infliction of the punch. However, a defendant can be guilty of this offence without physically coming into contact with another person. In *Fagan v Commissioner of Police for the Metropolis*,[6] the defendant was sat in his car when a police officer came up to him and told him to move the vehicle elsewhere. The defendant then reversed his car and accidentally rolled it onto the officer's foot. Unsurprisingly, the officer (very forcefully) told him to remove the car from his foot immediately. The defendant then proceeded to swear at the officer and turned the engine off, leaving the car on the officer's foot. The defendant was convicted of battery and appealed against his conviction. On appeal, the defendant's argument centred on the fact there could not be an offence because he omitted to act, ie move the car when told, and therefore he was lacking the requisite *mens rea* (or intention) when the incident occurred. The court agreed that there needed to be a physical act and ultimately that the act could not be committed by omission (or failing to act). However, the court said that when the defendant refused to move the car from the officer's foot, that established a continuing act of battery and therefore his appeal was dismissed.

Whilst this case indicates that physical harm is required to satisfy the courts, what is the position if the harm is psychological rather than physical? *R v Ireland and Burstow*[7] provides the answer. In *Ireland*, the defendant and the victim were previously involved in a short romantic relationship which was ended by the victim. Upon hearing the news of the break-up, the defendant was unhappy and began to harass the victim over the course of several months. This harassment included making silent phone calls, sending the victim hate mail, and appearing unexpectedly, all of which the victim said caused her psychiatric injury. The question for the court was whether or not psychiatric injury could be classified as bodily harm. The court answered in the affirmative and the defendant was convicted of assault. The court held that there was 'no reason why something said should be incapable of causing an apprehension' and that words (or silence, as in *Ireland*) can suffice to cause immediate personal violence.

So far we have mentioned the word 'apprehend' in our case law analysis, but can an assault be committed when there is no apprehension of violence, eg the other person does not expect the violence to arise? The short answer is no; the complainant must expect the violence to come, and the leading case on this topic is the very sad case of *R v Lamb*.[8] Here, two young friends were messing around and playing a game of Russian roulette with a gun. They knew it was loaded but did not believe that the bullet was in the firing chamber. They did not realise that by firing the gun, the chamber would rotate. Whilst joking, the defendant pointed the gun at

6. [1969] 1 QB 439.
7. [1998] AC 147.
8. [1967] 2 QB 981.

the victim and pulled the trigger. Unbeknownst to the defendant and victim, the chamber was indeed loaded and the victim was killed. The defendant appealed against his conviction, arguing that there was no *actus reus* present for the offence as neither child thought the chamber was loaded and therefore there was no apprehension on the part of the victim. The Court of Appeal agreed and the conviction was quashed. So, for a defendant to be found guilty of this offence, it is imperative that the victim expected the unlawful violence to come.

5.4.1 Assault

In order to be convicted of assault, the *actus reus* and *mens rea* need to be present, and these elements can be broken down as follows:

Actus reus

- *The act.* Something needs to be done to another.
- *Apprehend.* The victim needs to think they are in danger, although the likelihood of that danger manifesting itself is not relevant.
- *Immediate.* The apprehension of the assault needs to happen soon, but it does not need to be an instantaneous threat. Standing outside someone's home and threatening them through the window is sufficiently immediate, even if the defendant would have to gain entry to a locked home to assault the victim.[9] For this reason, it is often said that the apprehension should be 'imminent'.
- *Unlawful personal violence.* Something is inflicted upon another which they did not consent to. However, it is only the anticipation that matters.

Mens rea

The *mens rea* of assault is intention to cause the victim to apprehend unlawful personal violence or being reckless as to whether such apprehension is caused.[10]

If intention cannot be shown, it will be enough if the prosecution can prove that the defendant was reckless in their conduct as to whether such apprehension would be caused. This test is laid out in the case of *R v Cunningham*,[11] where the court provided a two-limb test for recklessness. The defendant would be said to have been reckless if:

- the defendant foresaw the possibility that the victim would apprehend immediate and unlawful violence; and
- the defendant took that risk anyway.

Cunningham recklessness provides something of a safety net for the prosecution. It allows it to charge defendants who did not intend to cause any harm but nevertheless took a risk in doing so, regardless of the consequences.

9. *Smith v Chief Superintendent of Woking Police Station* (1983) 76 Cr App R 234.
10. *Fagan v MPC* [1969] 1 QB 439.
11. [1957] 2 QB 396.

5.4.2 Battery

Whereas assault rests on the notion of 'apprehension', the offence of battery requires the actual infliction of unlawful force. The seminal case that defines the offence is *R v Williams (Gladstone)*,[12] where Lord Lane CJ defined the offence as 'an act by which the defendant, intentionally or recklessly, applies unlawful force to the complainant [or victim]'. Again, we can cite the case of *Collins v Wilcock*,[13] where the court held that the merest touch might amount to a battery. However, this touch needs to go 'beyond generally acceptable standards of conduct'.[14] This means that if you are on a packed underground platform waiting for a tube, a slight bump into a stranger is unlikely to amount to a battery. However, it is important to note that any touching that goes beyond our acceptable standards of conduct does not need to be hostile or aggressive.[15]

The force used to commit a battery can be direct or indirect. An example of direct force would be the defendant punching or touching the victim and, generally, it will be pretty clear where direct force has been used. Indirect force is a little more opaque. In *R v Clarence*,[16] Stephen J commented:

> If a man laid a trap for another into which he fell …, the man who laid it would … be guilty of … an assault as soon as the man fell in.

In essence, the court needs to be certain that the defendant has taken an action to apply force to the victim, even if this was indirectly applied. To make this point clearer, here are a few further examples. In *R v Martin*[17] a man placed a bar across the exit door of a theatre, turned out the lights to the exit, and shouted 'fire!', resulting in the injury of several members of the audience. The defendant was convicted of battery. In *DPP v K (a Minor)*[18] a schoolboy tipped acid into a bathroom hand dryer in order to conceal the theft of the acid from a teacher. The air nozzle was pointing up and when the next pupil used the dryer, the acid was squirted in his face, causing permanent scarring.

Much like assault, the offence of battery cannot generally be committed by an omission – it requires a positive act, ie the defendant has to do something to harm the victim; they cannot do nothing. In *DPP v Santana-Bermudez*,[19] however, the suspect was asked if he had any sharp objects in his pockets prior to be being searched by a police officer. He denied that he did and the officer pricked her finger on a needle. The defendant was convicted in the magistrates' court of actual bodily harm. He was re-tried in the Crown Court and was acquitted on the basis that the *actus reus* was not satisfied because he had omitted to tell the officer there was a needle in his pocket. The prosecution appealed this decision, claiming that

---

12. *R v Williams (Gladstone)* [1987] 3 All ER 411.
13. [1984] 3 All ER 374.
14. ibid per Goff LJ.
15. *Faulkner v Talbot* [1981] 3 All ER 468.
16. (1888) 22 QBD 23.
17. (1881) 8 QBD 54.
18. [1990] 1 All ER 331.
19. [2004] Crim LR 471.

an omission could satisfying the *actus reus* of a battery. The Divisional Court stated that if a defendant creates a danger and exposes such danger to another person, there is a basis to say that the *actus reus* of the offence is satisfied, *if* the danger to the other person is reasonably foreseeable.

In order to be convicted of battery, the following elements are required:

Actus reus

• The infliction of unlawful force on another person.

Mens rea

• The defendant intends to inflict unlawful force on another person or is reckless as to the infliction of unlawful force.

5.5 Assault occasioning actual bodily harm

In order to be convicted of actual bodily harm (ABH) (contrary to s 47 of the Offences Against the Person Act 1861), the victim must suffer a certain level of injury. ABH is satisfied where the defendant commits the offence of assault *or* battery that causes the victim ABH. The Offences Against the Person Act 1861 does not define what ABH is. Section 47 merely states: 'Whosoever shall be convicted on indictment of any assault occasioning actual bodily harm shall be liable to be kept in penal servitude.' This section tells us that the offence could lead to a lengthy prison sentence for the defendant (a maximum of five years), but the courts have been left to interpret the meaning of bodily harm.

Assault or battery (see **5.4**) is called the base offence. That means that the *actus reus* and *mens rea* for assault/battery and ABH are identical. The difference is the harm that has been inflicted on another. For example, in the case of *R v Roberts*,[20] the defendant had met the victim at a party earlier in the evening and had offered to give her a lift to another party – which she accepted. During the journey, the defendant stopped at a remote location and attempted to make sexual advances which the victim refused. The defendant drove off at speed and when he tried to take off her coat, she decided to jump out of the moving car. She suffered a concussion and various cuts and bruises. The offence of battery was satisfied by the unwanted touching of the victim's clothes, but the severity was increased when the victim suffered cuts and bruises from jumping out of the car. The defendant was convicted of s 47 ABH, and the Court of Appeal dismissed his appeal on the basis that it is irrelevant that the defendant does not foresee that his conduct will lead to injuries that amount to ABH.

As we have said, it is the level of injury suffered that underpins the offence of ABH. It has been held that an offence will not amount to ABH where the injury is 'merely transient and trifling'.[21] In plain English, transient is defined as something that lasts for a short period of time – therefore it is not permanent. The word

---

20. (1972) 56 Cr App R 95.
21. *R v Donovan* [1934] 2 KB 498.

trifling means something that is unimportant or trivial. As such, not all injury can be readily described as ABH. In *R v Miller*[22] the court held that ABH could occur where 'any hurt of injury [is] calculated to interfere with the health or comfort of the [victim]'. As such, the following actions have been classified as ABH:

- Causing someone to fall unconscious. In *T v DPP*,[23] the defendant kicked the victim, causing them to lose consciousness for a brief period of time. The defendant was convicted of ABH.
- Cutting off a substantial part of someone's hair (perhaps surprisingly). In *DPP v Smith*[24] the defendant cut off the pony tail of his then girlfriend. He did not cause any physical injury to her body, and there were no cuts or bruises. The victim was emotionally upset and distressed. The court held that the cutting of hair did amount to ABH as the court interpreted the meaning of 'bodily' in the statute to include all parts of the human body, including that of the hair on one's scalp. Furthermore, by cutting off a substantial part of someone's hair, this could not be seen as merely transient or trifling. This was a significant act and the defendant was convicted.
- Psychiatric injury is capable of amounting to ABH or even GBH.[25]

Actus reus and *mens rea*

As discussed in this section, the *mens rea* of ABH is identical to assault or battery (intention or recklessness of assault or battery). There is an additional element to the *actus reus* – actual bodily harm. That means that in order to be convicted of the more serious ABH, the level of injuries have simply to be more than transient and trifling.[26]

5.6 Malicious wounding and inflicting grievous bodily harm

This offence is committed when a person, unlawfully and maliciously, either wounds another person, or inflicts grievous bodily harm (GBH) upon another person. The offence under s 20 of the Offences Against the Person Act 1861 is made out if the defendant foresaw that their actions would result in some form of bodily harm. Section 20 states: 'Whosoever shall unlawfully and maliciously wound or inflict any grievous bodily harm upon another person, either with or without a weapon or instrument, shall be guilty [of the offence].'

As under s 47, conviction for s 20 GBH carries a maximum sentence of five years' imprisonment. However, the greater the harm caused by the defendant, the greater the likelihood that the offence will be categorised as a s 20 offence.

In order to satisfy the *actus reus* of the offence, the defendant needs to wound the victim or inflict GBH.

---

22. [1954] 2 QB 282.
23. [2003] Crim LR 622.
24. [2006] EWHC 94 (Admin).
25. See *Ireland and Burstow* [1998] AC 147.
26. *Donovan* (n 21).

5.6.1 Wounding

What constitutes wounding? In a nutshell, the defendant must break the skin of the victim. A classic example of this would be stabbing another person. However, the offence does not have to be as serious as stabbing somebody. A defendant can be convicted of the s 20 offence if they split the lip of the victim in the course of punching them. However, a defendant needs to break every layer of skin – simply breaking the surface layer of the skin will not suffice as a wound.[27] Furthermore, the wound must have some external break. In *R v Wood*,[28] the defendant broke the collar bone of the victim, but there was no breaking of the skin and the court held that there was no wound. So any wound needs to be external in the first instance; a purely internal wound will not suffice.

5.6.2 Inflicting GBH

The Act does not define GBH. As with the other offences covered in this chapter, it has been left for the courts to define. In the case of *R v Smith*,[29] a policeman attempted to stop the defendant driving off with stolen goods. The officer jumped on to the bonnet of the car, and the defendant drove in an erratic manner to throw the officer from the car. The officer died and the defendant was convicted of murder. After having his conviction quashed by the Court of Appeal, the House of Lords reinstated the defendant's murder conviction and defined GBH to mean 'serious bodily harm'. However, serious bodily harm does not have to be permanent or life threatening,[30] and the case of *R v Hicks*[31] suggests that being briefly rendered unconscious would be enough to satisfy the GBH requirement.

5.6.3 Maliciously

The section states that any wounding or infliction of GBH has to be carried out maliciously. However, the courts have interpreted this to allow for reckless behaviour to suffice for GBH. The leading case on intention for s 20 is *R v Savage and Parmenter*.[32] This was a combined appeal of two similar yet distinct cases. In *Savage*, the defendant threw beer over her husband's ex-girlfriend, but in carrying out this act, the glass slipped from her hand and ended up cutting the victim's wrist. She claimed she had no intention of harming the victim in that way, but she was convicted of s 20 GBH. In *Parmenter*, the defendant injured his newborn son but explained that there was no intention to cause the injury; he just had little or no experience with small babies. Again, the defendant was convicted of inflicting GBH. In the joint appeal, the issue at hand was the necessary intention in order to be convicted of the malicious infliction of GBH.

---

27. *R v Morris* [2005] EWCA Crim 609.
28. (1830) 1 Mood CC 278.
29. [1961] AC 290.
30. *R v Bollom* [2004] 2 Cr App R 50.
31. [2007] EWCA Crim 1500.
32. [1992] 1 AC 699.

The court held that if the defendant intends to inflict some harm, or the defendant foresaw that their unlawful act *might* inflict some harm, then that will satisfy the court. As such, reckless behaviour will suffice if the defendant is aware that there is risk of harm to another person. As such, both appeals were dismissed and the defendants' convictions for GBH stood.

5.7 Wounding and causing grievous bodily harm with intent

To conclude this section on non-fatal offences against the person, we now look at s 18 of the Offences Against the Person Act 1861. The *actus reus* of this section is identical to that of s 20. However, *the mens rea* is different. The offence can only be committed with intention; recklessness is not sufficient. Therefore, should intention not be present, the act may satisfy a s 20 offence but not the s 18 offence. (For more in of how intention is defined, see below where we turn to the fatal offences of murder and manslaughter.)

5.8 Murder

When we set out the various non-fatal offences, we started with the least severe and worked up in severity. We did this because it is important to establish the base offence of any particular act. However, with fatal offences we start with the most severe and work down. That is because we have to establish whether the defendant had the requisite intention to commit the offence.

Despite the prevalence of legislation,[33] there is no statutory definition of murder. As such, we need to look to the common law and see how the courts define the act of murder. The most commonly used definition of murder stems from the 17th century *Institute of Laws*, written by Sir Edward Coke CJ. He states that:

> Murder is when a man of sound memory, and of the age of discretion, unlawfully killeth within any country of the realm any reasonable creation in *rerum natura* under the king's peace, with malice aforethought, either expressed by the party or implied by law, so as the party wounded or hurt etc die of that wound or hurt etc within a year and a day after the same.

This is a rather wordy statement using archaic language, so how do we define the contemporary offence of murder? To be found guilty of the offence of murder, the defendant needs to unlawfully kill another person under the Queen's peace and do so with the intention to kill or cause really serious harm (GBH).

5.8.1 *Actus reus*

The *actus reus* of murder is the unlawful killing of a person under the Queen's peace

---

33. The Homicide Act 1957 and the Corporate Manslaughter and Corporate Homicide Act 2007.

The offence of murder does not require someone to be murdered in a certain way, for example being shot or stabbed. Instead, the law allows for any conduct that causes the unlawful death of another person. Ultimately, the type of conduct causing death is immaterial.

This act needs to be carried out 'under the Queen's peace', and, as such, a soldier killing an enemy combatant during wartime will not be guilty of murder. However, if the killing is not carried out during battle, this may be considered as murder. In 2019, Sgt Alexander Blackman was convicted of murder when he shot dead a Taliban insurgent who had been injured in an air strike. In body cam footage, Blackman was heard muttering 'shuffle off this mortal coil, you c***' before shooting the wounded enemy at point blank range. He then stated, 'I just broke the Geneva Convention.' Blackman was sentenced to seven years' imprisonment, but the conviction was later reduced to manslaughter on the grounds of diminished responsibility (see below).

The victim needs to be a human being, and, under the law, an unborn child is not a person. In law, a human being is born when it is 'fully expelled from the womb'[34] and is alive.[35] If a defendant kills an unborn child, there are other crimes that may be committed but not murder.[36] The courts have also interpreted when someone stops being a person, and medical science has given the courts quite the problem. There is no set definition of when someone stops being a human, but if there is complete and irreversible non-function of the brain stem, it is likely that the courts will accept that the person is dead.[37] But if the person is in a persistent vegetative state, ie in a permanent coma, the person will not be considered dead and will remain a 'person' who is capable of being murdered.

This poses a problem for those people who are accused of so-called 'mercy killings', where they kill an ill person out of compassion. If a defendant kills someone under the auspices of a mercy killing, they are effectively bringing forward the death of that person and can be charged with murder. In *R v Inglis*,[38] a mother was convicted of the murder of her son who was in a permanent vegetative state. On appeal, the court reduced her minimum term to five years' imprisonment on the basis of a mercy killing, but she was still convicted of murder.

5.8.2 *Mens rea*

Coke used the term 'malice aforethought'. Basically, this means that the defendant needs some form of intention, but it does not need to be malicious. Furthermore, 'aforethought' does not necessarily mean any pre-planning or premeditation; the defendant simply needs to have intended to carry out of the act. The court has interpreted intention to come in two different forms; it can be direct or indirect (sometimes called oblique) intention.

---

34. *R v Poulton* (1832) 5 C & P 329.
35. *R v Reeves* (1839) 9 C & P 25.
36. See Infant Life (Preservation) Act 1929, s 1 and Offences Against the Person Act 1861, s 58.
37. *R v Bland* [1993] 1 AC 789.
38. [2011] 1 WLR 1110.

Direct intention

This is where the result of the act is the main aim or purpose. In *R v Moloney*[39] a stepfather and son were having a drunken race to see who could load a shotgun the quickest. The son won the race and his stepfather challenged him to fire the gun. He did so and his stepfather was killed instantly. At first instance, the defendant was convicted, and he appealed all the way to the House of Lords. The House of Lords allowed his appeal as there was no intent to kill or seriously harm his stepfather.

Indirect intention

A three-stage needs to be satisfied in order for the jury to find indirect intention. In *R v Woollin*[40] the defendant killed his child by throwing it against a hard surface. He claimed that it was not his intention to kill the child, but he was convicted of murder. At trial, the judge directed the jury that the defendant could be found guilty if they believed that the defendant knew his actions posed 'a substantial risk' of causing death or serious harm. The Court of Appeal agreed and the case went to the House of Lords, which ruled that the lower courts were wrong in their approach of using substantial risk. This threshold was too low and therefore the House of Lords created a three-limbed test:

(1) The result needs to be a virtual certainty.
(2) This virtual certainty needs to be recognised by the defendant.
(3) It is a decision for the jury to find the intention.

This is a far higher threshold than 'substantial risk'. It is not enough that the defendant believes that the result may occur or even that it is highly likely to occur – it needs to be virtually certain. This is an objective judgement. The second element is subjective in nature. The jury must believe that the defendant honestly believed that the result was not virtually certain. The final element is a question for the jury – if the result of the defendant's action was virtually certain, the defendant recognised that fact and carried on regardless, the jury are entitled to find that the defendant had indirect intention and can be convicted of murder.

5.8.3 Partial defences

There are three partial defences to murder that, if successful, will reduce a murder conviction to that of voluntary manslaughter.

Loss of self-control

Loss of self-control is governed by ss 54–55 of the Coroners and Justice Act 2009. This means that where intention is found, either direct or indirect, the level of the defendant's culpability could be lower if they are found to have lost self-control. An example would be where A finds out that B has been sexually abusing A's child and kills B; a partial defence of loss of self-control may be applicable. However, s 54(4) states that a considered desire for revenge will mean that the defendant has

---

39. [1985] 1 AC 905.
40. [1998] 4 All ER 103.

not lost self-control and therefore this partial defence would not be successful. In *R v Ahluwalia*[41] the defendant poured petrol over her abuser whilst he slept. She lit the petrol and he died as a result of the injuries he suffered. The court at first instance convicted the defendant of murder and she appealed. The Court of Appeal agreed with the trial judge's intimation that the loss of control needs to be both sudden and temporary. However, evidence existed that could give rise to an alternative defence of diminished responsibility, a re-trial was ordered and this defence was successful (see below). This case pre-dated the Coroners and Justice Act 2009, which has provided clarity on this particular issue.

In order for the partial defence to be successful, the defendant needs to show the presence of one of two 'qualifying triggers':

- *Fear of serious violence* (s 55(3)). This trigger means that the defendant was under a threat of serious violence to themselves or another person, such as their child. This requirement is subjective, meaning that the defendant needs to react to a genuine fear and this fear needs to be based on the fact that there is a threat of serious violence. It does not matter if the threat turns out not to be genuine; the defendant just needs to believe that the threat is genuine.
- *A sense of being seriously wronged by things said or done* (s 55(4)). This trigger is a fusion of both a subjective element (the defendant needs to have a sense of being seriously wronged) and an objective element (the feeling of being wronged must be objectively accepted by the jury). Therefore, the reaction of the defendant to the occurrence of the wrongdoing needs to be objectively reasonable. Interestingly, sexual infidelity is excluded from this sense of wrongdoing, and so a reaction to a partner's infidelity will not give rise to a qualifying trigger.[42]

If a defendant possesses either of the qualifying triggers, the final element that needs to be shown is that the reaction of the defendant was objectively plausible. This means that a person of the same sex, age, intellectual capacity and with a normal degree of tolerance would have reacted in the same or similar manner.[43]

Unlike the other partial defences discussed below, the burden of proof in such cases remains with the prosecution. This means that it has to disprove the defence beyond a reasonable doubt, once the defence has provided 'sufficient evidence' to the court that the defendant is entitled to run a loss of self-control defence.[44]

Diminished responsibility

As with loss of self-control, if a defendant can successfully raise a defence of diminished responsibility, their liability for murder will be reduced to voluntary manslaughter. The defence of loss of self-control is based on how the 'normal' person with the same personal characteristics of the defendant would act. Diminished responsibility takes the opposite approach. The defendant acted as

---

41. [1992] 4 All ER 889.
42. Coroners and Justice Act 2009, s 55(6)(c).
43. ibid s 54(1)(c).
44. ibid s 54(5).

they did because they were suffering from an abnormality of mental functioning; as such, this abnormality hindered their thought processes and impaired their decision-making capabilities. Section 2 of the Homicide Act 1957 (as amended by s 52 of the Coroners and Justice Act 2009) sets out the test for diminished responsibility:

(1) A person ('D') who kills or is a party to the killing of another is not to be convicted of murder if D was suffering from an abnormality of mental functioning which—

    (a) arose from a recognised medical condition,

    (b) substantially impaired D's ability to do one or more of the things mentioned in subsection (1A), and

    (c) provides an explanation for D's acts and omissions in doing or being a party to the killing.

(1A) Those things are—

    (a) to understand the nature of D's conduct;

    (b) to form a rational judgment;

    (c) to exercise self-control.

It is clear from the statutory wording that the defendant must have an abnormality of mental functioning. This means that there must be a link between a medical condition of the defendant impacting on their decision-making processes. In *R v Byrne*[45] it was held that an abnormality of the mind (the terminology under the old legislation) is a 'state of mind so different from that of ordinary human beings that the reasonable man would term it abnormal'.

This abnormality must stem from a recognised medical condition. This is rather opaque and open to interpretation as to what is 'recognised', but it is highly likely the court would rely on the World Health Organization's *International Statistical Classification of Diseases and Related Health Problems*. In *R v Dowds*[46] it was held that paedophilia would not be classified as a recognised medical condition. The condition needs to be shown as an impairment as regards to one of three circumstances:

(1) *To understand the nature of the defendant's conduct.* The Law Commission gave an example of a boy aged 10 who plays violent video games, loses his temper and kills another child when the child attempts to take a game from him. The boy shows no understanding that a person cannot simply be revived, as happens in video games such as *Call of Duty*.

(2) *To form a rational judgement.* The abnormality substantially impairs the defendant in forming a rational judgement. For example, someone who has been a victim of persistent domestic violence might claim their abuse clouded their ability to form a rational judgement when they killed their abuser.

(3) *To exercise self-control.* The defendant is impaired substantially from exercising self-control.

---

45. [1960] 2 QB 396.
46. [2012] EWCA Crim 281.

If one of these circumstances is present, the final element to satisfy is that the substantial impairment provides an explanation for the killing.[47] Ultimately, the abnormality of mental functioning needs to be the reason 'why' the defendant killed the victim in so far as causing or being a significant contributing factor in causing the defendant to carry out their conduct. The burden of proof rests on the defence when raising the partial defence of diminished responsibility. That means that the defence must prove on the balance of probabilities (greater than 50%) that the abnormality of mental functioning exists and the defendant satisfies the various limbs of the test.

Suicide pact

The final partial defence to murder is that of a suicide pact. This is governed by s 4 of the Homicide Act 1957, which states:

(1) It shall be manslaughter, and shall not be murder, for a person acting in pursuance of a suicide pact between him and another to kill the other or be a party to the other ... being killed by a third person.

(2) Where it is shown that a person charged with the murder of another killed the other or was a party to his ... being killed, it shall be for the defence to prove that the person charged was acting in pursuance of a suicide pact between him and the other.

(3) For the purposes of this section 'suicide pact' means a common agreement between two or more persons having for its object the death of all of them, whether or not each is to take his own life, but nothing done by a person who enters into a suicide pact shall be treated as done by him in pursuance of the pact unless it is done while he has the settled intention of dying in pursuance of the pact.

Like diminished responsibility, the burden of proof rests on the defence to prove the presence of a suicide pact, and there are two constitute elements that have to be proven on the balance of probabilities. First, the defendant and victim must have an agreement that they will die together, and, secondly, at the time the victim was killed, the defendant must intend to die as well.

5.9 Involuntary manslaughter

Unlike voluntary manslaughter, which rests on the fact that the defendant has a partial defence to murder and their culpability is reduced to manslaughter, this second form of manslaughter is concerned with offences where the victim dies as a result of the defendant's conduct, but there is no intention to kill or cause GBH. (The term 'involuntary' is something of a misnomer in that the offence does not require any form of involuntariness.)

Involuntary manslaughter requires the *actus reus* of murder to be completed, and therefore the defendant needs to carry out the unlawful killing of a human. The *mens rea* of murder, ie intention to kill, is not required for a conviction of

---

47. Homicide Act 1957, s 2(1B).

involuntary manslaughter. There are three types of involuntary manslaughter, and they will be discussed in turn:

- unlawful act manslaughter
- gross negligence manslaughter
- reckless manslaughter.

5.9.1 Unlawful act manslaughter

There are three component parts to unlawful act manslaughter that need to be present in order for the defendant to be convicted:

(1) an unlawful act

(2) that act is objectively dangerous

(3) that act causes the death of another.

As with all types of involuntary manslaughter, unlawful act manslaughter is a common law offence. As such, there is no statutory guidance on the offence, so we have to analyse the approach taken by the courts.

The unlawful act

The unlawful act is the base offence and has to be present. If the offence was lawfully committed, the defendant will not be convicted. In *R v Goodfellow*,[48] the defendant set fire to his house in order to show that he was under threat. Unfortunately, he unintentionally killed three members of his family and he was convicted of unlawful act manslaughter. This case illustrates the three constitute elements of the offence. First, setting fire to the home was an unlawful act; secondly, it was reasonably foreseeable that some harm would arise from the act; and, thirdly, the act caused the deaths of three people. The defendant in this case was convicted of unlawful act manslaughter.

Finally, the unlawful act must be fully completed. In *R v Lamb*[49] (see **5.4** above), it was impossible for the defendant to be convicted of unlawful act manslaughter as there was no unlawful act.

The act is objectively dangerous

When talking about something being objectively dangerous, we mean that a reasonable person would believe that the act is dangerous. It does not matter what the defendant thought; what matters is whether a reasonable person would think it was a dangerous act. In *R v Dawson*[50] three men attempted to rob a petrol station with an imitation gun and a pick axe handle. A 60-year-old man was working in the petrol station and, after the men fled, he had a heart attack and subsequently died. The three men were convicted of unlawful act manslaughter but appealed against their convictions. The Court of Appeal quashed their conviction on the basis that it would not be obvious to the reasonable person that the man had a heart condition, which brought on his fatal heart attack. As such, this did not

---

48. (1986) 83 Cr App R 23.
49. [1967] 2 QB 981.
50. (1985) Cr App R 150.

satisfy the second limb of the test. The *Dawson* ruling was affirmed by the court in *R v Church*,[51] which defined dangerousness as follows:

> The unlawful act must be such as all sober and reasonable people would inevitably recognise must subject the other person to, at least, the risk of some harm resulting … albeit not serious harm.

The offence must cause the death of another

The final element of unlawful act manslaughter is the requirement that the base offence must cause the death of the victim. In *AG's Reference (No 3 of 1994)*[52] the defendant stabbed his pregnant girlfriend who then gave birth prematurely, and the baby died a few months after being born. The defendant was charged with the murder of the child but was acquitted at his original trial. The Attorney General appealed to the House of Lords and the defendant was convicted of manslaughter. The three elements of unlawful act manslaughter were present in this case:

(1) The defendant committed an unlawful and dangerous act (the stabbing of his girlfriend).

(2) A reasonable person would think that some harm would arise from stabbing another.

(3) The death of the then unborn child was caused by his act.

The court held that it did not matter that the harm was original intended for the girlfriend rather than the unborn baby. As such, the defendant was convicted of unlawful act manslaughter.

5.9.2 Gross negligence manslaughter

Gross negligence manslaughter is a form of manslaughter which can punish someone for doing something grossly negligent. Unlike unlawful act manslaughter, a person may be liable for gross negligence manslaughter for failing to do something. The leading case in this area is *R v Adomako*.[53] The defendant was an anaesthetist who was responsible for a patient being administered a general anaesthetic during an operation. At some point during the operation, a tube became detached from the ventilator and the patient suffered a fatal heart attack. The defendant was convicted of gross negligence manslaughter. The House of Lords upheld the conviction as the defendant owed the victim a duty of care, which was breached, and the defendant's actions, which caused the death of the victim, were characterised as gross negligence. Each element need to be present in order to make out the offence of gross negligence manslaughter.

Duty of care

The prosecution will need to prove that the defendant owed the victim a duty of care. A duty of care is owed in straightforward cases, such as doctor to patient (as

---

51. [1966] 1 QB 59 at 70.
52. [1998] AC 425.
53. [1995] 1 AC 171.

in *Adomako*), carrier to passenger[54] and employer to employee.[55] Some situations are less obvious, but a duty may still be owed. In *R v Wacker*[56] the defendant was smuggling illegal immigrants into the UK in a lorry. He had closed the vent in the container which housed the immigrants, and 58 of the 60 immigrants suffocated and died. The defendant was convicted of gross negligence manslaughter.

In the case of *R v Evans,*[57] the victim's half-sister provided her with heroin, which the victim injected into her body herself. The defendant recognised that the victim was overdosing but did not seek medical help to assist the victim as she was scared of what would happen to her should the authorities get involved. The defendant was convicted of gross negligence manslaughter, and the Court of Appeal upheld the conviction. The Court affirmed the idea that a defendant owes someone a duty a care if they create a dangerous situation. This notion stems from the case of *R v Miller*[58] where a drunk vagrant fell asleep in a squat with a lit cigarette. He woke up to see the mattress on fire but took no steps to put the fire out; instead he walked to another room and went back to sleep. The court held that by creating a dangerous situation, the defendant was under a duty to take action once he knew the mattress was on fire. This assumption of duty did not rest on any subjective assessment of risk; it was an objective assessment of risk that the reasonable person would find the situation dangerous and would therefore be under a duty to act.

The breach of duty

After establishing that the defendant owes a duty of care, the prosecution then has to prove that this duty was breached. The question of whether or not there is a breach of duty centres on whether the conduct of the defendant falls below that of the reasonable person. Again, this is an objective rather than subjective approach. In a nutshell, would the reasonable person have acted differently to the defendant? If we return to the case of *R v Adomako,*[59] the question is whether a reasonable anaesthetist would have acted differently to the defendant. A failure of the defendant to meet the objective standard of the reasonable person will result in a breach of duty.

Causing death

The breach of duty must cause the death of the defendant. If we look at the two aforementioned cases of *Evans* and *Adomako*, in both cases, the reasonable person would have acted differently. In *Evans*, once the onset of an overdose was clear, the reasonable person would have sought medical intervention. By breaching her duty to her half-sister, Evans caused her death. The same can be said in *Adomako*; the reasonable person with the same training as the defendant would know that the

---

54. *R v Barker* [2003] 2 Cr App R (S) 110.
55. *R v Dean* [2002] EWCA Crim 2410.
56. [2003] QB 1207.
57. [2009] EWCA Crim 650.
58. [1983] 2 AC 161.
59. [1995] 1 AC 171.

ventilator was detached and have taken steps to rectify this error. As such, the defendant was found guilty of gross negligence manslaughter.

Grossly negligent

The final element that needs to be shown is that the act or omission of the defendant was grossly negligent. Lord McKay in *Adamako* stated that:

> The essence of the matter which is supremely a jury question is whether having regard to the risk of death involved, the conduct of the defendant was so bad in all the circumstances as to amount in their judgment to a criminal act or omission.

If the jury believe that the conduct of the defendant was so bad as to amount to a criminal act or omission, they are entitled to find the defendant guilty of gross negligence manslaughter.

5.9.3 Reckless manslaughter

The final type of involuntary manslaughter is reckless manslaughter. However, as Child and Ormerod point out, reckless manslaughter is very rarely prosecuted as cases of involuntary manslaughter will almost always satisfy the elements of unlawful act manslaughter or gross negligence manslaughter.[60] To be convicted of reckless manslaughter, a defendant must cause the death of another person by either an act or omission and be reckless to the fact that their act *could* cause death or GBH. Effectively, this is a safety-net offence which allows the prosecution to charge defendants who kill by omission (therefore unlawful act manslaughter is not suitable) or do not foresee a risk of death (therefore gross negligence manslaughter is not suitable).

5.10 Conclusion

This chapter has provided you with a brief introduction to both fatal and non-fatal offences against the person. You will cover all of these elements in your Criminal Law module and deal with a great number of the cases that we have covered in this chapter. Both fatal and non-fatal offences against the person are complex and intricate, but this chapter has aimed to allow a core understanding of what constituent elements are needed for the court to find a defendant guilty.

---

60. J Child and D Ormerod, *Smith and Hogan's Essentials of Criminal Law*, 4th edn (OUP, 2021).

6 Understanding Violent Crimes: Criminology

6.1 Introduction

Criminological theory has long attempted to explain the causes of delinquency and criminal activity, dating back to the 17th century when classical criminology endeavoured to understand crime and punishment. Classical criminologists, such as Beccaria and Bentham, believed that criminals choose to commit criminal acts in order to maximise pleasure and minimise pain – they weigh up the pros and cons of committing a criminal offence.[1] Today, criminology adopts a more contemporary approach, considering a number of internal and external influences, such as biology, genetics, brain development, mental illness, socialisation, the impact of structural inequality, and age. This chapter will therefore consider a number of explanations for violent crimes.

It will consider:

- understanding aggression in offenders;
- psychological and sociological explanations of violence;
- explanations of serial killing; and
- explanations of youth crime.

6.2 Understanding aggression in offenders

6.2.1 Introduction

Aggression is defined as 'any form of behaviour that is intended to injure someone physically or psychologically'.[2] There is no clear definition of the term aggression and therefore no real consensus about the parameters of aggression or violence. However, it is accepted that aggression does not have to involve physical force or violence. Subsequently, stalking or threats may amount to aggression. However, it is widely acknowledged that there are two types of aggression – hostile or expressive aggression and instrumental aggression. Hostile or expressive aggression involves an internal state of emotional arousal. This may occur in reaction to a provocation, a triggering frustrating event, such as losing a job or a failure in a relationship. It is characterised by an impulse to hurt or harm something or someone.[3] Examples

---

1. J Walker and J Boyeskie , 'The Discourse of Criminality: From Beccaria to Postmodernism' (2020) 12 *Journal of Theoretical and Philosophical* Criminology 37, 37.
2. L Berkowitz, *Aggression: Its Causes, Consequences and Control* (McGraw Hill, 1993) 3.
3. J Assaad and M Exum, 'Understanding Intoxicated Violence from a Rational Choice Perspective' in A Piquero and D Tibbetts (eds), *Rational Choice and Criminal Behavior: Recent Research and Future Challenges* (Routledge, 2002) 65–84.

include rapes or murder which invoke an emotional arousal in the offender. On the other hand, instrumental aggression is a more utilitarian form of aggression and is therefore not necessarily characterised by emotional arousal. It may manifest itself as a premeditated means of obtaining a goal or some desired reward, such as a property offence which does not involve the intention to harm a victim. Thus, anger is not a necessary, nor sufficient condition for aggression, and not all forms of aggression involve violence, but all forms of violence involve aggression.[4]

6.2.2 Biological approaches

Biological explanations have attempted to explain aggression amongst offenders. Biological approaches have suggested that murderers who suffered from childhood neglect may undergo biological abnormalities, such as an underdeveloped prefrontal cortex, which regulates impulsive behaviour, reasoning and making decisions. Such abnormalities subject the individual to a greater risk of carrying out homicide and other forms of violence.[5] This is further supported by research that suggests that murderers have variations in their brain structure, as Nichols established that murderers have less prefrontal cortex activity than non-murderers.[6] Subsequently, there is evidence to suggest that a person's biology and physical make-up may impact their behaviour and therefore the likelihood of their committing violent offences.

In particular, advances in science have suggested that alcoholism may have a profound effect on the prefrontal cortex.[7] Substance abuse remains among the most common mental disorders in the US, affecting one in 10 people.[8] Other biological explanations have attempted to account for violent behaviour through high correlations between alcoholism and violent offending. Assaad and Exum[9] suggested that the consumption of ethanol directly weakens the inhibitory process, allowing the individual's aggression to manifest due to the absence of conscious decision making. One in four incidents of violence[10] and 48% of homicides have been found to involve alcohol, suggesting that offenders who engage in violence are often intoxicated during the commission of the act.[11] Subsequently, it is

---

4. J Kuhns, M Exum, T Coldfelter and M Bottia, 'The Prevalence of Alcohol-Involved Homicide Offending: A Meta-Analytic Review' (2014) 18 Homicide Studies 251, 252.

5. K Heide and E Solomon, 'Biology, Childhood Trauma, and Murder: Rethinking Justice' (2006) 29 *International Journal of Law and Psychiatry* 220, 222.

6. D Nichols, 'Tell Me a Story: MMPI Responses and Personal Biography in the Case of a Serial Killer' (2006) 86 *Journal of Personality Assessment* 242, 242.

7. M Friese, L Gianotti and D Knoch, 'The Association Between Implicit Alcohol Attitudes and Drinking Behavior is Moderated by Baseline Activation in the Lateral Prefrontal Cortex' (2016) 35 *American Psychological Association* 837, 837.

8. K Morgenstern, E Labouvie, B McCrady, C Kahler and R Frey, 'Affiliation with Alcoholics Anonymous After Treatment: A Study of its Therapeutic Effects and Mechanisms of Action' (1997) 65 *J Consult Clin Psychol* 768, 677.

9. Assaad (n 3).

10. L Greenfeld, Washington, DC: US Department of Justice, *Alcohol and Crime: An Analysis of National Data on the Prevalence of Alcohol Involvement in Crime. Assistant Attorney General's National Symposium on Alcohol Abuse and Crime* (1998).

11. Kuhns (n 4) 252.

possible that alcohol consumption can have a biological impact on the offender, increasing the likelihood of aggressive behaviour.

6.2.3 Sociological approaches

Sociological explanations offer an insight as to why people may commit aggressive and violent crimes, as well as other offences. Examples include how pride, social status, hierarchy and masculinity may influence behaviour. Social psychology attempts to explain and understand how the thoughts, feelings and behaviours of individuals are influenced by the presence of others. It therefore links the social environment with a person's individual psychology. Social Learning Theory argues that behaviour can be learnt through observation and imitation of role models.[12] Thus, certain conditions conducive to learning aggressive behaviour are those in which a child has many opportunities to observe aggression. The observed behaviour is reinforced in the child exposed to the aggression. This involves operating conditioning of particular behaviour, which entails external reinforcement whereby an action is rewarded or punished. Such reward may make you more likely to repeat the action, whilst punishment may make you less likely to repeat behaviour. For example, if you stole a car and evaded capture, you may be more likely to do it again.

Moreover, other sociological approaches consider vicarious reinforcement as an explanation for aggressive behaviour. This entails observation of the punishment or reward of another's actions. Subsequently, Bandura's Bobo Doll Experiment suggested that children who are exposed to an aggressive model acted more aggressively than those exposed to a non-aggressive model, supporting the argument that if parents are aggressive, the child may imitate the behaviour.[13] This suggests that violent offenders may have learned to be engaged in aggressive and violent behaviour through imitating others' aggression towards each other. Examples include witnessing parents be aggressive towards each other or watching TV programmes or films which display aggression.

Sociological explanations of violence have also attempted to explain violent behaviour through vicarious reinforcement and the role of the media. Gentile and Walsh uncovered that American children (aged 2–18) spend an average of six hours a day with electronic media and seven hours a week on video games. Of a sample of 33 popular Nintendo and Sega games, 80% were violent in nature.[14] Subsequently, Huesmann et al concluded that viewing media violence is the main contributor to aggressive behaviour in children, adolescents and adults.[15] In particular, their study concluded that scenes in which children are able to identify

---

12. A Bandura, *Aggression: A Social Learning Analysis* (Prentice Hall, 1973).
13. A Bandura, D Ross and S Ross, 'Transmission of Aggression Through Imitation of Aggressive Models' (1961) 63 *Journal of Abnormal and Social Psychology* 575.
14. T Dietz, 'An Examination of Violence and Gender Role Portrayals in Video Games: Implications for Gender Socialization and Aggressive Behavior' (1998) 38 *Sex Roles* 425, 428.
15. L Huesmann, J Moise-Titus, C Podolski and L Eron, 'Longitudinal Relations Between Children's Exposure to TV Violence and their Aggressive and Violent Behavior in Young Adulthood: 1977–1992' (2003) 39 *Developmental Psychology* 201.

with the perpetrators of violence, or where the perpetrator gets rewarded for the violence, have the biggest effect on their interpretation of aggressive behaviour. Thus, sociological explanations have suggested that exposure to violent video games and other forms of violent media may lead to an increase in aggressive behaviour and thoughts amongst children that later manifest in their adult life. However, it is important to note that such studies are dated, and this issue has been deeply contested due to a lack of empirical evidence between the risk factor and aggressive or violent behaviour.

6.2.4 Conclusion

By understanding aggression, we can better understand violence and therefore violent crime. However, whilst the above approaches may provide an insight into aggressive offending behaviour, they are problematic due to being overly deterministic by neglecting the role of free will in behaviour. They are also reductionist in that they only accept biology or social contexts as an explanation, though behaviour may be better explained by a combination of biological, psychological and environmental factors.[16] However, it is clear that there are a number of approaches which attempt to explain aggression, particularly in the commission of violent offending.

6.3 Psychological and sociological explanations of violence

6.3.1 Introduction

Biology, personality and psychopathology have been argued to be intertwined. They help shape our attitudes and behaviours. By understanding psychological explanations of crime, we can better understand offenders, crime prevention, crime investigation and the treatment of offenders. Subsequently, psychological theories have attempted to explain crime and delinquency, with a focus on shaping policy in order to reduce the impact that psychology may have on the influence of the commission of crime. However, there is often an overlap between the psychological and sociological influences of crime.[17] This section will outline the psychopathology approach to explaining offending behaviour. It will also consider sociological explanations, such as loneliness or lack of self-control, in explaining crime and will evaluate their utility and accuracy in offering an explanation of offending behaviour.

6.3.2 Psychological explanations of violence

Psychopathology

Garner described a 'psychopath' as someone '... with a mental disorder characterized by an extremely antisocial personality that often leads to aggressive,

---

16. R Akers, *Criminological Theories: Introduction and Evaluation* (Routledge, 1999).
17. M Moore, 'Psychological Theories of Crime and Delinquency' (2011) 21 *Journal of Human Behavior in the Social Environment* 226, 226.

perverted, or criminal behavior'.[18] Thus, whilst psychopathology refers to the study of mental illness and its causes, it often carries an association with criminal activity. This field of study encompasses a range of biological, psychological and sociocultural processes and factors. Historical psychopathology even considered supernatural influences as a cause of mental illness. It encompasses the study of a range of disorders, such as anxiety, dissociative disorder, mood disorders such as depression and bipolar disorder, and schizophrenia, and personality disorders such as psychopathy, borderline personality disorder and obsessive-compulsive disorder. However, psychologists have struggled to define 'psychopathology'. Moreover, the DSM-IV states that 'no definition adequately specifies precise boundaries of the concept of "mental disorder"'.[19] Subsequently, if psychopathology cannot be defined, it is almost impossible to attribute it to a cause of crime. However, this has not limited attempts to apply psychopathology to the commission of crime.

Research suggests that there is a high prevalence of mental illness in the UK. The Mental Health Foundation UK published the findings of the 2014 Adult Psychiatric Morbidity Survey in 2016. It uncovered that one in five adults have considered taking their own life, around half of adults believe that they have suffered from a diagnosable mental health problem within their lifetime, but just a third of such adults received a diagnosis.[20] This illustrates that whilst thoughts of suicide are prevalent within the UK, there are limits to which adults are diagnosed with a recognised mental illness, restricting the ability to identify and provide treatment for mental health conditions. Moreover, research has identified a correlation between offending and the prevalence of mental illness amongst violent offenders.[21] Decades of research have attributed to an understanding of an over-representation of mentally ill patients throughout the criminal justice system in both the UK and the US.[22] In particular, one study found that 43% of young people aged 18 or younger on community orders had mental health disorders.[23]

In particular, developmental psychopathology uses an inter-disciplinary approach by integrating a number of frameworks, such as the sciences of human development, general systems theory, clinical psychology, psychiatry, sociology, paediatrics, neuroscience and behaviour genetics. This approach argues that early experiences can have an impact on mental health in adulthood. Thus, poor mental

---

18. B Garner, 'Psychopath' in *Black's Law Dictionary*, 8th edn (Thomson West, 2004) 1263.
19. D Stein, K Phillips, D Bolton, K Fulford, J Sadler and K Kendler, 'What is a Mental/Psychiatric Disorder? From DSM-IV to DSM-V' (2010) 40 *Psychol Med* 1759, 1762.
20. Mental Health Foundation, *Fundamental Facts About Mental Health 2016* (2016) 5: www.mentalhealth.org.uk/sites/default/files/fundamental-facts-about-mental-health-2016.pdf (accessed 4 May 2021).
21. A Baskin-Sommers, D Baskin, I Sommers, A Casados, M Crossman and S Javdani, 'The Impact of Psychopathology, Race, and Environmental Context on Violent Offending in a Male Adolescent Sample' (2016) 7 *Personality Disorders: Theory, Research, and Treatment* 354, 354.
22. S Calhoun, '"That's Just the Tip of It Because It Goes Deeper Than That": A Qualitative Exploration into the Role of Mental Illness in Offending Onset and Subsequent Offending Behavior' (2018) 29 *Criminal Justice Policy Review* 341, 342.
23. Mental Health Foundation (n 20) 34.

health or the identification of mental illness in adulthood may be a result of '…
problems in the early caregiving environment (e.g., maltreatment, neglect,
malnutrition, inconsistent care …'.[24] This may also include genetic or biological
abnormalities. It therefore argues that children who experience such vulnerability
in early life are more likely to be rejected by prosocial peers, perform poorly in
school and associate with deviant peers.[25] Thus, the theory argues that a mixture of
environmental and genetic factors may impact the development of a child which
may contribute to risk-taking behaviour, depression and delinquency. This may
manifest as anti-social behaviour in adolescence or adulthood which may amount
to criminal activity.

Thornberry et al maintain that crucial brain development in adolescence allows
for the development of cognitive capacity and the maturing of the prefrontal
cortex (the area of the brain which controls planning complex cognitive behaviour,
personality expression, decision making, and moderating social behaviour).
Subsequently, the presence of mental illness as a result of environmental and
biological influences in adolescence may increase the likelihood of the commission
of criminal behaviour in adulthood. This may be due to a lack of brain
development, which may inhibit decision-making and increase risk-taking,
ultimately influencing deviant and criminal activity.[26] However, whilst this
approach includes a multi-disciplinary framework, accounting for both
environmental and biological factors, it is deterministic by ignoring other factors
which may influence offending, such as environmental and biological factors and
the role of free will.

6.3.3 Sociological explanations of violence

Loneliness in childhood

An isolated and neglected childhood is argued to contribute to a number of
biological, social and psychological factors that inevitably could explain one's
offending due to its manifestation in numerous psychiatric diseases.[27] Loneliness
is argued to play a significant role in continuing violent and anti-social behaviour,
particularly where substance abuse is also present.[28] Martens argues that healthy
relationships are the breeding ground for empathy, and that an inadequate
bonding limits the chance of emotional development.[29] This maximises the
existence of deviant fantasies as a defence against rejection where others have

---

24. T Thornberry, P Giordano, C Uggen, M Matsuda, A Masten, A Donker and D Petechuk, Department of
Justice, *Explanations for Offending (Study Group on the Transitions between Juvenile Delinquency and
Adult Crime)* (2013) 18.

25. ibid 17–18.

26. ibid 20–21.

27. J McGraw, 'The First of All Evils' in S Wawrytko (ed), *The Problem of Evil. An Intercultural Exploration*
(Editions Rodopi BV, 2000) 145.

28. W Martens and G Palermo, 'Loneliness and Associated Violent Antisocial Behaviour: Analysis of the
Case Reports of Jeffrey Dahmer and Dennis Nilsen' (2005) 49 *International Journal of Offender Therapy
and Comparative Criminology* 298, 307.

29. W Martens, *Psychopathy and Remission* (Shaker Publishing, 1997) 45.

shown little interest in that person. Labelled as 'psychopaths', those who have experienced severe loneliness have found it to be the trigger in their severe anti-social behaviour and claimed that friendships may have prevented their violence.[30] Subsequently, it is possible that one's social environment can influence violent offending behaviour. However, researchers acknowledge that further study is necessary in order to understand the neurological and psychosocial correlations with loneliness. This therefore limits the validity and reliability of the theory.

Self-control

Low self-control has been argued to influence substance abuse which is linked to higher rates of offending. A lack of ability to resist the consumption of alcohol may increase the likelihood of reduced inhibitions in offenders. It has been suggested that such reduced inhibitions may influence the experiences of immediate gratification when committing a crime.

Hirschi's Social Control Theory argues that criminal activity may result due to a lack of social connections that would usually prohibit such activity through social constraints. It also argues that without these social constraints, the offender is able to commit the crime in order to directly satisfy themselves.[31] Burton et al[32] supported this theory as they established that even where measures of constraint are employed, low self-control has a significant effect on crime and deviance. Moreover, Felson and Staff suggest that a lack of control through consumption of alcohol may allow certain offenders to escape feelings of guilt for the commission of their crime as they may use the defence or excuse of intoxication to avoid responsibility.[33] Research has also suggested that murderers may resort to alcohol when there is a conflict between their moral resistance and their compulsion in order to ignore their feelings of guilt.[34] Low self-control may therefore explain how some offenders are able to commit an array of violent, sexual or property offences where the offender receives immediate gratification.

6.3.4 Conclusion

There are a number of psychological and sociological approaches which are able to explain the commission of violence, including psychopathology, loneliness in childhood and a lack of self-control. However, each of these approaches are reductionist as they only accept one explanation of the commission of violence, ignoring the interplay of biological, psychological and environmental factors. They are also deterministic as they neglect the role of free will or those who have experienced such influences but do not commit violent offences.

---

30. ibid 46.
31. M Gottfredson and T Hirschi, *A General Theory of Crime* (Stanford University Press, 1990) 27.
32. V Burton, F Cullen, D Evans and R Dunaway, 'Reconsidering Strain Theory: Operationalization, Rival Theories, and Adult Criminality' (1994) 46 *Journal of Quantitative Criminology* 213, 233.
33. R Felson and J Staff, 'The Effects of Alcohol Intoxication on Violent Versus Other Offending' (2010) 37 *Criminal Justice and Behaviour* 1343, 1346.
34. B Masters, *The Shrine of Jeffrey Dahmer* (Hodder and Stoughton Ltd, 1993) 127.

6.4 Serial killers: explaining serial murder

6.4.1 Introduction

We explored the influences on aggressive offending at **6.2**. But what makes a person commit serial murder? This section will attempt to explain the serial killer typologies which were introduced in order to categorise serial killers for the purpose of profiling them, therefore increasing the likelihood of catching them. It will then consider some of the biological, psychological and social explanations of violence discussed above, such as the effect of alcohol on the prefrontal cortex or an isolated childhood, applying them to a case study of the infamous serial killer, Jeffrey Dahmer.

6.4.2 A case study: Jeffrey Dahmer

Jeffrey Dahmer became a household name following his capture and confession in July 1991, after drugging, strangling and dismembering the bodies of 17 young black and Asian males in Milwaukee between 1978 and 1991. An American survey established that only 23% of participants could identify the location of the equator, yet 100% were able to identify Jeffrey Dahmer as the 'homosexual' and 'cannibalistic' serial killer.[35] June 1978 saw the murder of Steven Hicks – Dahmer's first murder victim. This would become the catalyst for a frenzy of sexual experimentation, dismemberment and even cannibalism of 16 other men across the subsequent 13 years. Boxes of muriatic acid, bagged hearts, muscles and vital organs, with three human heads in a freezer and an aluminium kettle containing human hands and genitals, recovered on 22 July 1991, provided just a transient insight into the callous crimes committed by Dahmer.[36]

So, what was Dahmer's modus operandi? Modus operandi (MO) is defined as 'the actions and procedures an offender engages in to commit crime successfully. It is a behavioural pattern that the offender learns as he or she gains experience in committing the offense.'[37] Dahmer consistently stalked local gay bars and shopping malls, pursuing potential prey. Offering money in exchange for nude photographs was Dahmer's method of enticement which would lure the victim back to his apartment – it was more often than not filled with the remains of other bodies.[38] Dahmer's first murder appears to have been more spontaneous and aggressive than his later offending as he bludgeoned Steven Hicks to death with a bat in response to Steven wanting to leave. The beginning of his murder frenzy almost nine years later appeared to be of a more calculated nature, particularly due to the excessive degree of planning.[39] This suggests that, as time passed, Dahmer's

---

35. R Tithecott, *Of Men and Monsters: Jeffrey Dahmer and the Construction of the Serial Killer* (University of Wisconsin Press, 1997) 4.

36. Masters (n 34) 33.

37. C Bartol and A Bartol, *Criminal Behavior: A Psychosocial Approach*, 8th edn (Pearson, 2008) 331.

38. R LaBrode, 'Etiology of the Psychopathic Serial Killer: An Analysis of Antisocial Personality Disorder, Psychopathy, and Serial Killer Personality and Crime Scene Characteristics' (2007) 7 *Brief Treatment and Crisis Intervention* 151, 157.

39. Masters (n 34) 105.

MO changed and became more consistent and predictable. Indeed, it has been agreed that the MO of an offender is a learned behaviour that can adapt over time in order to meet the offender's changing needs.[40]

The absence of Dahmer's father and the deteriorating mental state of his mother meant that Dahmer spent a lot of his childhood separated from his parents. As Dahmer spent the majority of his childhood isolated from society, the development of his prefrontal cortex could have been affected, which may have influenced his inability to empathise with others and control his compulsive sexual fantasies.[41] In addition, at **6.2.2** we explored the evidence which suggests that alcoholism may have a profound effect on the prefrontal cortex.[42] It is therefore possible that Dahmer's excessive drinking whilst he was in high school may have affected his brain development during adolescence, thus being linked to his violence in later life. This may explain Dahmer's offending behaviour as he remained largely intoxicated during everyday life – particularly during his offending.[43]

Dahmer's inability to form relationships may also have been influenced by what he had learned from his social environment. Observing his parents' aggressive arguments as a young child may have led to Dahmer's internal aggression as he felt oppressed from society.[44] Social Learning Theory argues that behaviour can be learnt through observation and imitation of role models.[45] Bandura's Bobo Doll Experiment suggested that children who were exposed to an aggressive model acted more aggressively than those exposed to a non-aggressive model, supporting the argument that if parents are aggressive, the child may imitate that behaviour.[46] This suggests that Dahmer learned to be aggressive towards others through imitating his parents' aggression towards each other.

Finally, serial killer typologies have been applied in order to explain Dahmer's offending behaviour. The earliest serial killer typology was introduced by the FBI in 1986. Ressler et al developed a dichotomy of typologies for 'serial murderers' in order to profile them.[47] Blau[48] defined profiling as 'a method of helping to identify the perpetrator of a crime based on an analysis of the nature of the offence and the manner in which it was committed'. Ressler et al categorised offenders as either organised or disorganised which determined the offender's characteristics and the crime scene characteristics based on crime scene evidence. For example, an organised killer would have good intelligence, engage in alcohol use and plan their

---

40. LaBrode (n 38) 155.
41. Masters (n 34) 170.
42. Friese (n 7) 837.
43. R Akers, *Criminological Theories: Introduction and Evaluation* (Routledge, 1999).
44. Masters (n 34) 210.
45. Bandura (n 12).
46. Bandura (n 13).
47. R Ressler, A Burgess, J Douglas, C Hartman and R D'Agostino, 'Sexual Killers and Their Victims: Identifying Patterns Through Crime Scene Analysis' (1986) 1 *Journal of Interpersonal Violence* 288, 292.
48. T Blau, 'Psychological Profiling' in T Blau (ed), *Psychological Services for Law Enforcement* (Wiley, 1994) 261.

offence, whilst a disorganised offender would live alone, become anxious during the crime, and depersonalise the victim.[49]

Limitations restrict the validity of this model as evidence has suggested that characteristics amongst serial killers *do* co-exist across both types. For example, Jeffrey Dahmer, the notorious 'Milwaukee Cannibal', had good intelligence, abused alcohol and planned his offending (which characterise an organised offender), but he lived alone, had an anxious mood during his crimes, and depersonalised the victims through dissolving their remains (disorganised).[50] This leaves the methodology of the dichotomy inconsistent as unpredictable behaviour patterns are possible.[51] Canter also raised the issue of the difficulty of identifying which features amongst the many variables of crime are most 'behaviourally important' on which the empirical findings can be built. These limitations render the dichotomy reductionist, as it simplifies complex characteristics present amongst serial killers into simple lists. Moreover, the approach is deterministic in that it assumes that specific characteristics will not co-occur across other typologies.

Holmes and Holmes[52] subsequently developed a typology in 1998 in which they devised four types of serial murderer: the power/control, missionary, hedonistic and visionary killers. The hedonistic killer is categorised into two sub-types: the lust killer and the thrill killer. Whilst lust killers commit murder for sexual gratification, a thrill killer offends for the excitement of the kill and loses interest once the victim is dead. Sex is a 'focal point' for lust killers, as the offender gains gratification from the commission of the crime, including any acts following the victim's demise. Offenders are organised and plan the offence in order to avoid detection.[53] Similarly to that of Ressler et al,[54] this typology lacks empirical testing as there is no suggestion as to how the offender would be assigned to one typology. This increases the likelihood that the typologies may co-occur, for example, characteristics such as aberrant sexual activity may overlap across the lust killer and the power/control killer.[55]

6.4.3 Conclusion

The case study of Jeffrey Dahmer suggests that there are a number of influencing factors on serial killing, including individual characteristics such as an organised or disorganised profile, an isolated childhood and the effect of alcohol on brain development. However, such influences alone cannot explain the commission of serial killing as lone approaches are reductionist and deterministic in nature. They

---

49. Ressler (n 47) 292.
50. Masters (n 34) 28.
51. D Canter, 'Offender Profiling and Investigative Psychology' (2004) 1 *Journal of Investigative Psychology and Offender Profiling* 1, 1.
52. R Holmes and S Holmes, *Serial Murder*, 2nd ed (Sage, 1998) 15.
53. D Canter and N Wentwink, 'An Empirical Test of Holmes and Holmes's Serial Murder Typology' (2004) 31 *Criminal Justice and Behavior* 489, 509.
54. Ressler (n 47) 292.
55. Canter (n 53) 510.

ignore the role of free will and only accept a single approach to explaining serial killing, ignoring other influencing factors which may better explain this type of violent offending. It is therefore likely that there are a number of psychological, social and biological influences on serial murder.

6.5 Explanations of youth crime

6.5.1 Introduction

It is recognised that there is a curvilinear relationship between age and crime, as offending is more common in adolescence and early adulthood than in childhood or later adulthood. This spike in criminal activity has attracted much discussion in criminology, with an emphasis on researching the causes of such delinquency.[56] In fact, in the US, offences committed by those aged 18–24 accounted for 28.7% of all recorded offences in 2016, despite this demographic representing only 11.2% of the general population.[57] This section will therefore explore the relationship with age and crime, considering the theory introduced by Hirschi and Gottfredson before moving on to explore the influence of violent video games on youth offending.

6.5.2 Hirschi and Gottfredson: age and crime

Hirschi and Gottfredson[58] identified the curvilinear relationship between age and crime in 1983. They uncovered that delinquency would commence in the early teenage years and peak in the early 20s before declining throughout adulthood. Moreover, they discovered that this curve was consistent across gender and race. As a result of the peak at this particular age, they concluded that the relationship is invariant and therefore cannot be explained by sociological or psychological variables. They therefore argued that 'because the shape of the age–crime curve is similar across time and place, there must be something inherent to offending that leads to its increase and then decline over the life course'.[59] In fact, they concluded that age has a direct effect on crime – the age itself is the influencing variable and is consequently the law of nature. Thus, they argued that ageing has an effect on the decline of criminal activity.

In support of this theory, in 2021, Snyder concluded that this curvilinear relationship of age and crime was consistent across decades – 1990, 2000 and 2010.[60] Moreover, Farrington[61] argued that in order to understand the

---

56. G Sweeten, A Piquero and L Steinberg, 'Age and the Explanation of Crime, Revisited' (2013) 42 *Journal of Youth and Adolescence* 921, 921–22.
57. M Rocque, C Posick and J Hoyle, 'Age and Crime' (2016) 1 *The Encyclopedia of Crime and Punishment* 1, 1.
58. T Hirschi and M Gottfredson, 'Age and the Explanation of Crime' (1983) 89 *American Journal of Sociology* 552, 522–84.
59. Rocque (n 57) 3.
60. H Snyder, Office of Justice Programs, Bureau of Justice Statistics, *Arrest in the United States, 1990–2010* (2021) 14.
61. D Farrington, 'Age and Crime' (1986) 7 *Crime and Justice* 189, 193.

relationship between age and crime, we must separate prevalence, frequency, period, and cohort effects. This includes assessing how many different people are offending at a given time, how frequently such people offend, factors relating to particular historical time points, and factors associated with a group of individuals who experienced similar events. After removing each of these factors when analysing the commission of crime across adolescence and early adulthood, Farrington's research indicated that the age–crime relationship was still prevalent.[62] Thus, this supports Hirschi and Gottfredson's theory that age has a direct effect on crime, regardless of other influencing factors, and is therefore invariable. However, this ignores other influences on the commission of youth crime. Subsequently, the next section will consider the effect that exposure to video games has on violent youth offending.

6.5.3 Youth offending and video games

We briefly considered the effect of video games and television as an influence on child offending at **6.2.3**. Sociological explanations suggested that aggressive behaviour in children is influenced by viewing violent material.[63] Huesmann et al concluded that this is the main contributor to aggressive behaviour in children, adolescences and adults,[64] particularly given their level of exposure to electronic media and video games in the US.[65]

The theoretical background of the relationship between exposure to violent media and youth offending suggests that such a factor enables us to predict violent or aggressive behaviour in adolescence or adulthood. This relationship has been found to persist when factors such as socioeconomic status, intellectual ability and a variety of parenting factors are controlled. Thus, academics widely accept that aggression and violent behaviour are unlikely to exist without predisposition to a number of factors, including exposure to violence or aggression in childhood.[66]

One case example of the effect of video games on violent youth offending involved the murder of Marie Smothers, a 78-year-old woman who lived in Louisiana, US. Smothers lived with an 8-year-old boy who was playing *Grand Theft Auto*, a popular but violent video game intended for players aged 18+. The young boy later found a pistol and shot Smothers in the back of the head, killing her. The police concluded that this killing was intentional and not an accident.[67] Whilst it is extremely rare for children of the age of 8 to commit murder, it was suggested that this violent act committed by a child of such a young age was influenced by exposure to the violent video game.

---

62. ibid 191.
63. S Smith, C Fergsuon and K Beaver, 'A Longitudinal Analysis of Shooter Games and their Relationship with Conduct Disorder and Self-Reported Delinquency' (2018) 58 *International Journal of Law and Psychiatry* 48, 48.
64. L Huesmann (n 15).
65. Dietz (n 14) 428.
66. Huesmann (n 15) 201.
67. Rocque (n 57) 1.

6.5.4 Conclusion

It is clear that there is a curvilinear relationship between age and crime.[68] Whilst Hirschi and Gottfredson have attempted to explain youth crime by suggesting that the age of the offender is the influence for such offending, this theory is reductionist as it only accepts age as an explanation of youth crime, ignoring the influence of biological, psychological and environmental factors. It is deterministic as it neglects the role of free will in youth offending. Moreover, whilst it is evident that video games may have an impact of the commission of violence amongst youths, once more, it is reductionist as it only accepts exposure to violent video games as an explanation of youth crime, ignoring the influence of biological, psychological and environmental factors. It is also deterministic as it neglects the role of free will in youth offending or youths that have been exposed to violent media but have not committed a crime in later life.

6.6 Chapter conclusion

It is evident that a number of approaches attempt to explain violent crimes – including biology, genetics, brain development, mental illness, socialisation and age.

There are a number of approaches which are able to explain aggression and the commission of violence, including psychopathology, loneliness in childhood and a lack of self-control. Moreover, the case study of Jeffrey Dahmer suggests that there are a number of influencing factors on serial killing, including individual characteristics such as an organised or disorganised profile, an isolated childhood and the effect of alcohol on brain development. Finally, the curvilinear relationship between age and crime, particularly youth offending, accepts age as an influencing factor and explanation of youth crime. Consequently, whilst such approaches may be criticised, they allow us not only to offer treatment to such offenders but to develop preventative measures against violent offending. Perhaps a more inter-disciplinary approach to understanding is required, which would encompass a range of biological, psychological and social approaches in order to better understand the commission of violent crime.

KEY POINTS AND SUMMARY

- By understanding aggression, we can better understand violence and therefore violent crime. However, although sociological and biological approaches may provide an insight into aggressive offending behaviour, they are problematic due to being overly deterministic and reductionist.
- There are a number of psychological and sociological approaches which are able to explain the commission of violence, including psychopathology, loneliness in childhood and a lack of self-control.

---

68. Sweeten (n 56) 921–22.

- A combination of biological, psychological and sociological approaches is best suited to explain serial offending and, in particular, serial killing. Moreover, serial killer typologies have been used in order to profile serial killers.
- Youth crime may be explained by the influencing factor of age alone. This explains the curvilinear relationship between age and crime.

STUDY QUESTIONS

- What approaches are able to explain displays of aggression?
- What effect can alcohol have on a person's offending behaviour?
- Why were the serial killer typologies criticised?
- What is the relationship between age and crime? In particular, what are the suggested influences on youth offending?

Understanding Sexual Offences: Law and Procedure

7.1 Introduction

This chapter considers sexual offences (in particular the offence of rape), governed by the Sexual Offences Act 2003, under the law in England and Wales. Currently, the criminal justice system is facing a crisis when dealing with cases in this area, especially in cases of rape. It was reported in October 2020 that 99% of rapes reported to the police in England and Wales in the year ending March 2020 resulted in no legal proceedings against the alleged attacker. *Sky News* questioned whether rape had become the 'perfect crime'. As such, this chapter will also look at reforms to how vulnerable and/or intimated witnesses can offer their best evidence in order to bring about justice. Further, the chapter will discuss whether those accused of sexual crimes ought to be provided with a degree of anonymity.

7.2 Rape

7.2.1 *Actus reus*

Section 1 the Sexual Offences Act 2003 sets out the offence of rape, and if a defendant is found guilty, they could be sentenced to life imprisonment. Section 1 states that:

(1) A person (A) commits an offence if—

    (a) he intentionally penetrates the vagina, anus or mouth of another person (B) with his penis,

    (b) B does not consent to the penetration, and

    (c) A does not reasonably believe that B consents.

It is important to note that to be convicted of a s 1 offence, the penetration needs to be done by using a penis. Any other body part or implement will not suffice for rape, but a defendant may in that case be charged with an offence under s 2 (assault by penetration). Therefore, only a male can be convicted of the offence of rape. Under s 79(3), a surgically constructed penis will suffice and therefore this would allow the prosecution to charge a post-operative transgender person with the offence of rape. Historically, the penis had to penetrate the vagina; however, the law has evolved to include the anus[1] and mouth.[2]

---

1. Criminal Justice and Public Order Act 1994, s 142.
2. Sexual Offences Act 2003, s 1.

Consent is an essential element of the offence, and it centres on the subjective mind of the victim. In *R v McFall*,[3] the defendant kidnapped the victim whom he had been living with. He suggested that he wanted to have sex and she consented, as she feared for the consequences of what might happen should she refuse. During the sexual intercourse, the victim made noises to intimate that she was enjoying sex, although these were faked. The defendant was charged with rape and convicted. The Court of Appeal upheld his conviction as, despite the signs and sounds that the victim consented to sex, she was subjectively not consenting.

Whether or not consent is present is a difficult area of law. This question will be left to the jury to decide, and owing to that difficulty there are three sections of the Act designed to help clarify matters for the jury:

- Section 76. This contains a set of conclusive presumptions that if proven by the prosecution will show that the victim did not consent to the sexual intercourse and the defendant did not reasonably believe the victim was consenting.
- Section 75. These presumptions are based on evidence. If these presumptions are made out by the prosecution, the defendant is required to provide some evidence to counter them. If the defendant fails to do so, that will establish that the sexual intercourse was non-consensual and the defendant did not reasonably believe the victim was consenting.
- Section 74. This section offers an imprecise definition of consent.

Conclusive presumptions about consent (s 76)

Section 76 states:

> (1) If in proceedings for an offence to which this section applies it is proved that the defendant did the relevant act and that any of the circumstances specified in subsection (2) existed, it is to be conclusively presumed—
>   (a) that the complainant did not consent to the relevant act, and
>   (b) that the defendant did not believe that the complainant consented to the relevant act.
>
> (2) The circumstances are that—
>   (a) the defendant intentionally deceived the complainant as to the nature or purpose of the relevant act;
>   (b) the defendant intentionally induced the complainant to consent to the relevant act by impersonating a person known personally to the complainant.

As ever, the case law provides an illustration of how this section is to be interpreted. The first case we examine pre-dates the Sexual Offences Act 2003 by some 80 years. Nevertheless, it paints a clear picture of how the courts interpret the idea of belief in consent.

In *R v Williams*[4] the defendant was a vocal coach who taught people to sing. The victim was a 16-year-old girl, and the defendant convinced her to let him 'try something' to improve her singing voice. This 'improvement' involved him having

---

3. [1994] Crim LR 226.
4. [1923] 1 KB 340.

sex with her. He was subsequently charged with rape and convicted. His conviction was upheld on appeal as he was deceptive as to the nature of the act to improve her singing voice. The victim thought she was consenting to improve her voice, not to have sexual intercourse. Therefore any consent was undermined by the defendant's deception. However, this area of law is not as clear as it sounds. In *R v Dica*[5] the defendant knew he was HIV-positive and had sex with two people, infecting them with the disease. It was clear to the court that neither of the victims would have consented to sex with the defendant had they known he was HIV-positive. At trial, he was acquitted of rape but convicted of an offence against the person. His appeal was successful, and the court clarified that being deceptive as to a disease does not amount to deception as to the 'nature and purpose of the act'. In *Williams* the deception concerned the nature of act – the victim thought that allowing the defendant to penetrate her vagina with his penis would improve her singing voice. In *Dica*, the 'nature' of the act was still sexual intercourse, but for gratification. The court believed that being deceptive as to one's health status did not undermine the victim's consent.

Evidential presumptions (s 75)

If the case facts do not fall within the conclusive presumptions outlined in s 76, the court will examine if they fall within the evidential presumptions in s 75. This section contains a number of rebuttable presumptions – this means that the jury will find a lack of consent *unless* the defendant can offer evidence that challenges the presumption that there was no consent to sexual intercourse.

Section 75(1) states:

> (1) If in proceedings for an offence to which this section applies it is proved—
> (a) that the defendant did the relevant act,
> (b) that any of the circumstances specified in subsection (2) existed, and
> (c) that the defendant knew that those circumstances existed,
> the complainant is to be taken not to have consented to the relevant act unless sufficient evidence is adduced to raise an issue as to whether he consented, and the defendant is to be taken not to have reasonably believed that the complainant consented unless sufficient evidence is adduced to raise an issue as to whether he reasonably believed it.

Section 75(2) provides a list of six circumstances where a rebuttable presumption of a lack of consent will arise:

(a) 'any person was, at the time of the relevant act or immediately before it began, using violence against the complainant or causing the complainant to fear that immediate violence would be used against him'. In the case of *R v Dagnall*[6] the defendant dragged the complainant from the road stating that he would rape her. She responded by saying 'do what you like, so long as you do

---

5. [2004] EWCA Crim 1103.
6. [2003] EWCA Crim 2441.

not harm me'. It is clear that this would not be consensual sex, and the defendant would not be able to rebut the presumption of a lack of consent.

(b) 'any person was, at the time of the relevant act or immediately before it began, causing the complainant to fear that violence was being used, or that immediate violence would be used, against another person'. An example of how this presumption would arise would centre on the threats to another. Should a defendant threaten to harm the victim's child, unless the victim has sex with him, this would fall under this provision.

(c) 'the complainant was, and the defendant was not, unlawfully detained at the time of the relevant act'. An example of this presumption is where a hostage is forced to have sex with their captor. This is uncontroversial and would be difficult to rebut.[7]

(d) 'the complainant was asleep or otherwise unconscious at the time of the relevant act'. Again, this is relatively self-explanatory. However, should the defendant present evidence that the victim had a desire or fantasy to have sex whilst she was asleep, the defendant might be able to rebut the presumption of a lack of consent.

(e) 'because of the complainant's physical disability, the complainant would not have been able at the time of the relevant act to communicate to the defendant whether the complainant consented'. If physical disability means that the complainant cannot communicate her consent to the defendant, the prosecution will be able to make the presumption that the act was non-consensual. This presumption is limited to a physical disability, and being intoxicated through drink or drugs would not allow the presumption to be used.

(f) 'any person had administered to or caused to be taken by the complainant, without the complainant's consent, a substance which, having regard to when it was administered or taken, was capable of causing or enabling the complainant to be stupefied or overpowered at the time of the relevant act'. This final scenario deals with the concept of date-rape, where the defendant drugs the complainant without their knowledge, eg by spiking their drink. This presumption will apply if the illicit substance is given to the victim without their knowledge. If the victim becomes intoxicated of their own free will, this presumption will not apply.

Definition of consent – capacity and freedom (s 74)

Section 74 of the Sexual Offences Act 2003 provides a broad definition of what consent is. If the presumptions in s 75 and 76 do not apply (or they are rebutted by the defendant in the case of s 75), the defendant could still be liable for rape so long as a lack of consent has been established. Section 74 defines consent as follows: 'a person consents if he agrees by choice, and has the freedom and capacity to make that choice'.

---

7.   See *R v David T* [2005] EWCA Crim 2668.

The definition offered by s 74 clearly states that the victim has to consent by choice. In *R v Jheeta*[8] the defendant sent the victim text messages from an anonymous phone purporting to be a police officer. The defendant told the victim that she should continue having sex with him in order to avoid a fine for causing distress. It was clear that the victim was not consenting through 'choice'. The Court of Appeal held that the deception had undermined the victim's consent by use of s 74 (even though there was no deception as to the nature or purpose of the act).

As well as having free choice, ie not being forced into something for the gratification of another person, the consent needs to be made by a person possessing the relevant capacity. In *R v C*[9] the victim had a history of mental disorders, which gave rise to sporadic episodes and delusions of irrational fear for her safety. She became friends with the defendant who supplied her with crack cocaine. He also forced her to perform oral sex on him and an acquaintance. The victim claimed that she only consented because she feared for her safety. The court convicted the defendant, but the Court of Appeal quashed the conviction and said that her capacity was not undermined by her condition. The House of Lords reinstated the conviction, suggesting that her mental condition prevented her from making a real choice.

As well as capacity, the victim must have the freedom to choose whether or not to engage in sexual relations. The term freedom is not defined within the Act but is defined in the *Oxford English Dictionary* as 'the state or fact of being free from servitude, constraint, inhibition etc'.[10] This means there can be no constraints on a person's consent, for example being forced to engage in sexual acts out of fear for one's safety or because of a deception (these circumstances would be covered by the presumptions discussed above). However, what about other constraints that might invalidate consent. In *F v DPP*[11] the victim agreed to sexual intercourse on the basis that the defendant would not ejaculate inside her. During penetration, the defendant told his wife that she was 'his' and he could do whatever he wanted. As such, he decided not to withdraw and ejaculated inside her. The question here was whether or not going back on such an agreement during sex could amount to rape. The court held that negating a promise not to ejaculate inside the victim could be held to remove freedom of choice and thus negate consent. The court suggested that this would not extend to cases where there has been a premature or accidental ejaculation.[12]

It is important to note that cases on the freedom and capacity to provide informed consent will be dealt with on a case-by-case basis by the jury. However, the cases of *F* and *Assange* provide an indication of how the jury might interpret the notion of freedom of choice.

---

8. [2007] EWCA Crim 1699.
9. [2009] 1 WLR 1786.
10. www.oed.com/view/Entry/74395?rskey=DwPMa4&result=1#eid (accessed 25 June 2021).
11. [2013] EWCA 945 (Admin).
12. See also *Assange v Swedish Prosecution Authority* [2011] EWHC 2849 (Admin) for a case concerning the prerequisite to use a condom.

7.2.2 *Mens rea*

The *mens rea* of rape has two elements: (1) the penetration must be intentional; and (2) the defendant does not reasonably believe that the victim consents. In order to satisfy the first component, it is relatively straightforward to establish intentional penetration. In *R v F*[13] the court took a dim view of the suggestion that a man could penetrate someone whilst unconscious, maintain an erection and ejaculate whilst waking up.

However, the second limb might be a little more problematic. Although the case pre-dates the Sexual Offences Act 2003, *R v Morgan*[14] provides an example of what might be classified as reasonable belief in consent. In this case, the defendant and others had sex with the victim. They were told by her husband that she wanted to have sex with a group of men and that any resistance she might show would highlight that she was enjoying it; and the more she resisted, the greater her enjoyment. Each defendant was charged with and convicted of rape. Their appeals were eventually dismissed by the House of Lords which stated that a belief of consent does not have to be reasonable, so long as it is honest. The House of Lords founds that no jury would find their honest belief in consent to be true. The Sexual Offences Act 2003 takes this further by explicitly stating that there needs to be a reasonable belief in consent.[15] Ultimately, the jury will have to consider whether a defendant (a) believed that the complainant consented (subjective); if so (b) reasonably believed it (objective). The jury are entitled to consider 'all the circumstances' to determine reasonableness, for example age, sexual experience and learning disabilities.[16]

7.3 Conviction rates and reform

In the introduction to this chapter, we stated that the criminal justice system is plagued with problems in terms of bringing sexual offenders to justice. The conviction rates for rape are at an all-time low, and this section will now look at reforms to the process in order not only to improve conviction rates but also to provide cathartic justice to those who have been subjected to sexual assaults.

Cases of sexual assault can be highly traumatising for victims; they can feel vulnerable, distressed and anxious when giving evidence in court. The Home Office Report, *Speaking up for Justice*,[17] described how the personal circumstances of the witnesses reflected their ability to give evidence, and failure to deal with these issues could undermine the outcome of the case. This is especially true for child victims of sexual assault and, as such, the Youth Justice and Criminal Evidence Act (YJCEA) 1999 was enacted to ensure that child complainants can give their best evidence possible. Under s 16 of the YJCEA 1999, a child witness,

---

13. [2014] EWCA Crim 878.
14. [1976] AC 182.
15. Sexual Offences Act 2003, s 1(1)(c).
16. ibid, s 1(2).
17. Interdepartmental Working Group, June 1998.

and any witness whose quality of evidence is likely to be diminished because they are suffering from a mental disorder, have significant impairment of intelligence and social functioning or have a physical disability or disorder, are entitled to assistance. The scope of the Act goes wider, and an adult can also be classed as an 'intimidated witness' and benefit from a range of special measures. An 'intimidated witness' is defined under s 17 of the YJCEA 1999 as one whose 'evidence ... is likely to be diminished by reason of fear or distress ... in connection with testifying in the proceedings'. For the purpose of this section, both adults and children may be classed as vulnerable or intimidated witnesses (VIWs), and we will now discuss the range of measures available to them.

There have always been concerns about the lack of sensitivity to the needs of VIWs in sexual offences cases, particularly in relation to children. ChildLine stated that 'there was little understanding of the child's lack of knowledge of court procedures and no real recognition of the stress that giving evidence in court put on a child'.[18] The YJCEA 1999 was introduced to provide a range of special measures that can be used in aiding and facilitating VIWs (ss 23–30). Special measures are a series of legislative provisions that are designed to help VIWs in the traumatic trial process by relieving stress and changing the way evidence is gathered and given in court. However, to receive the benefits of special measures in court proceedings, two hurdles must be overcome: (a) a person involved in the case must be eligible as defined under s 16 or s 17 of the YJCEA 1999; and (b) a trial judge must exercise their discretion to implement special measures. This discretion can only be exercised where the court is of the opinion that the measures are likely to improve the quality of the evidence given. However, it remains the case that certain witnesses will not be entitled to such suitable provisions and will continue to be failed by the court system.

One measure available to courts is the use of screens to shield the witness from the defendant.[19] This is designed to reduce anxiety and trauma, particularly if the defendant is known to the VIW. Early evidence suggests that this measure is a positive step as '81% of VIWs found screens helpful'.[20] However, there is a risk that this may offend the fair trial rights of the defendant. Arguably, a screen may give rise to unconscious bias in the jury; they could infer that the defendant behind the screen is a 'monster' whom the witness simply cannot face – without listening to all of the evidence. Section 32 goes some way to mitigating this issue. A judicial warning needs to be given to the effect that the screen should not be taken as justifying such a conclusion.

Another measure provided by the court is outlined in s 24, which allows for evidence to be given via a 'live link'. Effectively, this means that the evidence will be provided by a live television feed into the courtroom. There is a presumption that this special measure will be used throughout proceedings, which will allow for

---

18. ChildLine, 'Going to Court: Child witnesses in their own words' (1996).
19. Youth Justice and Criminal Evidence Act 1999, s 23.
20. B Hamlyn et al, 'Are Special Measures Working? Evidence from surveys of vulnerable and intimidated witnesses' (Home Office, 2004).

real time responses. It has been found that '90% of VIWs found live links helpful'[21] in terms of reducing the anxiety and fear of giving evidence. It ought to be noted that the live link does not prevent the defendant seeing the witness; this is something that surprises and worries many VIWs who, when they realise this, sometimes opt for screens instead.[22] This could be problematic for some VIWs, as they might struggle with the thought of being viewed by a defendant, which in turn might cause an element of stress and therefore diminish the quality of their evidence.

A further special measure (s 25) allows for evidence to be given in private, which means that the judge has the power to remove the public from the court room. This reduces the number of 'unnecessary' people in court and allows for pressure to be lessened on the VIW; it also mitigates potential intimidation that may occur. Hamlyn et al concluded that 'of the small group of 32 witnesses for whom the gallery had been cleared ... most said they found it helpful'.[23] Complainants can also apply for the removal of wigs and gowns under s 26, whereby the judiciary and barristers will dispense of them during witness evidence. This section is typically used in cases involving a child witness, as the removal of such regalia may be effective in lowering stress and intimidation in this unfamiliar environment. Majeed-Ariss suggests that this has 'an impact ... that it produces a less formal situation'.[24] Hamlyn et al found that 'most VIWs who gave evidence with wigs and gowns removed appreciated this, and that many not offered this facility would have accepted'.[25] However, this special measure 'was nearly always refused' in practice,[26] and the Home Office has doubted its effectiveness.[27]

Section 27 of the YJCEA 1999 provides for a video recording of an interview of the witness to be admitted as evidence-in-chief. This is as a substitute for giving 'live' evidence in a court room, which will release the pressure and stress put on VIWs. This measure was supported by Hamlyn et al's study which discovered that '90% of VIWs found pre-recorded evidence-in-chief helpful',[28] implying that it enhanced the quality of evidence offered by VIWs. However, this positivity is not universally accepted. This special measure raises fair trial questions, but it may also be susceptible to criticism because of technological complications. Hamlyn et al's study shows that in one case 'the interviewing officer was constantly obscuring the view of the witness by excessive gesture',[29] which therefore diminished the quality of that evidence. It was concluded that their evidence would have been more beneficial to the jury had it been live. These problems may cause the witness to feel

---

21. ibid [14].
22. A Wade, 'Stories in Court' (1998) *Child & Fam LQ* 179.
23. Hamlyn (n 20) [14].
24. R Majeed-Ariss, '"Could do better": Report on the use of special measures in sexual offences cases' (2021) 21(1) *Criminology and Criminal Justice* 89–106 at 92.
25. Hamlyn (n 20) [14].
26. ibid [22].
27. ibid [23].
28. ibid [14].
29. ibid.

as though they have been failed by the court as they had trusted the interviewing officer to be professionally trained in this area. For a trial to be negatively impacted by something as simple as the interviewing officer not being spatially aware is very disappointing.

A further measure to enable VIWs to give their best evidence and reduce pressure on them is set out in s 28 of the YJCEA 1999. Where a direction under s 27 is given, the direction may also provide for 'any cross-examination of the witness, and any re-examination, to be recorded by means of a video recording'. However, there are questions of fair trial rights concerning this particular measure. In *R v PMH*,[30] the defendant argued that his right to a fair trial was breached, as the judge had not warned the jury on the limitations imposed on cross-examination. The complainant's body and lower face were not visible as a result of a fault with the recording. However, Hallett LJ concluded that 'Parliament has provided for this procedure in section 28 ... and those who are accustomed to it report that, if operated properly, it can work well. It does not undermine the defendant's right to a fair trial.' When using pre-recorded evidence in practice, it was observed that 'factors such as the choice of camera perspective may bear careful scrutiny for their potential to influence jurors' assessments of witness credibility'.[31] This could potentially affect whether or not trials are conducted fairly, and there should be more awareness around conclusions juries could draw from technical issues. Due to these issues, it could be argued that the court system is still continuing to fail VIWs; however, from the evidence above, it is clear that this type of special measure is important in aiding VIWs.

During the examination of a witness, an intermediary may be appointed by the court under s 29 of the YJCEA 1999 to aid the witness in giving evidence. Their function is to communicate the questions asked to the witness, so they are fully understood by the witness, and to feed back the answers given. Intermediaries are provided with specific training and have unique knowledge of the witness, providing VIWs with a more comfortable environment and making communication clearer so that they can provide their best evidence. This section is only available for witnesses eligible under s 16. Intermediaries must be registered by the Witness Intermediary Scheme, and it is imperative that they perform their role 'faithfully', as they are the only person in the courtroom that will understand what the VIWs is 'saying'. The Ministry of Justice stated, 'They will not alter the question put or answer given in the first instance but may if required offer an alternative form of question to facilitate understanding.'[32]

This special measure has been viewed as particularly effective by VIWs and the judiciary. In *R v Watts*[33] the court stated, 'The use of intermediaries forms an

---

30. [2018] EWCA Crim 2452.
31. V Munro, 'The impact of the use of pre-recorded evidence on juror decision-making' (Scottish Government, 2018): www.gov.scot/publications/impact-use-pre-recorded-evidence-juror-decision-making-evidence-review-9781788516679/ (accessed 1 July 2021).
32. Ministry of Justice, 'Achieving Best Evidence in Criminal Proceedings' (2011).
33. [2010] EWCA Crim 1824.

integral part of the structure of the special measures regime.'[34] Without the use of an intermediary, no evidence would have been adduced from the VIW. This is further evidenced by Plotnikoff and Woolfson, who quote a prosecutor who states that 'we could not have got the evidence out without the intermediary'.[35]

Ultimately, these measures are designed to obtain the best evidence possible from the witness and to reduce the rate of attrition (that is the rate of cases that drop out of the criminal justice system) as witnesses will feel more supported, thus continuing with the trial and contributing to a positive outcome.

It must be noted that the accused is excluded from most of these measures, save for the use of intermediaries and the giving of evidence via live link. This ultimately begs the question that if the idea of the measures is to obtain the best possible evidence, to ensure a fair trial, we should also require the best evidence from the defendant.

7.4 Suspect anonymity

Arguably, being accused of a sexual offence is the most stigmatising of all offences. With the advent of 24-hour rolling news channels and the rise of social media, it has never been more easy for a suspect or defendant to be tried in the court of public opinion. Couple this concern with the idea that there is 'no smoke without fire', should we protect the identity of the suspect until either the point of charge or conviction?

Suspect anonymity is not a recent concept, and historically we have continually altered our approach to it. The Helibron Committee first introduced the notion of anonymity in 1975,[36] and based on these recommendations, Parliament brought forward a Bill to afford anonymity to complainants in rape cases. During the report stage of the Bill, the Standing Committee voted to extend the measures to defendants,[37] and therefore the Sexual Offences (Amendment) Act 1976 introduced anonymity for both complainants and defendants in rape cases.[38] However, anonymity was only afforded to defendants, not suspects; thus anonymity was only available from the charging stage to conviction.[39] Defendant anonymity in rape cases was repealed in 1988[40] and is now a privilege only extended to complainants in sexual offence cases,[41] with the only exception being pre-charge anonymity for teachers.[42]

---

34. per Mackay J.
35. J Plotnikoff and R Woolfson, 'The Go-Between: Evaluation of Intermediary Pathfinder Projects' (NSPCC/The Nuffield Foundation, 2007) 29.
36. Home Office, *Report of the Advisory Group on the Law of Rape* (Cmnd 6352, 1975) para 163.
37. Home Affairs Committee, *Sexual Offences Bill (fifth report)* (HC 2002-03, 639) para 68.
38. s 4 and s 6.
39. Home Affairs Committee (n 37) para 77.
40. Criminal Justice Act 1988, s 158(5).
41. Sexual Offences (Amendment) Act 1992, s 2.
42. Education Act 2011, s 13.

We said in the opening to this section that there is a particular stigma attached to sexual offences.[43] However, this is something that the Criminal Law Revision Committee disagreed with. It maintained that being accused of rape was no different from being accused of other crimes.[44] Rumney disagreed with this contention, arguing that society does not necessarily draw the distinction between those who are *convicted* and those who are *suspected* of a criminal offence.[45] Therefore, it ought to be essential to evaluate how social stigma in sexual offences cases affects both false allegations and the presumption of innocence of those accused of these crimes.

Advocates in favour of suspect and defendant anonymity argue that it is necessary to protect individuals from social stigma in cases of false allegations. Henriques argues that anyone can be the subject of a false allegation, as it only takes one accusation for an individual's reputation to be tarnished.[46] Christine Hamilton, who was arrested with her husband on false sexual offences claims, noted the fact that the stigmatisation was almost never-ending. She said that 'it can destroy lives',[47] despite the fact that she was never formally charged with an offence. This was reiterated by Lord Paddick, who said that the public assume 'there is no smoke without fire if the police go as far as arresting an individual',[48] suggesting in the case of sexual offences that being a suspect is enough to be assumed guilty. Lady Brittan, the wife of the late Leon Brittan (a victim of Carl Beech's false allegations), experienced this stigmatisation, having to arrange for security to be present at her husband's funeral.[49] This highlights not only the effect social stigma has on the suspect but also the shadow impact that it has on their family. Furthermore, defendants of sexual offences also face social stigma. They find that their reputation is often ruined and struggle to find work post-acquittal as details of their trial remain available online.[50] This enforces the argument that 'If you throw mud it sticks',[51] suggesting that both suspect and defendant anonymity is needed. This is the reason that teachers are afforded pre-charge anonymity as the possibility of a false allegation could destroy a teacher's career.[52] Though it might be inconsistent to suggest that a teacher's career could be destroyed by a

43. Baroness Stern, *The Stern Review* (Home Office, 2010) 41.
44. Home Affairs Committee (n 37) para 70.
45. Rumney et al, 'Rape, Defendant Anonymity and Evidence-Based Policy Making' (2013) 76 *MLR* 109, 126–27.
46. R Henriques, 'An Independent Review of the Metropolitan Police Service's handling of non-recent sexual offence investigations alleged against persons of public prominence' (October 2016).
47. Home Affairs, *Anonymity in rape cases* (HL 2012) 8.
48. HL Deb 1 March 2019, vol 796, col 418.
49. 'Carl Beech: "VIP abuse" accuser jailed for 18 years', BBC News (July 2019): www.bbc.co.uk/news/uk-49130670 (accessed 25 June 2021).
50. C Hoyle, N-E Speechley, and R Burnett, 'The Impact of Being Wrongly Accused of Abuse in Occupations of Trust: Victims' Voices' (University of Oxford Centre for Criminology, 2016): www.law.ox.ac.uk/sites/files/oxlaw/the_impact_of_being_wrongly_accused_of_abuse_hoyle_et_al_2016_15_may.pdf at 32 (accessed 25 June 2021).
51. Baroness Stern (n 43) 41.
52. HC Deb 1 March 2011, cols 43–100.

false accusation, whilst if you are a plumber or a postal worker you are somewhat impervious to the accusations.

Social stigma also affects the presumption of innocence. Lord Paddick suggested that 'in the eyes of the public, people are no longer considered to be innocent until proven guilty',[53] indicating that the court of public opinion is more prevalent today than ever before, which is why anonymity should be granted. Academics have suggested that in the modern day there exists a presumption of guilt towards the defendant, due to the nature of sexual offences and the associated stigma.[54] A BBC reporter highlighted this difficulty when interviewing a man, 'John', who stated, 'from the moment my name was in the public domain, my life changed'.[55] Even after the trial, 'John' was forced to move due to the stigmatisation he suffered, despite being acquitted, clearly suggesting the need for both suspect and defendant anonymity. Whilst the Criminal Law Revision Committee in 1984 considered whether introducing defendant anonymity in order to achieve equality between the parties was a 'superficial'[56] argument, this view may now appear somewhat outdated. Baroness Walmsley argued that the media's evolution and coverage of news, from when defendant anonymity was first introduced, has changed dramatically.[57] Modern-day access to news online means that once a name is in the media, the damage is done and, to the world, suspects and defendants may be presumed guilty.[58] Therefore, to maintain their right to the presumption of innocence, both suspects and defendants should be granted anonymity.

A further argument for the reintroduction of anonymity stems from the idea that there is little-to-no public vindication should the case be discontinued or the defendant be acquitted at trial. Suspects, who are accused but never formally charged, will never benefit from public vindication, because their case never progresses to trial.[59] This means they never get 'their day in court' to highlight their innocence, and arguably they ought to be afforded the protection of anonymity. Additionally, an acquittal does not necessarily bring public vindication. Wolchover and Heaton-Armstrong argue that defendants who are acquitted are not necessarily cleared because they are found to be innocent; rather the prosecution did not meet the evidential threshold of proving the case beyond reasonable doubt.[60] They argue that the notion that innocent defendants receive vindication is a 'hollow' argument.[61]

---

53. HL Deb 1 March 2019, vol 796, col 418.
54. K Corteen and R Steele, 'A Criminal Injustice System? Sex Offender Suspects and Defendants' (2018) 39 *Liverpool Law Review* 265.
55. V Kearney, 'Sexual assault cases: Guilty until proven innocent?' (*BBC News* (Northern Ireland), 17 November 2018).
56. Home Affairs Committee (n 37) para 70.
57. HL Deb 2 Jun 2003, cols 1090–1092.
58. HL Deb 1 March 2019, vol 796, col 418.
59. Home Affairs Committee (n 37) para 12.
60. D Wolchover and A Heaton-Armstrong, 'Rape defendant anonymity: part 2' (2012) 176 *Criminal Law and Justice Weekly* 7.
61. ibid.

Finally, it may be argued that suspects and defendants should be granted anonymity for their own safety, as those accused of criminal offences are more at risk of self-harm.[62] Jay Cheshire committed suicide at 17, just months after being falsely accused of rape,[63] and 'Rhys', who was accused of a sex crime, said he felt suicidal as 'being dead was a preferable alternative to having to be falsely accused'.[64] The impact an accusation had in these cases clearly highlights the need for suspect anonymity, as a matter of welfare. Crucially, in a Covid-19 era, with growing delays in the criminal justice system, suspects are placed in a state of limbo.[65] In May 2019 the Crown Court backlog was 33,660 cases; however by May 2020, the backlog had grown to 40,900 cases.[66]

However, anonymity for suspects and defendants is not without its pitfalls. There is an argument that suspect anonymity might hinder an investigation. It was not until ITV broadcast 'Exposure: The Other Side of Jimmy Savile' that victims of Savile came forward to report their abuse.[67] The documentary detailed the allegations of five women, but after the broadcast hundreds came forward in reporting their abuse by Savile.[68] Additionally, many of Savile's victims have contended that if it had not been for the publicity surrounding the documentary, they would not have spoken up about their assaults.[69] Therefore, if anonymity was granted, serious and repeat sexual offenders might never be held accountable for their actions, and justice would not be given to those victims of sexual crimes. This highlights the difficulty faced by legislators in terms of balancing the rights of those accused of crimes and the rights of those subjected to those crimes.

The intrusive and distressing nature of sexual offences is not being downplayed in this section; it is imperative that victims feel confident in reporting allegations of sexual offences. It might appear inconsistent to grant anonymity to suspects and defendants in sexual offences, but no other criminal offences suffer the stigma attached to allegations of sexual offences. The fact that an individual's name may reach newspaper headlines before they have been charged may lead to a suspect being tried in the court of public opinion. Arguably, this defeats due process safeguards on the presumption of innocence. This debate is one that is sure to run, but it is clear that there are no easy answers to the question of whether there should be a regime of suspect and defendant anonymity.

---

62. Rumney et al (n 45) 129.
63. 'I am not a rapist', BBC: www.bbc.co.uk/iplayer/episode/p08pldr0/i-am-not-a-rapist (accessed: 25 June 2021).
64. Hoyle (n 50) 32.
65. Criminal Justice Natters, Interview with Liam Allan: www.youtube.com/watch?v=8kaylCpUH7Q&t=50s (accessed 25 June 2021).
66. Justice Select Committee, 'Coronavirus (COVID-19): The impact on courts' (UK Parliament, 30 July 2020): https://publications.parliament.uk/pa/cm5801/cmselect/cmjust/519/51905.htm#_idTextAnchor006 (accessed 25 June 2021).
67. K Lampard and E Marsden, 'Themes and lessons learnt from NHS investigations into matters relating to Jimmy Savile' (2015): https://assets.publishing.service.gov.uk/government/uploads/system/uploads/attachment_data/file/407209/KL_lessons_learned_report_FINAL.pdf (accessed 25 June 2021) 6.
68. ibid.
69. W Turvill, 'Mark Williams-Thomas: Without Savile exposure, Harris and Clifford victims would never have come forward', Press Gazette (2014): www.pressgazette.co.uk/mark-williams-thomas-if-savile-was-still-alive-he-harris-and-clifford-would-still-be-free/ (accessed 25 June 2021).

chapter

8 Understanding Sexual Offending: Criminology

8.1 Introduction

It is widely accepted that there is a discrepancy in sexual offending – the majority of sexual offences consist of men carrying out sexual violence against women. Research suggests that one in five women are subjected to sexual violence at least once in their lifetime – this is not limited to class, race, age or geographical location.[1] Moreover, research shows that the majority of sex offences are committed by men.

This chapter will consider the following:

- the paradigm of gender-based violence;
- theories of sexual offending;
- societal construction of deviant behaviour; and
- contemporary challenges for lawyers and criminologists.

8.2 Paradigm of gender-based violence

8.2.1 Introduction

A 'paradigm' refers to a pattern or model. Thus, the paradigm of gender-based violence takes the view that violence against women is displayed in order to maintain the patriarchy – a social system that sees men as privileged and as oppressors of women. Gender-based violence can take the form of, but is not limited to, sexual violence, domestic violence, sex trafficking, honour killings, female genital mutilation and child marriage. Gender is a social construct which consists of masculinity and femininity. Feminism has offered a 'paradigm', in which it acknowledges that men hold power advantages over women in a patriarchal society. Feminism argues that domestic and sexual violence are displayed to enable men to maintain a power advantage over women. Thus, the feminism paradigm concludes that sexual violence supports the male enterprise, and, as a result, females are viewed as defensive and reactive.[2]

8.2.2 Feminism and gender-based violence

Feminists maintain that misogyny has encompassed sexual harassment, violence against women and sexual objectification, which can be traced back to ancient

---

1. A Grubb and E Turner, 'Attribution of Blame in Rape Cases: A Review of the Impact of Rape Myth Acceptance, Gender Role Conformity and Substance Use on Victim Blaming' (2012) 17 *Aggression and Violent Behaviour* 443, 443.
2. D Dutton and T Nicholls, 'The Gender Paradigm in Domestic Violence Research and Theory: Part 1 – The Conflict of Theory and Data' (2005) 10 *Aggression and Violence Behaviour* 680, 683.

Greek mythology.[3] 'Misogyny' is derived from the ancient Greek word 'mīsogunía', which means hatred towards women. Misogyny has taken form in a number of ways throughout history – the patriarchy, male privilege, gender discrimination, the belittling of women and violence against women. Subsequently, feminism across history and cultures has shared a common goal – to dismantle the patriarchy and promote social equality of gender.[4]

In 16th century England, rape was portrayed as an expression of men's 'lustful desires' and 'pleasures'.[5] In contrast, female sexual activity was regarded as a sin[6] and consequently connotated with blame and dishonour. Thus, this gender-based construction of sexual activity contributed to a lack of disclosure of consensual sexual intercourse but also, importantly, of non-consensual sexual intercourse throughout history. This also facilitated the prevalence of sexual violence by protecting men, as women were reluctant to report sexual violence due to the implications of sin.[7]

Modern feminism consists of an argument that 'in order to stop men's use and women's experiences of violence on the personal level, structures of gender inequality at the societal level must change'.[8] It argues that there still exists a power imbalance between men and women, which facilitates sexual violence as a result of gender inequality. This inequality is prevalent in family, political, economic and other social institutions. Thus, when women have a lower status than men, it is likely that men will engage in sexual violence in order to maintain such power.[9]

8.2.3 Gender-based violence and criminal justice

The Sexual Offences Act 1956[10] became the first piece of legislation that would govern sexual offences exclusively. However, there was dissatisfaction with such legislation; for example, marital rape was not recognised as an offence in this Act. With the second wave of feminism commencing in the 1960s, feminists campaigned, *inter alia*, for women's rights surrounding the law which arguably permitted male sexual violence against women.[11] Consequently, since the 1970s, England and Wales has seen radical change in how the law governs sexual offences.[12] Though the majority of the 1956 Act (exclusive of ss 33 to 37) was repealed in 2004 by the Sexual Offences Act 2003,[13] reform had been slow, with

---

3.   K Srivastava, S Chaudhury, P Bhat and S Sahu, 'Misogyny, Feminism and Sexual Harassment' (2017) 26 *Industrial Psychiatry Journal* 113, 113.
4.   ibid 114.
5.   M Sommerville, *Sex and Subjection: Attitudes to Women in Early Modern Society* (Arnold, 1995) ch 5.
6.   G Walker, 'Rereading Rape and Sexual Violence in Early Modern England' (1998) 10 *Gender & History* 1, 5.
7.   ibid.
8.   C Yodanis, 'Gender Inequality, Violence Against Women, and Fear: A Cross-National Test of the Feminist Theory of Violence Against Women' (2004) 19 *Journal of Interpersonal Violence* 655, 655.
9.   ibid 656–57.
10. Sexual Offences Act 1956 (c 69).
11. Srivastava (n 3) 112.
12. J Temkin, '"And Always Keep A-hold of Nurse, For Fear of Finding Something Worse": Challenging Rape Myths in the Courtroom' (2010) 13 *NCLR* 710, 710.
13. Sexual Offences Act 2003.

legislation reflecting attitudes in society which had ceased to prevail.[14] (Despite these more recent reforms, rape has failed to shed its label of being less likely to progress from reporting to prosecution and conviction than any other type of offence.[15])

One example of slow reform was the reluctance of the legislature to recognise marital rape as a criminal offence. The 1975 case of *DPP v Morgan*[16] was notorious in illustrating the lack of recognition the criminal justice system had for marital rape. The case involved a man encouraging his friends to have sexual intercourse with his wife. He told his friends that if she resisted, that was just a pretence, and therefore they should carry on. Though the friends of the defendant were convicted of rape, the defendant was acquitted.[17] The law did not protect women from martial rape and, in fact, left wives subject to sex on demand[18] – a breach of Article 5 of the European Convention on Human Rights (the right to liberty and security).[19]

Case law took the first step towards the abolition of marital rape in 1991. The case of *R v R*[20] involved a husband and wife who had separated. The husband subsequently broke into the wife's new home and attempted to have sex with her without her consent.[21] The judge held that 'the time has now arrived when the law should declare that a rapist remains a rapist subject to the criminal law, irrespective of his relationship with his victim'.[22] The Labour Party proposed a Bill which would criminalise marital rape, arguing that the law was outdated and did not reflect the 'reality of marriage'.[23] It was not until 1994 that Parliament enacted the legislation,[24] criminalising marital rape and recognising gender-based sexual violence.

Today, it is clear that legislation is more likely to acknowledge the paradigm of gender-based violence. The offence of rape refers to a penis penetrating a vagina, mouth or anus without consent.[25] Therefore, women cannot legally commit rape as a penis does not form part of the female anatomy. This recognises the gender discrepancy within sexual violence – that male violence against women is the most common form of gender-based violence.[26] Moreover, there are a number of women's shelters and welfare support groups aimed at female victims of sexual

---

14. R Griffith, 'Sexual Offences Act 2003: Key Concepts' (2010) 18 *British Journal of Midwifery* 524, 524.

15. R Wright, 'A Note on Attrition of Rape Cases' (1984) 25 *British Journal of Criminology* 399, 399.

16. [1975] UKHL 3.

17. ibid.

18. F Banda, 'If You Buy A Cup, Why Would You Not Use It? Marital Rape: The Acceptable Face of Gender Based Violence' 109 *AJIL Unbound* 321, 321.

19. Convention for the Protection of Human Rights and Fundamental Freedoms (European Convention on Human Rights, as amended) (ECHR).

20. *R v R* [1992] UKHL 12.

21. ibid.

22. ibid.

23. HC Deb 21 February 1990, vol 167, col 945.

24. HL Deb 14 June 1994, vol 555, col 1630.

25. Sexual Offences Act 2003, s 1(1).

26. L Ellis, *Theories of Rape: Inquiries into the Causes of Sexual Aggression* (Hemisphere Publishing Company, 1989) 3.

violence.[27] However, whilst there are other offences which encompass female sexual violence,[28] the law can be criticised for assuming that the offence of rape can only be perpetrated by men. It should also be acknowledged that men sexually victimise other men.

8.2.4 Conclusion

It is clear that whilst misogyny was first recognised in ancient Greece, it remains prevalent in today's society. Feminism argues that the power imbalance between men and women, with women holding a lower social status, is an influence on sexual violence against women. This imbalance was arguably ignored by the criminal justice system for centuries. However, whilst we see a more progressive approach to criminalising male sexual violence against women in the modern day, this chapter will outline that such attitudes prevail.

8.3 Theories of sexual offending

8.3.1 Introduction

Modern theories which attempt to explain sexual offending have considered a number of different influences on such behaviour. These include:

- genetic predispositions;
- adverse developmental experiences, eg abuse, rejection, attachment difficulties;
- psychological dispositions/trait factors, eg empathy deficits, attitudes supportive of sexual assault, deviant sexual preferences, emotional skill deficits and interpersonal problems;
- social and cultural structures and processes; and
- contextual factors, such as intoxication and severe stress.

This section will consider the Integrated Theory of Sexual Offending (ITSO) and theories of aggression in relation to sexual offending.

8.3.2 Aggression and sexual violence

It is generally accepted by academics[29] that those who endorse sexually aggressive behaviours are more likely to respond less empathically to rape complainants, leaving the complainant to feel at blame for the act of sexual violence committed against them. Additionally, those who commit sexual violence often engage in victim-blaming behaviour.[30]

Aosved and Long argue that it is possible that cultural attitudes may influence tolerance of male aggression against women, facilitating sexual violence as opposed to preventing it.[31] An individual's sex and self-reported physical

---

27. Temkin (n 12) 715.
28. For example, the offences of assault by penetration and sexual assault.
29. N Kibble, and A Aosved and P Long. See n 30 and n 31.
30. N Kibble, 'R. v D: Rape: Rape Within a Relationship - Delayed Allegations - Summing Up' [2009] *Crim LR* 590, 591.
31. A Aosved and P Long, 'Co-occurrence of Rape Myth Acceptance, Sexism, Racism, Homophobia, Ageism, Classism, and Religious Intolerance' (2006) 55 *Sex Roles* 481, 481.

aggression have been found to significantly predict rape myth acceptance.[32] As such, Lainer suggests that eradicating rape myths may lead to individuals being less likely to engage in and be accepting of sexually aggressive behaviour, consequently reducing the rate at which sexual offences are committed (see **8.5.1** and **8.5.2** for context and definition of rape myths).[33]

Moreover, Bhogal and Corbett's study offers two hypotheses surrounding the relationship between aggression and rape myth acceptance.[34] They hypothesized that sex, physical aggression, verbal aggression, anger and hostility, both collectively and individually, significantly influence rape myth acceptance. Additionally, they hypothesized that the male participants would exhibit significantly higher levels of rape myth acceptance than the female participants. The results supported the hypotheses, suggesting that males are considerably more likely to endorse rape myths than females. Furthermore, males were found to display significantly higher levels of aggression than females. Thus, physical aggression and sex were found to be the only significant predictors of rape myth acceptance.[35] This is further supported by Nunes et al, who discovered that the most aggressive participants had more opaque attitudes towards rape, suggesting that there exists a strong correlation between aggression and rape myth acceptance.[36]

Bhogal and Corbett's study is one of the limited studies that offers a rationale for not only rape myth acceptance but its relationship with aggression. It suggests that socialisation and exposure to aggression towards women in the media may provide an explanation for the correlation between rape myth acceptance and aggression.[37] For example, research has indicated that those who play videogames which display violence against women have increased levels of rape myth acceptance.[38] This supports Beck et al's hypthosis that video games, such as *Grand Theft Auto*, which display sexist images of women and include scenes of violence against women, particularly sex workers, may increase the existence of rape myths among young males.[39]

Moreover, Ellis argues that 'Social Learning Theory' is able to explain the correlation between high levels of aggression and high acceptance of rape myths, as individuals are taught gender roles and gender-appropriate behaviour through the process of socialisation.[40] Such processes occur when persons are subjected, in society, the family environment, and the mass media, to frequent displays of

---

32. M Bhogal and S Corbett, 'The Influence of Aggressiveness on Rape-Myth Acceptance Among University Students' (2016) 23 *Psychiatry, Psychology and Law* 709, 709.
33. C Lainer, 'Rape-Accepting Attitudes' (2001) 7 *Violence Against Women* 876, 876.
34. Bhogal (n 32) 709.
35. Bhogal (n 32) 711–13.
36. L Nunes, C Hemann and K Ratcliffe, 'Implicit and Explicit Attitudes Toward Rape are Associated with Sexual Aggression' (2013) 28 *Journal of Interpersonal Violence* 2657, 2675.
37. Bhogal (n 32) 713.
38. ibid.
39. V Beck, S Boys, C Rose and E Beck, 'Violence Against Women in Video Games: A Prequel or Sequel to Rape Myth Acceptance?' (2012) 27 *Journal of Interpersonal Violence* 3016, 3017 and 3023.
40. Ellis (n 26) 3.

violence towards women. This creates a tolerance to violent behaviour, allowing violence against women to become normalised. Moreover, this may also provide an explanation for the lack of reporting, as women may internalise the belief that violence against them is acceptable. Such research suggests that literature regarding rape myth acceptance has taken a positive shift towards explaining the existence of negative attitudes towards rape. This offers the potential for prevention schemes which aim to reduce the existence of rape myth acceptance in aggressive males[41] – the main perpetrators of sexual violence.[42]

8.3.3 Integrated Theory of Sexual Offending

Ward and Beech argue that whilst theories of sexual offending have attempted to take account of a number of influencing factors, there is a key flaw – 'the majority of theories … tend to focus on the surface level of symptomology and fail to take into account the fact that human beings are biological or embodied creatures'.[43] This ignores underlying factors, such as brain development, and only pays attention to more observable factors, such as attachment difficulties. Subsequently, a more integrated approach encompassing a number of different factors is required in order to adequately explain the commission of sexual violence.

The Integrated Theory of Sexual Offending (ITSO) was first introduced by Marshall and Barbaree in 1990. They acknowledged the disparity in influencing factors in explaining sexual offending and suggested that a more integrated approach was necessary in order to account for all influencing factors.[44] The ITSO suggests that the commission of sexual violence is influenced by a number of factors: brain development (including evolution, genetic variations and neurobiology) and ecological factoring (including social and cultural environment, personal circumstances, physical environment). Thus, this theory takes an integrated approach in explaining sexual offending. It suggests that a number of influencing factors are responsible for the commission of sexual violence, advocating a multi-disciplinary approach in explaining such behaviour.[45]

Biological influences

This element of the ITSO suggests that a genetic disposition to aggressive behaviour may contribute to sexual offending. It is widely accepted that biology has played a part in sexual behaviour in order for the human race to continue its existence. Thus, biological approaches assume that evolution has influenced sexual violence by executing displays of aggression in order to achieve sexual goals. However, Mashall and Barbaree acknowledge that this explanation 'does not mean

---

41. ibid.
42. Grubb (n 1) 443.
43. T Ward and A Beech, 'An Integrated Theory of Sexual Offending' (2006) 11 *Aggression and Violent Behaviour* 44, 45.
44. W Marshall and H Barbaree, 'An Integrated Theory of the Etiology of Sexual Offending' in W Marshall, W Lamon and H Barbaree (eds), *Handbook of Sexual Assault* (Springer Science and Business Media, 1990) 257–275.
45. Ward (n 43) 44.

that the display of these behaviors should be accepted as inevitable, nor does such an argument in any way excuse someone for engaging in particular behaviors'.[46]

Childhood experiences

This element of the ITSO argues that poor socialisation, particularly in the context of violent parenting, will facilitate the use of aggression in later life. This could result in resentment and hostility which may manifest itself in sexual violence. This approach also suggests that early development experiences (more so during puberty) may influence a 'strong desire to engage in sex and aggression'.[47] Thus, there are many childhood experiences that may explain the commission of sexual violence in adolescence or adulthood.

Social context

This approach to sexual offending suggests that social experiences may influence sexual offending as a result of poor parenting which leads to children seeking guidance from media sources. Marshall and Barbaree suggest that such media convey misleading messages to youths which may attribute to low self-esteem. This low self-esteem may influence a quest for a sense of power, which ultimately results in the display of sexual aggression in order to maintain such power and control.[48]

Situational factors

Finally, the ITSO argues that situational factors may influence sexual offending. This suggests that environmental factors play a key role in sexual offending. One example is that the excessive consumption of alcohol may influence the commission of sexual violence. One study suggested that in 70% of rapes, police were able to demonstrate that the offender had consumed alcohol.[49] Thus, this suggests that reduced inhibitions may increase the presence of underlying aggression which influences the commission of sexual violence.[50]

8.3.4 Conclusion

It is widely accepted that there are a number of influencing factors on the commission of sexual violence. Theories of understanding aggression argue that the presence of aggression can explain male sexual violence against women. However, this approach alone cannot account for violent sexual behaviour. Thus, the ITSO encompasses a range of influences, such as brain development and ecological factors.

---

46. Marshall (n 44) 258.
47. ibid 261.
48. ibid 265.
49. M Christie, W Marshall and R Lanthier, *Report to the Solicitor General of Canada, Ottawa: A Descriptive Study of Incarcerated Rapists and Pedophiles* (1979).
50. Marshall (n 44) 269.

8.4 Societal construction of deviant behaviour

8.4.1 Introduction

There are a range of different factors which may contribute to a societal construction of deviant behaviour and, in particular, sexual deviant behaviour. Subsequently, this section will outline the influences of sexism and pornography on the commission of sexual violence, which have been argued to correlate with violent sexual behaviour.

8.4.2 Sexism and its relationship with sexual violence

Victims of rape experience stereotyping which is influenced by extra-legal information, for example, their clothing, appearance, general attractiveness, lifestyle, relationship status and previous sexual relationships.[51] Such attitudes typically derive from sexism, which reflects attitudes about the way that women should behave.[52] Furthermore, Lonsway and Fitzgerald have suggested that stereotypes towards women are associated with a higher level of rape myth acceptance – an influencing factor common amongst male university students.[53]

Feminism suggests that male sexual violence towards women is utilised in order to instil fear into women for the purpose of control.[54] Fear of sexual assault therefore limits women's freedom, creating a dependency on men. For example, research has suggested that many women avoid going out late at night or going to certain places for fear of sexual violence.[55] Hostile sexism refers to negative stereotyping of gender roles.[56] It is contended that such sexism justifies men's power – women are rewarded for conforming with traditional gender roles that seek to serve men.[57] Research suggests that hostile sexism encompasses stereotypes of female rape victims, contributing to the justification of sexual violence.[58] Bohner and Schwarz argue that rape myths specifically 'put women at a disadvantage', highlighting the sexist nature of stereotypes about rape.[59] Stoll et al's regression analysis established that those who hold attitudes which conform

---

51. S Koepke, F Eyssel and G Bohner , '"She Deserved It": Effects of Sexism Norms, Type of Violence, and Victim's Pre-Assault Behavior on Blame Attributions Toward Female Victims and Approval of the Aggressor's Behavior' (2014) 20 *Violence Against Women* 446, 447.
52. ibid.
53. K Lonsway and L Fitzgerald, 'Attitudinal Antecedents of Rape Myth Acceptance: A Theoretical and Empirical Re-examination' (1995) 68 *Journal of Personality and Social Psychology* 704, 704.
54. Srivastava (n 3) 113.
55. D Abrams, G Viki, B Masser and G Bohner, 'Perceptions of Stranger and Acquaintance Rape: The Role of Benevolent and Hostile Sexism in Victim Blame and Rape Proclivity' (2003) 84 *Journal of Personality and Social Psychology* 111, 111.
56. P Glick and S Fiske, 'The Ambivalent Sexism Inventory: Differentiating Hostile and Benevolent Sexism' 70 *Journal of Personality and Social Psychology* 491, 491.
57. Koepke (n 51) 447.
58. Abrams (n 55) 111.
59. G Bohner and N Schwarz, 'The Threat of Rape: Its Psychological Impact on Nonvictimized Women' in D Buss and N Malamuth, *Sex, Power, Conflict: Evolutionary and Feminist Perspective* (Oxford University Press, 1996), 162–75.

with gender-blind sexism are more likely to accept common rape myths.[60] This is supported by Aosved and Long, who found that sexism has the highest influence on rape myth acceptance. Although gender did not influence the relationship between other oppressive belief systems and rape myth acceptance, results of their 2006 study indicated that men have a higher rate of endorsement of rape myths than women.[61] Thus, it is evident that certain attitudes towards women and their behaviour have an influence on beliefs about sexual violence.

Abrams et al conducted a unique four-study investigation in order to establish the relationship between different types of sexism and different scenarios of rape.[62] The first study suggested that participants with benevolent sexist attitudes were more likely to engage in victim-blaming towards an acquaintance rape scenario than hostile sexists. The second study established that those with hostile sexist attitudes were more likely to demonstrate a proclivity to commit acquaintance rape. The third study highlighted that those who endorsed benevolent sexist attitudes attributed blame to the victim due to a perception of the victim having behaved inappropriately. The final study discovered that those with hostile sexist attitudes suggested that victims of rape wanted to have sex with the rapist. Thus, it was concluded that different types of sexism generate different attitudes and perceptions towards rape and sexual violence. These findings have significant psycho-legal implications as acquaintance rape is much more common than stranger rape.

8.4.3 Pornography and its relationship with sexual violence

Pornography is defined by the *Oxford Dictionary of English* as 'printed or visual material containing the explicit description or display of sexual organs or activity, intended to stimulate sexual excitement'.[63] Exposure to pornography has grown across the globe in recent decades.[64] Moreover, a number of studies have suggested that viewing pornography is most prevalent amongst men who are aged 18–25.[65] Thus, research began to explore the relationship between viewing pornography and its effect on men's attitudes and behaviour.[66] Not only has such research demonstrated that increased exposure to pornography has a strong correlation with the acceptance of rape myths, but it has also demonstrated a 'strong behavioural intent to rape'.[67] This suggests that men who are exposed to pornography are more likely to commit sexual violence. Moreover, men who have

---

60.   L Stoll, T Lilley and K Pinter, 'Gender-Blind Sexism and Rape Myth Acceptance' (2017) 23 *Violence Against Women* 28, 28.

61.   Aosved (n 31) 481.

62.   Abrams (n 55) 121–22.

63.   *Oxford English Dictionary*, 'Definition of Pornography'.

64.   G Dines, 'The Big Business of Pornography' in D Guinn (ed), *Pornography: Driving the Demand in International Sex Trafficking* (Captive Daughters Media, 2007).

65.   S Boies, 'University Students' Uses of and Reactions to Online Sexual Information and Entertainment: Links to Online and Offline Sexual Behaviour' (2002) 11 *Canadian Journal of Human Sexuality* 77, 78.

66.   K Foubert, M Brosi and S Bannon, 'Pornography Viewing among Fraternity Men: Effects on Bystander Intervention, Rape Myth Acceptance and Behavioral Intent to Commit Sexual Assault' (2011) 18 *Sexual Addition and Compulsivity* 212, 213.

67.   ibid 219.

committed sexual violence against women have been found to have been influenced by pornography, and many have in fact viewed pornography prior to the commission of sexual violence.[68] Thus, exposure to pornography has been identified as a large influencing factor on rape myth acceptance and victim-blaming behaviour. Furthermore, 19% of participants in one study admitted to viewing rape pornography.[69]

8.4.4 Conclusion

It has been shown that both sexism and pornography have a relationship with the commission of sexual violence. This suggests that there are a number of environmental and societal factors that may influence the justification and even commission of violent sexual behaviour. Sexism and exposure to pornography may therefore pose a profound threat to achieving justice for victims of sexual violence, particularly as research has suggested that benevolent sexist attitudes heavily influence the criminal justice system.[70] It is important that such attitudes are challenged in order to reduce the prevalence of sexual offences.

It should be noted that there is conflicting opinion in this field as some researchers have suggested that the consumption of pornography is irrelevant to sexism, and other studies have found no relationship between pornography consumption and sexual violence.

8.5 Contemporary challenges for lawyers and criminologists

8.5.1 Introduction

Temkin suggests that only 30% of those subjected to sexual violence report it to the police – leaving a potential 70% of sexual offences unreported.[71] In addition to the low reporting rate, the charging rate of cases of all sexual offences was just 3.2% in the year ending 2020.[72] This may be a direct result of 'attrition' – case drop-out in a number of instances throughout the process of the criminal justice system.[73] The Ministry of Justice identified a gap in the understanding of the decision-making process during the investigation and prosecution of rape.[74] Incidences of attrition typically occur due to: victims' failure to report the rape; complainants' withdrawal of the allegation; the police unwilling to proceed; the CPS not charging; and juries

---

68. M Allen, D D'Alessio and K Brezgel, 'A Meta-Analysis Summarizing the Effects of Pornography II: Aggression After Exposure' (1995) 22 *Human Communication Research* 258, 260.

69. Foubert (n 66) 222.

70. L Holmstrom and A Burgess, *The Victim of Rape* (Transaction, 1991).

71. Home Office, The Stern Review, *A Report by Baroness Vivien Stern CBE of an Independent Review into How Rape Complaints are Handled by Public Authorities in England and Wales* (2010) 9.

72. Home Office, *Crime Outcomes in England and Wales 2019 to 2020* (2020) 13.

73. S Lea, U Lanvers and S Shaw, 'Attrition in Rape Cases: Developing a Profile and Identifying Relevant Factors' (2003) 43 *British Journal of Criminology* 583, 583.

74. Ministry of Justice, M Burton, R McLeod, V de Guzmán, R Evans, H Lambert and G Cass, *Understanding the Progression of Serious Cases Through the Criminal Justice System: Evidence Drawn from a Selection of Casefiles* (2012) 2.

not returning a guilty verdict.[75] Subsequently, this poses challenges to lawyers and criminologists when prosecuting sexual violence.

8.5.2 The influence of rape myths on prosecuting and convicting sexual offences

The concept of rape myths was introduced by the disciplines of sociology and feminism in the mid-1970s, which recognised that certain cultural beliefs not only supported but perpetuated male sexual violence against women.[76] Brownmiller first described 'rape myths' as '[the] cannons of the dirty jokesters. They deliberately obscure the true nature of rape.'[77] The earliest comprehensive definition of 'rape myths' was proposed by Burt in the 1980s, who defined them as 'prejudicial, stereotyped, or false beliefs about rape, rape complainants, and rapists'.[78] Lonsway and Fitzgerald expanded this definition in 1994 by commenting on the relationship of gender and rape myths. They defined rape myths as 'attitudes and beliefs that are generally false but widely and persistently held, and that serve to deny and justify male sexual aggression against women'.[79] They argued that such myths serve cultural practices, such as the sexual victimisation of women.[80]

Rape myths are therefore identified as a barrier to conviction rates for rape yet remain prevalent throughout the process of investigating and convicting sexual offences.[81] Rape myths are described as perceptions of how 'real' complainants of rape should behave.[82] By manipulating jurors' interpretations of evidence, they shift the blame from the perpetrator to the complainant, justifying sexual violence.[83] Moreover, rape myths suggest that the offender is male and the complainant is female, consequently influencing the slow recognition of male rape complainants.[84] The offence of rape carries a connotation of blame unlike any other offence. For example, Dame Alison Saunders maintained that a victim of

---

75. J Brown, C Hamilton and D O'Neill, 'Characteristics Associated with Rape Attrition and the Role Played by Scepticism or Legal Rationality by Investigators and Prosecutors' (2007) 13 *Psychology, Crime and Law* 335, 355.

76. D Payne, K Lonsway and L Fitzgerald, 'Rape Myth Acceptance: Exploration of Its Structure and Its Measurement Using the Illinois Rape Myth Acceptance Scale' (1999) 33 *Journal of Research in Personality* 27, 27.

77. S Brownmiller, *Against Our Will: Men, Women and Rape* (Simon and Schuster, 1975) 312.

78. M Burt, 'Cultural Myths and Supports for Rape' (1980) 38 *Journal of Personality and Social Psychology* 217, 217.

79. K Lonsway and L Fitzgerald, 'Rape Myths: In Review' (1994) 18 *Psychology of Women Quarterly* 133, 134.

80. Lonsway (n 53) 704.

81. S Dinos, N Burrowes, K Hammond and C Cunliffe, 'A Systematic Review of Juries' Assessment of Rape Victims: Do Rape Myths Impact on Juror Decision-making?' (2014) 43 *IJLCJ* 36, 36.

82. M Carr, A Thomas, D Atwood, A Muhar, K Jarvis and S Wewerka, 'Debunking Three Rape Myths' (2014) 10 *Journal of Forensic Nursing* 217, 217.

83. J Temkin, J Gray and J Barrett, 'Different Functions of Rape Myth Use in Court: Findings From a Trial Observation Study' (2016) 13 *Feminist Criminology* 205, 205.

84. W Scott, '"Men Cannot Be Raped" Correlates of Male Rape Myth Acceptance' [2018] *Journal of Interpersonal Violence* 1, 2.

burglary would not be asked 'what have you done to deserve that?'[85] Yet, a suggestion of blameworthiness on the part of the victim often surrounds the commission of sexual violence.[86] Thus, complainants may feel that they are to blame for the assault.[87] The literature suggests that misinformed attitudes surrounding the circumstance not only of the sexual offence but of the reporting of the offence largely contribute to attrition and a lack of reporting.[88]

8.5.3   Examples of rape myths

Rape myths expect that the complainant does all they can to fight off the attack,[89] despite the definition of rape making no reference to either force or violence.[90] In reality, 81% of complainants (from a sample of 317 victims of sexual violence) did not actively resist their attack.[91] 43% of victims did not attend a hospital until at least 12 hours following the assault.[92] Although these statistics challenge the myth regarding injuries during a sexual assault, juries remain susceptible to internalising beliefs that complainants will sustain injuries during their attack. As a result, absence of injury to the complainant frequently fails to convince jurors of the truth of the alleged assault.[93] As we have seen, a juror may believe that the victim consented to sex when there is an absence of resistance,[94] as common perceptions assume the complainant was not trying hard enough to prevent an attack.[95] Thus, this poses a barrier to prosecution lawyers when attempting to obtain a conviction for rape.

Whilst false allegations feature in only 2–8% of rape cases,[96] another example of a common rape myth is the misconception that complainants tend to fabricate the attack as a mechanism to undermine the suspect.[97] This casts doubt on the credibility of their account, implying that the complainant is lying, which may impact the likelihood of a conviction.[98] A complainant's perception of the criminal process has also been argued to have an effect on reporting – they fear

---

85.   A Saunders, 'Sexual consent is simple. We should all be clear what constitutes rape' (2015): www.theguardian.com/commentisfree/2015/sep/23/sexual-consent-rape-prosecution-myth-consentis (accessed 5 May 2021).

86.   Grubb (n 1) 443.

87.   K Temkin, *Rape and the Legal Process* (Sweet and Maxwell, 1987).

88.   R Venema, 'Making Judgments: How Blame Mediates the Influence of Rape Myth Acceptance in Police Response to Sexual Assault' [2016] *Journal of Interpersonal Violence* 1, 2.

89.   Temkin (n 83) 5.

90.   Sexual Offences Act 2003, s 1.

91.   Carr (n 82) 217.

92.   ibid.

93.   Burt (n 78) 217.

94.   K Jenkins, 'Rape Myths and Domestic Abuse Myths as Hermeneutical Injustices' (2017) 34 *Journal of Applied Philosophy* 191, 201.

95.   O Smith and T Skinner, 'How Rape Myths Are Used and Challenged in Rape and Sexual Assault Trials' (2017) 26 *Social and Legal Studies* 441, 444.

96.   C Gunby, A Carline and C Beynon, 'Regretting It After? Focus Group Perspectives on Alcohol Consumption, Non-consensual Sex and False Allegations of Rape' (2013) 22 *Social & Legal Studies* 87, 90.

97.   Temkin (n 83) 2.

98.   ibid.

their complaint will not be believed as a result of others endorsing rape myths.[99] Moreover, 23% of offences recorded in 2019/20 were described as 'non-recent offences' (offences that had taken place more than 12 months prior to being recorded).[100] Subsequently, such delay might attribute to a belief that the complaint has been fabricated. It is apparent that misconceptions surrounding reporting may ultimately contribute to the main cause of attrition – lack of reporting.

8.5.4 Conclusion

It is clear that historic misogynistic attitudes continue to exist. Literature suggests that over two-thirds of cases reported to the police do not reach prosecution, with just half of those prosecuted resulting in a conviction.[101] Whilst these statistics indicate vast obstacles to criminal justice, the biggest issue in fact refers to the highest incidence of attrition – the lack of reporting. It is apparent that rape myths, which surround delayed reporting, lack of injury, and lack of resistance, remain prevalent across society. Such attitudes are inherently problematic, yet are deeply held by individuals.[102] It is indicated that such behaviour could be a result of cultural influences which tolerate sexual violence against women.[103] Thus, such lack of reporting distorts the true crime figures.

8.6 Chapter conclusion

It is evident that gender-based violence is prevalent in today's society. Feminism argues that the power imbalance between men and women, with women holding a lower social status, is an influence on sexual violence against women. Whilst we have seen progression in challenging sexist attitudes within the criminal justice system, it is evidence that such attitudes prevail in wider society. Though there are a number of approaches which attempt to explain sexual offending behaviour, it is likely that the ITSO is the most appropriate approach as it signposts a number of influencing factors – biological, social and situational factors and childhood experiences. Moreover, the number of influencing factors on the endorsement of rape myths, such as sexism, aggression, exposure to pornography and other oppressive beliefs, suggest that the prevalence of rape myths is not unique to an understanding of the criminal justice system and is therefore an issue within wider society.

---

99. Temkin (n 12) 710.
100. Office for National Statistics, *Crime in England and Wales: Year Ending March 2020* (2020) 8.
101. Home Office, L Kelly, J Lovett and L Reagan, *A Gap or a Chasm? Attrition in Reported Rape Cases* (2005) 5.
102. ibid 55.
103. M Koss and T Dinero, 'Predictors of sexual aggression among a national sample of male college students' (1988) 528 *Annals of the New York Academy of Sciences* 11, 11.

KEY POINTS AND SUMMARY

- Feminism argues that the power imbalance between men and women, with women holding a lower social status, is an influence on sexual violence against women. This imbalance was arguably ignored by the criminal justice system for centuries and prevails today.
- Though approaches to understanding aggression are able to explain sexual offending, the ITSO is the most appropriate approach as it signposts a number of influencing factors – biological, social and situational factors and childhood experiences.
- Literature has established that sexist attitudes and exposure to pornography have a relationship with sexual offending – they justify sexual violence. Thus, this societal construction has allowed for deviant behaviour.
- The endorsement of rape myths has a significant impact on the criminal justice system by discouraging victims of sexual violence from reporting their assault to the police. Moreover, literature suggests that such attitudes are prevalent in today's society, posing a barrier to criminal justice.

STUDY QUESTIONS

- How does feminism explain gender-based violence?
- Why do Marshall and Barbaree criticise previous approaches to explaining sexual violence?
- How do high levels of aggression correlate with the commission of sexual violence?
- What are 'rape myths'? Why do they pose challenges to lawyers and criminologists?

Contemporary Issues in Law

9.1 Introduction

This chapter will examine four new criminal offences that have been created since 2015. We will look at the issues surrounding coercive control, upskirting, revenge porn and, arguably the most contentious development in recent criminal law, the fixed penalty notice for breaching Covid-19 restrictions. We aim to look at the genesis of these offences, the problems that led to their creation and how they operate in the sphere of criminal law. The chapter will show you that criminal law is sometimes reactionary (there is a problem that needs fixing so the law fixes it) and sometimes preventative (the problem might occur, so the police need powers to stifle the potential problem). Coercive control, upskirting and revenge porn fall under the reactionary model, whereas fixed penalty notices for Covid-19 breaches can be viewed as a preventative power. Both can be claimed to be legitimate and proportionate; this chapter will examine if they are.

9.2 Coercive control

In 2013, the Government revised its definition of domestic violence and abuse to include elements of coercive control. The definition of domestic violence and/or domestic abuse is as follows:

'Any incident or pattern of incidents of controlling coercive or threatening behaviour, violence or abuse between those aged 16 or over who are or have been intimate partners or family members, regardless of gender or sexuality.'

This can encompass, but is not limited to, the following types of abuse:

1. psychological
2. physical
3. sexual
4. financial
5. emotional

'Controlling behaviour is a range of acts designed to make a person subordinate and/or dependant by isolating them from sources of support, exploiting their resources and capacities for personal gain, depriving them of the means needed for independence, resistance and escape and regulating their everyday behaviour.'

'Coercive behaviour is: an act or a pattern of acts of assaults, threats, humiliation and intimidation or other abuse that is used to harm, punish, or frighten their victim.'[1]

Section 76 of the Serious Crime Act 2015 created a new statutory offence of controlling or coercive behaviour in an intimate or family relationship:

(1) A person (A) commits an offence if—

    (a) A repeatedly or continuously engages in behaviour towards another person (B) that is controlling or coercive,

    (b) at the time of the behaviour, A and B are personally connected,

    (c) the behaviour has a serious effect on B, and

    (d) A knows or ought to know that the behaviour will have a serious effect on B.

(2) A and B are 'personally connected' if—

    (a) A is in an intimate personal relationship with B, or

    (b) A and B live together and—

        (i) they are members of the same family, or

        (ii) they have previously been in an intimate personal relationship with each other.

There are two ways in which it can be proved that the defendant's behaviour has a 'serious effect' on the victim:

(4) A's behaviour has a 'serious effect' on B if—

    (a) it causes B to fear, on at least two occasions, that violence will be used against B, or

    (b) it causes B serious alarm or distress which has a substantial adverse effect on B's usual day-to-day activities.

So, to be found guilty of the offence, this behaviour needs to occur either repeatedly or continuously and have a 'serious effect' on the victim. The prosecution 'should be able to show that there was intent to control or coerce someone'.[2]

With regards to s 76(4)(a) – the behaviour has a serious effect on the victim if it causes the victim to fear that violence will be used against them on at least two occasions – there is no specific requirement in the Act that the activity should be of the same nature.

CPS guidance goes on to provide some examples of what would be a 'substantial adverse effect on [the victim's] usual day-to-day activities' under s 76(4)(b). These include but are not limited to:

- Stopping or changing the way someone socialises
- Physical or mental health deterioration

---

1. CPS, Domestic Abuse Guidelines for Prosecutors (28 April 2020): www.cps.gov.uk/legal-guidance/domestic-abuse-guidelines-prosecutors (accessed 25 June 2021).

2. CPS, Controlling or Coercive Behaviour in an Intimate of Family Relationship (20 June 2017): www.cps.gov.uk/legal-guidance/controlling-or-coercive-behaviour-intimate-or-family-relationship (accessed 25 June 2021).

- A change in routine at home including those associated with meal times or household chores
- Attendance record at school
- Putting in place measures at home to safeguard themselves or their children
- Changes to work patterns, employment status or routes to work.

Upon conviction of this offence, the defendant may be sentenced to a maximum of five years' imprisonment (should the case be heard in the Crown Court), a fine or both. If the case is heard in the magistrates' court, the defendant could be sentenced to six months' imprisonment, a fine or both.

The prosecutor will need to consider the cumulative effect of the controlling or coercive behaviour and examine its impact to ascertain if this pattern of behaviour could lead to fear that violence, or serious alarm of distress, might be incurred by the victim. There are many facets to consider when examining if the behaviour can be classed as controlling. The CPS guidance goes on to provide some examples of what might be relevant controlling behaviour:

- Isolating a person from their friends and family
- Depriving them of their basic needs
- Monitoring their time
- Monitoring a person via online communication tools or using spyware
- Taking control over aspects of their everyday life, such as where they can go, who they can see, what to wear and when they can sleep
- Depriving them access to support services, such as specialist support or medical services
- Repeatedly putting them down such as telling them they are worthless
- Enforcing rules and activity which humiliate, degrade or dehumanise the victim
- Forcing the victim to take part in criminal activity such as shoplifting, neglect or abuse of children to encourage self-blame and prevent disclosure to authorities
- Financial abuse including control of finances, such as only allowing a person a punitive allowance
- Control ability to go to school or place of study
- Taking wages, benefits or allowances
- Threats to hurt or kill
- Threats to harm a child
- Threats to reveal or publish private information (e.g. threatening to 'out' someone)
- Threats to hurt or physically harming a family pet
- Assault
- Criminal damage (such as destruction of household goods)
- Preventing a person from having access to transport or from working
- Preventing a person from being able to attend school, college or University

- Family 'dishonour'
- Reputational damage
- Disclosure of sexual orientation
- Disclosure of HIV status or other medical condition without consent
- Limiting access to family, friends and finances

This list is not exhaustive, so other types of behaviour could be classed as coercive and controlling.

How prevalent is coercive and controlling behaviour?

In the year ending March 2020, there was a 9% increase in the number of domestic abuse-related crimes in England and Wales.[3] There were 758,941 offences recorded by the police. Of that figure, 24,856 offences concerned coercive or controlling behaviour. This makes up 3.2% of all claims of domestic abuse. Rather startlingly, this is an increase of 16,679 (149%) on the year ending March 2019. This is clearly a growing area of concern and one that has likely become worse due to the enforced lockdowns during the Covid-19 pandemic.

The Sally Challen case

Sally Challen was convicted of murdering her husband in 2010. However, in August 2020, she had her conviction quashed by the Court of Appeal and a retrial ordered. The Court heard evidence regarding Challen's state of mind, but, more importantly, the Court considered the issue of her being subjected to coercive control. She met her husband when she was 15 and he was 21. During the early part of their relationship, Challen challenged her husband about seeing another woman. He responded to this challenge in a violent manner; he dragged her down the stairs of the home and threw her out of the front door. Her son claims that this behaviour scared her for the rest of her life and created a culture of 'fear and dependency over the next 40 years'.[4] Her husband isolated her from her family and friends and controlled whom she could see as well as the household finances and her movements. At the time of her original trial in 2010, coercive control was not recognised by the law. In 2017, the campaign group, *Justice for Women*, submitted new grounds of appeal, centring on how the coercive behaviour of her husband led to Challen's response in killing him. The Court ordered a retrial, but the prosecution accepted that a diminished responsibility defence was likely to succeed and therefore accepted her plea of manslaughter. Challen was released from prison as she had already served the imprisonment tariff.

9.3 Upskirting

Upskirting is the practice of taking a picture up a person's skirt without their knowledge. Remarkably, this was not a criminal offence until 2019. In 2017, Gina

---

3. www.ons.gov.uk/peoplepopulationandcommunity/crimeandjustice/articles/ domesticabuseandthecriminaljusticesystemenglandandwales/november2020#main-points (accessed 25 June 2021).

4.   www.theguardian.com/society/2020/jun/07/coercive-control-sally-challen-domestic-abuse-bill (accessed 25 June 2021).

Martin was watching the band, *The Killers*, at a gig in Hyde Park, London. During the performance, a man put his phone between her legs and took a picture. Upon discovery of this act, she informed the police but was told that upskirting was not a specific offence and the case was closed. Martin took to social media to highlight what had happened to her and her post went viral, with many women sharing similar experiences. Wera Hobhouse MP then brought a private members' bill which called for the offence to be created. The Bill was initially blocked, but it eventually succeeded and the Voyeurism (Offences) Act 2019 came into force. The Act, which inserted a new s 67A into the Sexual Offences Act 2003, makes it an offence for someone to operate a camera beneath the clothing of the victim, with the intention of enabling the defendant or another person to observe the victim's genitals or buttocks (whether exposed or covered by underwear) or their underwear. The purpose of taking the picture can be twofold. First, it could be for obtaining sexual gratification, or secondly it could be to cause humiliation, alarm or distress to the victim. If convicted of this offence in the magistrates' court, a defendant may be imprisoned for up to 12 months and receive a fine. If convicted in the Crown Court, a defendant may be sentenced to a maximum of two years' imprisonment.

9.4 Revenge porn

Much like the other offences covered in this chapter, revenge porn is a relatively new phenomenon. The Ministry of Justice defines revenge porn as the sharing of private, sexual materials, either photos or videos, of another person, without their consent and with the purpose of causing embarrassment or distress.[5] The guidance highlights that this offence can be committed on- or offline, and so images can be shared traditionally via physical photographs or electronically. This includes uploading material to websites as well as sharing via a mobile device. A photograph or film is 'private' if it shows something that is not of a kind ordinarily seen in public. Sexual material not only covers images that show the pubic region, but anything that a reasonable person would consider to be sexual, so this could be a picture of someone who is engaged in sexual behaviour or posing in a sexually provocative way.

The term 'revenge porn' was born out of global press coverage in 2010. However, it is arguably too narrow a definition. McGlyn and Rackley suggest that a better term would be 'image-based sexual abuse' as this covers the nature of harm associated with the non-consensual sharing of private sexual images (see further below).[6]

Revenge porn is a global problem. In 2007, a man in Virginia non-consensually filmed his girlfriend performing sex acts and copied this recording onto a number of DVDs. Motivated by the woman breaking off their relationship, he distributed

5. www.gov.uk/government/publications/revenge-porn-be-aware-b4-you-share (accessed 25 June 2021).
6. C McGlynn and E Rackley, 'Not "Revenge Porn", but Abuse: Let's Call it Image-based Sexual Abuse', *Inherently Human: Inherently Brief*, vol 41, 15 February 2016.

the DVDs, along with the woman's contact information, on random car windscreens.[7]

With the explosive rise of digital technology, it is not surprising that the internet plays a vital role in the proliferation of revenge porn. In 2010, a website, *Is Anyone Up?*, featured thousands of private images of non-consenting males and females. The images were accompanied by their social media profiles. The site's founder had refused to take the images down, claiming he was not responsible for the sharing of images as he had created a consent form, which the submitter had to agree to, which meant they assumed responsibility for the images and subsequent comments. This site closed down in 2012 after the FBI opened an investigation. This issue unsurprisingly reached the UK, and by 2014 the UK Safer Internet Centre found that there were approximately 30 websites displaying revenge porn in the UK. Some of these were free to access and others operated on a pay-per-view basis.

The impact of revenge porn can have 'devastating consequences'[8] for the victim. There are myriad consequences associated with this act. Victims have reported suffering anxiety and panic attacks;[9] others have lost their jobs or suffered varying forms of harassment, meaning they had to move schools, homes or jobs.[10] Furthermore, this could have an impact on future relationships, as well as relationships with family and friends.[11]

The dissemination of private images and materials is now a criminal offence in England and Wales, under s 33 of the Criminal Justice and Courts Act 2015, and carries a maximum sentence of two years' imprisonment. The Act states that it is an offence for a person to disclose a private sexual photograph or film if the disclosure is made without the consent of an individual who appears in the photograph or film, and with the intention of causing that individual distress. As such, the sharing must be with the intention of causing distress, otherwise the criminal offence will not be completed. It is important to note that the law is not retrospective; this means that a person who shared such images prior to the enactment of the 2015 Act cannot be retrospectively convicted.

In 2019, the BBC reported that the law was not working as intended, claiming that one in three allegations made by a complainant ended up being withdrawn.[12] Unlike reporting of a sexual offence, the complainant in a revenge porn case is not provided with anonymity. The North Yorkshire Police and Crime Commissioner started a petition to change the law so that complainants could be afforded anonymity, but, despite attracting over 15,000 signatures, the law has not been

---

7. News Briefs, 'Former Boyfriend Pleads No Contest Over Sex DVDs' (Chesterfield Observer, 25 April 2007).
8. J Mitchell 'Censorship in Cyberspace: Closing the Net on Revenge Porn' (2014) 25(8) *Ent LR* 283, 283.
9. DK Citron and MA Franks, 'Criminalizing Revenge Porn' (2014) 49 *Wake Forest Law Review* 350.
10. MA Franks 'Adventures in Victim Blaming: Revenge Porn Edition' (Concurring Opinions blog, February 2013).
11. Z Franklin, 'Justice for Revenge Porn Victims: Legal Theories to Overcome Claims of Civil Immunity by Operators of Revenge Porn Websites' (2014) 102 *Cal Law Rev* 1303, 1307.
12. www.bbc.co.uk/news/uk-england-44411754 (accessed 25 June 2021).

changed. The importance of having anonymity when making an allegation is clear. Victims may feel they are further abused by having their name dragged through the mud. The BBC interviewed 'Lydia', who said she was with her partner for 12 months before ending the relationship. During sex with her ex-partner, Lydia would sometimes be blindfolded so she had no idea that he was taking videos of her. To her shock, she received an email from a woman she did not know saying that there were explicit photos of her online. Lydia visited the website, typed in her name and saw numerous pictures of herself. Her ex-partner was sentenced to six months' imprisonment, but Lydia did not think that was long enough and said that she felt like she was 'molested … [it was] like I was raped.'[13]

It is arguable that the term 'revenge porn' should be changed, as suggested by McGlyn and Rackely. By calling the offence 'porn,' it implies that the victim is in some way to blame. Whilst it is outside the scope of this short section, there is a great deal of victim blaming in the criminal justice system and it appears to be no different in this case.[14] For the year ending September 2020, a government-funded helpline had received 2,050 reports of revenge porn, marking a 22% increase on the previous year.[15] It could be argued that the Covid-19 lockdown has meant more people carrying out this offence online, but, regardless, it shows that the issue of revenge porn is real and that there should be more support available to victims and a greater awareness that the sharing of private images is a criminal offence.

9.5 Breach of Covid-19 restrictions

With the advent of the global pandemic, the UK Government took the invasive step of restricting the liberty of its citizens by ensuring they stayed at home and did not mix with others (save for certain circumstances), in order to beat the spread of infection that was ripping through the country. These restrictions were called 'lockdowns' and that's effectively what they were. People were instructed to stay at home so that infection levels could be reduced and kept as low as possible. To ensure compliance with the lockdown, the police were given the power to issue a fixed penalty notice to any individual who broke the rules. The Coronavirus Act 2020 gave the police the legal duty to enforce the rules. The police could issue a fine starting at £200 (in England and Northern Ireland) and £60 (in Wales and Scotland) and rising to £10,000 for the most serious breaches.

The problem with the use of the fixed penalty notice is the distinct lack of oversight. It rests basically on the opinion of the police officer; there is almost no oversight or supervision from the authorities in relation to the penalty. In practice, Sanders, Young and Burton suggest that the use of penalty notices for disorder

13. ibid.
14. See LK Thacker, 'Rape Culture, Victim Blaming and the Role of the Media in the Criminal Justice System' (2017) *Kentucky Journal of Undergraduate Scholarship*, Vol 1, Issue 1, Article 8: https://encompass.eku.edu/kjus/vol1/iss1/8 (accessed 25 June 2021).
15. www.theguardian.com/world/2020/sep/16/uks-revenge-porn-helpline-registers-busiest-year-on-record (accessed 25 June 2021).

(PNDs) is 'not about prosecutions but about controlling suspect populations and should be viewed as part of a wider goal to increase surveillance and curb anti-social behaviour'.[16]

An example of this lack of oversight has been cited in Johnston and Smith's textbook, *Criminal Procedure and Punishment*,[17] where one of the authors witnessed at first hand an example of curbing anti-social behaviour. In December 2008, Millwall played Bristol Rovers at the New Den. Bristol Rovers equalised late in the game to level the game at 2–2, and, unsurprisingly, the goal sparked joyous scenes amongst the travelling fans. One of the author's group witnessed a police officer push over a fan, which caused him to topple back into the seats. Incensed with that he had witnessed, the member of the group told the police officer that he would be filing an official complaint. Within minutes, three officers marched up the stand to arrest the group member for being drunk and disorderly in a public place and subsequently issued a PND. Whilst this is one anecdotal example, it does point to the idea that 'attack is the best form of defence'. As such, the officer felt under threat from the group member and elected to quash that threat by using the power of arrest. Ultimately, the use of this power allows the police to 'get a result' but does not allow any further scrutiny from those in authority and very little due process protection for the offender.[18]

So, how would the police use these new powers, which are devoid of scrutiny, during a time when citizens were being required to stay at home? The answer is mixed – of course, if people complied with the rules, they would not have been issued a Covid-19 fine, but as we will see from the examples below, there was a great deal of latitude afforded to the police in dealing with lockdown breakers. The National Police Chief's Council stated that, 'The overwhelming majority of people are abiding by these rules and police chiefs are not asking for any further restrictions. Our approach across the country remains the same – to *engage* with people, *explain* the rules, *encourage* them to go home and finally, if we have to, we will use *enforcement*'[19] (the 'four Es'). What this means is that the police will attempt to engage with individuals and explain the rationale for their powers and how they might use them against a person, before encouraging them to go home and avoid a fine, before finally using the powers given to them to enforce the rules. However, this appears utterly unrealistic. Do the police have the time (or resources) to engage, explain and encourage people not to breach the rules? We think this notion is highly dubious, and it comes as no surprise that so many Covid-19 fines were issued. Since the start of the lockdown, some 93,000 fines had been issued in England and Wales.[20] The Joint Committee on Human Rights suggested that there were 'significant concerns' about the validity of the fines, the inadequacy of the review and appeal process, the size of the penalties and the

---

16. A Sanders, R Young and M Burton, *Criminal Justice,* 4th edn (OUP, 2010) 409.

17. 2nd edn (Hall and Stott, 2020).

18. ibid at 258.

19. https://news.npcc.police.uk/releases/coronavirus-policing-approach-remains-to-use-enforcement-as-last-resort (accessed 25 June 2021).

20. www.bbc.co.uk/news/uk-56890540 (accessed 25 June 2021).

criminalisation of those who could not afford to pay. Worryingly, 18% (279) of individuals who were charged were actually charged incorrectly.[21] This calls into question the validity of all the Covid-19 fines that have been issued.

In Sheffield, the police handed out more than £34,000 in fines after breaking up a party with 150 students in attendance. The organisers were each fined £10,000 and more than 30 fines of £800 were issued.[22] A student in Bournemouth was also fined £10,000 after he ignored repeated warnings not to host events in his student accommodation.[23] In January 2021, two men were each given a £10,000 fine for organising a mass snowball fight in Leeds.[24] Two fans of Bram Stoker's book, *Dracula*, were each fined when they carried out a road trip to visit the place of Dracula's (fictional) arrival in the UK.[25] Our final example is of a man driving from Luton to Devizes to visit a McDonald's restaurant – even through the Wiltshire town does not have one! He travelled over 100 miles from his home and was fined £200.[26]

These case studies have highlighted the difficulty faced by the police. Some involved large scale gatherings and mixing of different households; others involved being too far from home with no good reason. But to return to the charging errors, if 18% of people were incorrectly charged, we can assume that a number of people would have been incorrectly given a Covid-19 fine, especially if the guidance on the 'four Es' was not being followed (despite it being unrealistic). A solicitor's daughter was given a fixed penalty notice when she was caught at a get-together with eight other people. The solicitor explained that the police were 'overbearing and aggressive' and did not follow the guidance of engage, explain, encourage and enforce.[27]

There are growing calls to review every fine issued for a Covid-19 breach. Harriet Harman, the chair of the Joint Committee on Human Rights, said:

> Swift action to make restrictions effective is essential in the face of this terrible virus. But the government needs to ensure that rules are clear, enforcement is fair and that mistakes in the system can be rectified. None of that is the case in respect of Covid-19 fixed penalty notices … [t]hose who can't afford to pay face a criminal record along with all the resulting consequences for their future development.[28]

It will be interesting to see how this plays out, as it has long been said that the lack of scrutiny around fixed penalty notices has been concerning and that more

---

21. www.cps.gov.uk/cps/news/cps-review-findings-first-year-coronavirus-prosecutions (accessed 25 June 2021).
22. www.bbc.co.uk/news/uk-england-south-yorkshire-55950930 (accessed 25 June 2021).
23. www.bbc.co.uk/news/uk-england-dorset-55362290 (accessed 25 June 2021).
24. www.bbc.co.uk/news/uk-england-leeds-55845582 (accessed 25 June 2021).
25. www.bbc.co.uk/news/uk-england-york-north-yorkshire-56346828 (accessed 25 June 2021).
26. www.bbc.co.uk/news/uk-england-wiltshire-55695408 (accessed 25 June 2021).
27. www.bbc.co.uk/news/uk-56890540 (accessed 25 June 2021).
28. www.theguardian.com/uk-news/2021/apr/27/all-covid-fines-in-england-should-be-reviewed-mps-say (accessed 25 June 2021).

oversight is needed. It appears that there has been a large number of Covid-19 fines issued incorrectly, and this is something that requires an urgent review.

9.6 Concluding thoughts

This chapter has highlighted the notion that criminal law is an evolving feast. Actions that were once not illegal, although morally questionable, have become illegal and subject to criminal sanction. For revenge porn and upskirting, this is a perfectly legitimate response to a long-standing problem that required the intervention of the criminal law. The same can be said for the offence of coercive controlling behaviour. Arguably, in all of these examples, the law was extremely slow to react and ought to have reacted quicker.

However, when the law does react in a swift manner, there are questions about proportionality and legitimacy. Take fixed penalty notices for breaching Covid-19 restrictions, where questions remain about the clarity of the guidance to allow the police to use their powers proportionality. Some of the examples covered clearly warranted a fine, but did they all warrant a fine? It is worrying to see that 18% of those charged with an offence (because they did not pay the fine) were incorrectly charged. Perhaps the police misused or misunderstood their powers. We have written earlier about police legitimacy, and nothing threatens legitimacy more than the misuse or overuse of power. Powers given to the police need to be well thought out and clear to avoid a crisis of legitimacy. We are confident that as you go through your academic journey, there will be new criminal offences that are not illegal at the time of writing. We hope that any new police powers are clear; both for the officer using the power and the citizen subjected to the power.

Contemporary Issues in Criminology

10.1 Introduction

Contemporary issues in modern society pose great challenges to crime and criminology. The internet has had a largely positive impact on society, enabling more simple means to socialise, research, shop and communicate.[1] However, the development of technology has also facilitated the commission of crime. It not only increases the scale to which a crime can be committed, but it may hinder investigative practices.

This chapter will consider:

- the nature of the online space
- the online space and its enabling of criminal behaviour
- the offence of revenge porn
- the offence of online fraud
- globalisation and the expansion of criminal opportunity.

10.2 Understanding the nature of the online space

10.2.1 Introduction

Computers were first introduced in the 1950s and then became commercially exploited in the 1980s. Thus, the internet was born, revolutionising the way that we live. In particular, Jaishankar argues that 'e-commerce has changed the patterns of marketing and sales behavior and the banking sector enabled its growth. In addition, the entrance of social media has brought people together.'[2] Subsequently, trade and communication became globalised through the nature of the online space. However, this revolutionary piece of technology was not introduced without risks – the internet began to facilitate a new type of crime, known as cyber crime.[3]

10.2.2 Criminology and cyber crime

Whilst the phenomenon of cyber crime began to grow as technology developed, criminologists were reluctant to research this new type of online crime. Other disciplines, such as computer science, began to develop new fields such as

---

1. N Akdemir, B Sungur and B Barsaranel, 'Examining the Challenges of Policing Economic Cybercrime in the UK' [2020] *Güvenlik Bilimleri Dergisi* 113, 114.
2. K Jaishankar, 'Cyber Criminology as an Academic Discipline: History, Contribution and Impact' (2018) 12 *International Journal of Cyber Criminology* 1, 1.
3. ibid.

information security and cyber forensics, but criminology was slow on the uptake. Subsequently, in 2007, Jaishankar founded the academic discipline of 'Cyber Criminology'.[4] Jaishankar defines this discipline as 'the study of causation of crimes that occur in the cyberspace and its impact in the physical space'.[5] This discipline takes a multi-disciplinary approach combining criminology, sociology, psychology, victimology, information technology and computer or internet sciences. Moreover, cyber crime encompasses a number of different offences, including illicit gambling, online fraud, revenge porn, making and distributing indecent images of children, and terrorism.[6] Whilst this discipline is relatively new, it has attracted a wealth of research which has allowed for the development of new theories.[7] Thus, criminology began to view 'cyber crime' as a new type of criminal activity, and thus a new theory was developed in order to explain why such crime was occurring.

10.2.3 Space Transition Theory and cyber crime

Jaishankar developed a theory which attempts to explain the phenomenon of cyber crime. It is defined as 'the movement of persons from one space to another' (eg, from physical space to cyberspace and vice versa). Space Transition Theory argues that people behave differently when they move from one space to another.'[8] This theory therefore stipulates that the transition from the physical world to the online world has allowed for the development of a new type of crime that would not be committable without the online space. Thus, the online space has allowed for the transition of crime in a new context.

Jaishankar refers to elements of Arbak's model of crime which argues that:

a) individuals feel varying degrees of self-reproach on engaging in criminal activities;

b) they are generally concerned with their social status in the society, based on others' perceptions of their values; and

c) in making their decision, they calculate the social and material risks of being a criminal against the comfort of living as a law-abiding citizen.[9]

In summary, a person who may experience feelings of guilt is less likely to endorse a criminal lifestyle. However, this theory only considers criminality in the physical space.

The Space Transition Theory of Cyber Crime considers that:

1. Persons with repressed criminal behavior (in physical space) have a propensity to commit crimes in cyberspace that they otherwise would not commit due to their status and position;

---

4. K Jaishankar, 'Cyber Criminology: Evolving a Novel Discipline with a New Journal' (2007) 1 *International Journal of Cyber Criminology* 1, 1.
5. ibid, para 1.
6. K Jaishankar, *Cyber Criminology: Exploring Internet Crimes and Criminal Behaviour* (CPR Press, 2011).
7. ibid xxviii.
8. ibid xxviii.
9. E Arbak, 'Social Status and Crime' (2005): www.researchgate.net/publication/5089515_Social_Status_and_Crime (accessed 17 May 2021) 1.

2. Identity flexibility, dissociative anonymity, and lack of deterrence factors in cyberspace provide the offenders with the means to commit cyber crime;

3. Criminal behavior of offenders in cyberspace is likely to be imported to physical space, and criminal behavior in physical space may be exported to cyberspace as well;

4. Intermittent ventures of offenders to cyberspace and the dynamic spatiotemporal nature of cyberspace give offenders an escape;

5. (a) Strangers are likely to unite together in cyberspace to commit crimes in physical space; and (b) associates in physical space are likely to unite to commit crimes in cyberspace;

6. Persons from closed societies are more likely to commit crimes in cyberspace than persons from open societies;

7. And the conflict between the norms and values of physical space and the norms and values of cyberspace may lead to cyber crimes.[10]

Accordingly, Jaishankar argues that such individuals may behave differently in the online space – 'individuals moved to cyber space, they are least concerned about their status because there is no one to watch and stigmatize them'.[11] For example, individuals who would not take the risk of physical theft might now consider committing online fraud. This suggests that the element of anonymity in the online space has the potential to encourage the commission of cyber crime, consequently posing barriers to criminal justice as cyber crime continues to increase on a global scale.

10.2.4 Conclusion

It has become clear that whilst the introduction of the internet has provided a number of benefits to society, it also has potential to facilitate and even encourage the commission of crime. Jaishankar's Space Transition Theory of Cyber Crime suggests that the removal of identity and lack of detection in the online space can therefore facilitate the commission of cyber crime, where such individuals would not take the risk of committing such crime in the physical space.

10.3 The online space and its enabling of criminal behaviour

10.3.1 Introduction

The previous section discussed a new and emerging theory which has attempted to explain the phenomenon of cyber crime. This section will therefore consider two types of online spaces which nurture the commission of crime – the world of pornography and the introduction of the infamous 'dark web'.

---

10. K Jaishankar, *Space Transition Theory of Cyber Crimes* in F Schmallager and M Pittaro (eds), *Crimes of the Internet* (Prentice Hall, 2008) 292–93.
11. K Jaishankar, 'Space Transition Theory of Cyber Crimes' [2008] *Cyber Criminology and Cyber Forensics* 1, 6.

10.3.2 The online world of pornography and its relationship with crime

Pornography is defined by the *Oxford Dictionary of English* as 'printed or visual material containing the explicit description or display of sexual organs or activity, intended to stimulate sexual excitement'. Exposure to pornography has grown across the globe in recent decades.[12] A number of studies have suggested that viewing pornography is most prevalent amongst men who are aged 18–25. This age group is most likely to be engaging with the development of technology and therefore the advancement in the online space.[13] Subsequently, it is evident that the online space has allowed for globalised access to pornography on a large scale.

Research began to explore the relationship between viewing pornography and its effect on men's attitudes and behaviour.[14] Not only has such research demonstrated that increased exposure to pornography has a strong correlation with the acceptance of rape myths, but it has also demonstrated a 'strong behavioural intent to rape'.[15] This suggests that men who are exposed to pornography are more likely to commit sexual violence. Moreover, men who have committed sexual violence against women have been found to have been influenced by pornography, and many have in fact viewed pornography prior to the commission of sexual violence.[16] Furthermore, 19% of participants in one study admitted to viewing rape pornography.[17] Consequently, literature has established a relationship between exposure to pornography and the commission and justification of sexual violence (though other studies dispute this). Further, the online space permits access to an endless volume of pornography, which has the potential not only to influence the commission of violence, but in fact may also display acts of sexual violence.[18]

10.3.3 The growing presence of the 'dark web'

The dark web, in basic terms, is an online network that is not retrievable by a simple *Google* search. Moreover, the dark web is not a single place – 'it is a concept that describes several online networks, just like the concept of social media describes thousands of different websites and platforms.'[19] Whilst such sites are not necessarily illegal, they can benefit those who wish to engage in illicit activity online. Such illicit activity on the dark web may include access to malware, account

---

12. G Dines, 'The Big Business of Pornography' in D Guinn (ed), *Pornography: Driving the Demand in International Sex Trafficking* (Captive Daughters Media, 2007).

13. S Boies, 'University Students' Uses of and Reactions to Online Sexual Information and Entertainment: Links to Online and Offline Sexual Behaviour' (2002) 11 *Canadian Journal of Human Sexuality* 77, 78.

14. K Foubert, M Brosi and S Bannon, 'Pornography Viewing among Fraternity Men: Effects on Bystander Intervention, Rape Myth Acceptance and Behavioral Intent to Commit Sexual Assault' (2011) 18 *Sexual Addition and Compulsivity* 212, 213.

15. ibid 219.

16. M Allen, D D'Alessio and K Brezgel, 'A Meta-Analysis Summarizing the Effects of Pornography II: Aggression After Exposure' (1995) 22 *Human Communication Research* 258, 260.

17. Foubert (n 14) 222.

18. Boies (n 13) 78.

19. B Beckstorm and M Brady, *Casing Light on the Dark Web: A Guide for Safe Exploration* (Rowman and Littlefield, 2019) 3.

information, fake passports, weapons, illegal drugs, abusive pornography and endangered animals.[20] Subsequently, there is an increase in the number of people that have access to such illicit material and products on a global scale. Moreover, there is evidence to suggest that this has increased the ability of young people, even children, to access this online illicit world.[21] Therefore, it is apparent that there are a number of ethical issues which surround the existence of the dark web.

Due to frequent advances in technology, it may become possible for an online offender to hide their IP address which would locate the offender. This poses huge barriers to police investigations as the police are unable to identify the source of the illegal activity. In some cases, this has meant that authorities have had to resort to more traditional approaches to policing, such as undercover work.[22] Investigators may infiltrate organised crime groups in order to collect information on the users of a particular site before commencing a crackdown on such illicit material or products.[23] However, such undercover work may not always be successful, leaving a vast network of criminals operating undetected online. This hinders criminal justice as such offenders are not able to be identified, investigated, prosecuted or convicted.

10.3.4 Conclusion

It is evident that the growing nature of the online space allows for the distribution of illicit materials and products. Whilst some online material, such as pornography, may be legal, it is clear that its easy access may correlate with the commission of other types of offences, such as the offence of rape. Moreover, it is apparent that advances in technology can conceal the identity of online offenders, encumbering the potential for such offenders to be reprimanded by the criminal justice system.

10.4 Revenge porn and sextortion

10.4.1 Introduction

Revenge porn refers to the act of sharing intimate images or videos of someone, either on- or offline, without their consent with the intention of causing distress.[24] The phenomenon of 'revenge porn' is relatively new. This is ultimately due to technological developments in the online space.[25] It is now effortless to take, send and share illicit photographs on a global scale. Moreover, it is just as simple to send such photographs on to another person or persons without the knowledge of the

---

20. ibid 83.

21. F Hsu and D Marinucci (eds), *Advances in Cyber Security: Technology, Operations and Experiences* (Fordham University Press, 2013) 113.

22. Beckstorm (n 19) 84–85.

23. Federal Bureau of Investigation, *Operation Disarray: Shining a Light on the Dark Web* (2018): www.fbi.gov/news/stories/operation-disarray-040318 (accessed 17 May 2021).

24. Revenge Porn Helpline, *What Is Revenge Porn?* (2021): https://revengepornhelpline.org.uk/ (accessed 17 May 2021).

25. S Bates, 'Revenge Porn and Mental Health: A Qualitative Analysis of the Mental Health Effects of Revenge Porn on Female Survivors' (2017) 12 *Feminist Criminology* 22, 22.

person who took the photograph. Subsequently, there has been a spike in the phenomenon of revenge porn, with its victims suffering a number of physical, mental, emotional, social and financial effects.

10.4.2 The impact on victims of revenge porn

Sexual assault refers to non-consensual touching of a sexual nature.[26] Whilst revenge porn does not encompass physical touching, it has been argued that those who are subjected to revenge porn suffer similar effects to those who are subjected to sexual assault.[27] Sexual assault has been found to have a significant impact on the mental health of its victims. In fact, one study established that 80% of victims of sexual assault suffered from serious mental illness following the assault.[28] Moreover, the National Women's Study in the USA discovered that victims of sexual assault were more likely to suffer from mental illness than those who had not been subjected to sexual assault. Thus, this study attempted to eliminate any other influencing factors, establishing a strong correlation between sexual assault and a decline in mental health.[29] Further, Kamal and Newman established that between 80–93% of victims of revenge porn suffered from emotional distress. This included but was not limited to depression, anxiety, PTSD, suicidal thoughts, paranoia, guilt, embarrassment and shame, trust issues, and feelings of insecurity.[30] Subsequently, it is clear that revenge porn has the ability to inflict a similar psychological impact on its victims as other types of sexual violence.

10.4.3 Victim-blaming in the context of revenge porn

Though research suggests that there is an enormous psychological impact on the victims of revenge porn,[31] such victims may be subjected to victim-blaming. Victim-blaming is the act of attributing blame to the victim of a crime. It is common in cases of sexual violence and involves '[blaming] the victims for their own fates'.[32] This shifts the blame from the perpetrator to the complainant, with the purpose of justifying sexual violence.[33] Subsequently, complainants may feel that they are responsible for the sexual violence they have been subjected to.[34]

---

26. Sexual Offences Act 2003, s 3.
27. S Khadr, V Clarke, K Wellings, L Villalta, A Goddard, K Welch, S Bewley, T Kramer and R Viner, 'Mental and Sexual Health Outcomes Following Sexual Assault in Adolescents: A Prospective Cohort Study' (2018) 2 *The Lancet: Child and Adolescent Health* 621, 660.
28. ibid.
29. D Kilpatrick, National Violence Against Women Prevention Research Centre, *The Mental Health Impact of Rape* (2000): https://mainweb-v.musc.edu/vawprevention/research/mentalimpact.shtml (accessed 17 May 2021).
30. M Kamal and W Newman, 'Revenge Pornography: Mental Health Implications and Related Legislation' (2016) 44 *Journal of the American Academic of Psychiatry and the Law* 359, 364.
31. ibid.
32. M Lerner and D Miller, 'Just World Research and the Attribution Process: Looking Back and Ahead' (2013) 85 *Psychological Bulletin* 1030, 1030.
33. J Temkin, J Gray and J Barrett, 'Different Functions of Rape Myth Use in Court: Findings From a Trial Observation Study' [2016] *Feminist Criminology* 1, 1.
34. K Temkin, *Rape and the Legal Process* (Sweet and Maxwell, 1987).

In the context of revenge porn, the offence may be perceived as 'naiveté rather than gender-based violence'.[35] This belief is common where the perpetrator is an ex-partner – a recurrent characteristic in cases of revenge porn. Subsequently, victims of revenge porn may be reluctant to report the offence to the authorities through fear of disbelief. Bothamley and Tully argue that this may have a 'harmful impact on the judicial process, beginning at initial detective questioning which may or may not end in prosecution of a perpetrator'.[36]

Moreover, whilst research conducted by Bothamley and Tully[37] suggested that victims of revenge porn are generally not blamed, it concluded that men are much more likely to engage in victim-blaming than women. In addition, males rated police intervention as unnecessary and perceived that victims of revenge porn were less likely to suffer a psychological impact.[38] This is concerning, particularly as male sexual violence against women is the most common form of sexual violence.[39] Consequently, it is evident that the psychological impact of revenge porn may not be adequately understood, which suggests a pressing need to raise awareness of the effect that revenge pornography has on its victims.

10.4.4 Challenges to policing and criminal justice

The nature of the online space has posed many challenges to policing and criminal justice. Through the development of technology, it is becoming more and more difficult to track the origin of an image and where that image has been shared. Research suggests that the training of police officers is often not up-to-date and therefore does not adequately equip them with the skills required to combat the use of the online space to commit sexual offences such as revenge porn.[40] There is also a concern that policing a virtual world will keep officers at their desks and therefore off the street (as opposed to 'real policing').[41] Moreover, the resources required to investigate cyber crime are enormous. Due to current budget cuts, the police need to delegate the finances available to them. Subsequently, it is possible that the investigation of online sexual offending may not receive the resources necessary to carry it out effectively.[42] It is therefore clear that the online space poses barriers to criminal justice due to its rapid development and its need for expertise.

---

35. N Henry and A Powell, 'Beyond the "Sext": Technology-Facilitated Sexual Violence and Harassment Against Adult Women' (2015) 48 *Australian and New Zealand Journal of Criminology* 104, 104.
36. S Bothamley and R Tully, 'Understanding Revenge Pornography: Public Perceptions of Revenge Pornography and Victim Blaming' (2017) 10 *Journal of Aggression, Conflict and Peace Research* 1, 3.
37. ibid 1.
38. Bothamley (n 36) 7.
39. N Kibble, 'R. v D: Rape: Rape Within a Relationship - Delayed Allegations - Summing Up' [2009] *Crim LR* 590, 591.
40. A Powell and N Henry, 'Policing Technology-Facilitated Sexual Violence Against Adult Victims: Police and Service Sector Perspectives' (2018) 28 *Policing and Society* 292, 304.
41. ibid.
42. Powell (n 40) 303.

10.4.5 Conclusion

Whilst revenge porn is contextually different to the offence of sexual assault, it is clear that there are similarities in the impact that such an offence has on its victims. Though there is insufficient evidence to suggest that victims of revenge porn are subjected to significant victim-blaming, it is clear that victims may be reluctant to report an offence to the police. Moreover, for those who choose to report the offence, there are barriers to the police investigation due to the online nature of the offence.

10.5 Fraud

10.5.1 Introduction

This section will explore the investigation frameworks that attempt to combat the growing phenomenon of online fraud. Academic study has considered the offence of fraud, and white-collar crime more broadly, since the mid-20th century. In fact, criminology became interested in the study of 'business deviance' as early as 1939. This chapter will analyse how the online space has enabled the commission of the 'white-collar' crime of fraud.

10.5.2 Who commits online fraud?

Early criminology in this field considered fraud and white-collar crime to be determined by characteristics such as occupation, class and social status – people in senior positions within society would commit fraud. Such theories did not consider poverty as an adequate explanation for this type of crime.[43] Today, there are no reliable theories which attempt to explain who commits fraud, or how or why.[44] It is acknowledged that fraud is a very complex crime committed by different people for different reasons. However, it is widely accepted that the development of technology has exacerbated and in fact encouraged the commission of this type of offence.[45]

10.5.3 The nature of online fraud

Throughout history, crime has been considered as a 'face-to-face' event whereby the victim and offender are in close proximity.[46] However, the development of technology has allowed further avenues for communication across the globe, thus facilitating crime in the online space. Holt, Burruss and Bossler maintain that 'personal finance and commerce has also shifted to online transactions, providing consumers with more choices in products, price points, and methods of payment'.[47] Subsequently, this allows for victimisation in the online space. Online

---

43. A Doig, *Fraud* (Willan, 2013) 1.
44. ibid 55.
45. C Cross, '"Oh We Can't Actually Do Anything About That": The Problematic Nature of Jurisdiction for Online Fraud Victims' (2019) 20 *Criminology and Criminal Justice* 358, 358.
46. ibid.
47. T Holt, G Burruss and A Bossler, 'An Examination of England and Welsh Constables' Perceptions of the Seriousness and Frequency of Online Incidents' (2019) 29 *Policing and Society* 906, 906.

fraud victimisation is defined by Cross, Smith and Richards as relating to 'an individual who has responded through the use of the internet to a dishonest invitation, request, notification or offer by providing personal information or money which has led to the suffering of a financial or non-financial loss of some kind'.[48] Though open to scrutiny, research suggests that 5% of all UK citizens experienced some type of bank card fraud between 2014 and 2018.[49] Moreover, online fraud is estimated to have cost UK banks £60.4 million in 2013 alone.[50] These statistics demonstrate the significance and prevalence of online fraud.

10.5.4 Challenges in policing fraud

Cross argues that one of the most pressing challenges in policing online fraud is the issue of multiple jurisdictions. An offender in one country may commit fraud against a victim in another country. This offender may even deposit this money in a third or fourth country. This creates barriers to policing as it reduces the ability for a police force in one jurisdiction to investigate, arrest and prosecute alleged offenders.[51] In 2011, the National Cyber Security Strategy recognised the role that local law enforcement has to play in investigating and preventing cyber crime such as online fraud. In addition, the strategy placed emphasis on the role of national intelligence agencies in order to combat international hacking and fraud. However, victims of online fraud felt dissatisfied with this approach.[52]

Consequently, Her Majesty's Inspectorate of Constabulary (HMIC) identified local police constables as key players in the police response to cyber crime and online fraud in 2017.[53] HMIC subsequently restructured the previous Action Fraud agency (the primary reporting mechanism for economic cyber crimes) in order to 'improve reporting and increase the triage of cases depending on the offence to improve the response to victim'.[54] Its hope was to increase the number of serious economic offences directed to local agencies for investigation, with the goal of increasing the number of arrests for cyber crime and offences such as online fraud.[55] However, there is no current literature which has assessed the effectiveness of this scheme.

Moreover, the nature of the online space poses barriers to police investigations. The virtual environment in which the offence of fraud can be committed may require forensic expertise in order to locate the offender or where the offence took place. Despite this, there is limited funding for the technological resources

---

48. C Cross, R Smith and K Richards, 'The Challenges of Responding to Victims of Online Fraud' (2014) 474 *Trends and Issues in Crime and Criminal Justice* 1, 1.

49. Office for National Statistics, *Overview of Fraud Statistics: Year Ending March 2016* (2016): www.ons.gov.uk/peoplepopulationandcommunity/crimeandjustice/articles/overviewoffraudstatistics/yearendingmarch2016 (accessed 17 May 2021).

50. Holt (n 47) 906.

51. Cross (n 45) 358.

52. Holt (n 47) 909.

53. Her Majesty's Inspectorate of Constabulary (HMIC), *State of Policing: The Annual Assessment of Policing in England and Wales 2016* (2017).

54. Holt (n 47) 907.

55. HMIC (n 53).

required to investigate complex online fraud.[56] Furthermore, as previously signposted, the potential for online fraud to be committed across a number of jurisdictions may limit the ability of the police to effectively investigate the offence.[57]

10.5.5 Conclusion

It is clear that whilst the commission of online fraud is relatively frequent in comparison to other offences, its complex nature poses huge barriers to policing. Although there is no current literature which has assessed the impact of Action Fraud, it is evident that due to the ability for online fraud to be committed across a number of jurisdictions, there is a need for an international policing response to combatting online fraud.

10.6 Globalisation and the expansion of criminal opportunity

10.6.1 Introduction

Giddens defines 'globalisation' as 'the intensification of worldwide social relations linking distant localities in such a way that local happenings are shaped by events occurring many thousands of miles away and vice versa'.[58] Giddens identifies four dimensions of globalisation:

- the world capitalist economy
- the nation-state system
- the world military order
- industrial development.[59]

10.6.2 Globalisation and organised crime

The world capitalist economy refers to the global economy as businesses develop national influence and begin to operate on a larger international scale. Therefore, the process of globalisation refers to the growth of an increasingly global economy.[60] McLuhan introduced the term 'global village', which describes the process of temporal and spatial 'shrinkage' due to the growth of advanced telecommunications and the greater ease of travel. This enables greater movement and improved long-distance communication in a global society[61] – air travel, smartphones and social media allow the world to appear smaller. It is much easier to engage in global business deals, permitting businesses to expand internationally. But how does globalisation link with criminology?

Open borders and increased international trade have created opportunities for criminals to not only move freely around the world (or even move their products),

---

56. Akdemir (n 1) 120.
57. Cross (n 45) 358.
58. A Giddens, *The Consequences of Modernity* (Stanford University, 1990) 64.
59. A Giddens, *Modernity and Self-Identity* (Polity Press, 1991) 70–75.
60. U Beck, *What Is Globalisation?* (John Wiley and Sons, 2018) 24.
61. M McLuhan, *The Gutenberg Galaxy* (Routledge, 1962) 8.

but to launder the money obtained from the proceeds of crime. In addition, increased poverty in developing countries has enabled the exploitation of the poor, as organised crime groups (OCGs) offer low-income citizens increased earnings in exchange for illicit conduct. Finally, the development of technology and transport allows OCGs to move through borders and to communicate more easily.[62] For example, encrypted messaging services allow OCGs to communicate without detection from authorities.[63]

This global economy is therefore characterised by free trade, free capital trade and the exploitation of cheaper international labour. The ease of movement and communication has not only enabled legitimate businesses to develop on a national scale, but it has assisted OCGs in expanding their territory. Thus, globalisation can allow OCGs to traffic people or drugs as a result of easier communication and movement, cheaper labour, transparent borders and political unrest.[64]

10.6.3 Globalisation and drug trafficking

The United Nations Office on Drugs and Crime (UNODC) defines drug trafficking as 'a global illicit trade involving the cultivation, manufacture, distribution and sale of substances which are subject to drug prohibition laws'.[65] This definition therefore recognises that the production and sale of certain substances is legal in certain countries or states and therefore that it may not amount to drug trafficking. For example, the cultivation, manufacture, distribution and sale of cannabis is legal in the state of California.[66]

The World Drug Report 2019 suggests that there were an estimated 271 million people who had used drugs in the previous year, accounting for 5.5% of the global population.[67] In fact, the consumption of drugs has increased by 30% since 2009.[68] Moreover, the report states that 585,000 people died from drug use in 2017 alone, demonstrating the significant impact that drug abuse can have on health.[69] This highlights the sheer scale of the consumption of illicit drugs and also the demand for this illegal trade.

95% of the world's illicit drugs are cultivated in what are known as the Afghanistan network, the Golden Triangle network and the Mexico–Columbia network.[70] However, this section will give particular focus to the opiate trade in

---

62. Beck (n 60) 24.
63. ibid.
64. ibid 30.
65. United Nations Office on Drugs and Crime, UNODC, *Drug Trafficking* (2021): www.unodc.org/unodc/en/drug-trafficking/ (accessed 17 May 2021).
66. CA.GOV, *California Cannabis Portal* (2021): https://cannabis.ca.gov/laws-regulations/ (accessed 17 May 2021).
67. United Nations Office on Drugs and Crime, *World Drug Report 2019* (2019): https://wdr.unodc.org/wdr2019/prelaunch/WDR19_Booklet_1_EXECUTIVE_SUMMARY.pdf (accessed 17 May 2021) 9.
68. ibid.
69. ibid 3.
70. J Milternburg, 'Supply Chains for Illicit Products: Case Study of the Global Opiate Production Networks' (2017) 5 *Cogent Business and Management* 1,1.

Afghanistan. The opium poppy (Papaver somniferum) is grown in Afghanistan by local farmers and processed into heroin. Not only is the climate right for the cultivation of such a product, but the OCGs take advantage of cheap labour in this developing country. The history of conflict in Afghanistan has left farmers in economic hardship.[71] OCGs are therefore able to exploit these circumstances by offering farmers work in the production of heroin – at a fraction of the value of the drugs. It is estimated that between 360–610 tonnes of heroin were exported from Afghanistan in 2018 alone.[72] Consequently, it is evident that globalisation has increased the availability of illicit drugs on a global scale as a result of free movement through borders and the ease of communication through technology. OCGs are able to take advantage of those in developing countries and exploit them for their labour in order to generate their own (much greater) profits.

10.6.4 Globalisation and human trafficking

In 2000, the Palermo Protocol provided the first ever worldwide definition of human trafficking: 'The recruitment, transportation, transfer, harbouring or receipt of persons, by means of the threat or use of force or other forms of coercion, of abduction, of fraud, of deception, of abuse of power or of a position of vulnerability or of the giving or receiving of payments or benefits to achieve the consent of a person having control of another person, for the purpose of exploitation.'[73] The definition stipulates that exploitation shall include 'the exploitation of the prostitution of others or other forms of sexual exploitation, forced labour or services, slavery or practices similar to slavery, servitude or the removal of organs'.[74] This is a very wide definition which attempts to tackle the wide range of actions that may amount to exploitation.

It is estimated that human trafficking, a modern form of slavery, affects up to 40.3 million people globally.[75] This would make human trafficking the second most valuable transnational crime in the world, with a value up to $2.5 billion per year.[76] However, it is difficult to measure the scale of human trafficking accurately due to the secrecy of organised crime. Victims of human trafficking within national borders may be sold for up to $250. However, victims trafficked across international borders can be sold for up to $25,000.[77] This highlights the

---

71. L Paoli, V Greenfield and P Reuter, *The World Heroin Market: Can Supply Be Cut?* (Oxford University Press, 2009).

72. United Nations Office on Drugs and Crime, *World Drug Report 2018* (2018): www.unodc.org/wdr2018/prelaunch/WDR18_Booklet_1_EXSUM.pdf (accessed 17 May 2021) 8.

73. United Nations Human Rights, Office of the High Commissioner, *Protocol to Prevent, Suppress and Punish Trafficking in Persons Especially Women and Children, Supplementing the United Nations Convention against Transnational Organized Crime* (2000): www.ohchr.org/en/professionalinterest/pages/protocoltraffickinginpersons.aspx#:~:text=(a)%20%22Trafficking%20in%20persons,giving%20or%20receiving%20of%20payments (accessed 17 May 2021).

74. ibid.

75. HM Government, Department of Justice, *2017 UK Annual Report on Modern Slavery* (2017) 44.

76. United Nations Office on Drugs and Crime, UNODC, *Global Report on Trafficking Persons 2020* (2020): www.unodc.org/documents/data-and-analysis/tip/2021/GLOTiP_2020_15jan_web.pdf (accessed 17 May 2021).

77. ibid 12.

discrepancy between national and international crime, as international trafficking is much more valuable. Globalisation therefore allows trafficking across national borders in order for OCGs to obtain a higher profit. It is able to facilitate OCGs who engage in human trafficking, as they utilise cheaper labour, transparent borders and political unrest.[78]

10.6.5 Conclusion

Whilst the theory and process of globalisation does not specifically refer to criminal activity, it is clear that globalisation has had a significant impact on different types of organised crime. OCGs are able to utilise a number of elements, such as open borders, increased international trade, increased poverty, and the development of technology in order to enable their international criminal activities.

10.7 Chapter conclusion

It has become clear that whilst the introduction of the internet has provided a number of benefits to society, it also has the potential to facilitate and even encourage the commission of crime. The Space Transition Theory of Cyber Crime suggests that the removal of identity and lack of detection in the online space are factors in the enabling of cyber crime. Moreover, whilst some online material may be legal, in the case of pornography, it is clear that its easy access may correlate with the commission of offences such as rape. Advances in technology are also able to conceal the identity of online offenders, encumbering the potential for such offenders to be reprimanded by the criminal justice system. For those who choose to report offences, such as revenge porn or online fraud, there are barriers to the police investigation due to the online nature of the offence. Furthermore, the internet has successfully aided the process of globalisation. This has had a significant impact on different types of organised crime, once again posing barriers to criminal justice.

KEY POINTS AND SUMMARY

- The internet has provided a number of benefits to society; it also has the potential to facilitate and even encourage the commission of crime.
- Online material, such as pornography, may be legal, but it is clear that its easy access may correlate with the commission of other types of offences, such as the offence of rape.
- Online offences, such as revenge porn and online fraud, may be difficult to investigate due to the online nature of the offence.
- Globalisation has been facilitated by the introduction of the internet, having a beneficial impact for OCGs.

---

78. Beck (n 60) 30.

STUDY QUESTIONS

- What is the Space Transition Theory of Cyber Crime? What are its key arguments?
- How might legal pornography encourage or influence the commission of crime?
- Can you identify any barriers to prosecuting online offences such as revenge porn or online fraud?
- How does globalisation facilitate crimes committed by organised crime groups?

FINAL NOTE

We said at the start of the book that you are embarking on a wonderful degree in which you will study a myriad of topics in both criminology and law. In the introduction, we tried to give you a flavour of some of the core skills you will need on this degree, with the ability to reference being a key skill to master.

We have also tried to provide you with a framework of the core issues you will cover. From the start of the process, we examined the actors in the criminal justice system and the differing roles that they play. We then moved onto a similar topic but through a criminological lens, where we examined the need for social control and diversity, representation and accountability in the criminal justice system. We critiqued the legal powers of the police in terms of how they are allowed to stop and search a citizen, arrest them and hold them in custody. We then subjected those powers to a criminological critique by looking at the idea of 'cop culture' and what influences the decision making of the police.

We sought to understand violent crimes in terms of the hierarchy of violent offences, which started with assault and battery and continued up to murder. We looked at the physical and mental elements required to complete these offences. In trying to understand violent offenders, the criminology element of your degree will allow you to understand *why* people commit crimes, and we have tried to tackle that in this book by analysing explanations of violence through the lens of psychology and sociology.

The book then attempted to understand the notion and prevalence of sexual violence. Whist the book could only tackle the issues surrounding rape, we examined the offence itself and how the justice system seeks to ensure complainants give their best evidence possible at trial by the use of special measures. We questioned whether suspects deserve anonymity during this process because of the stigma attached to allegations of rape. There is no easy or straightforward answer to that question – perhaps this is something you will answer through your academic journey.

Finally, the book looked at contemporary issues in law. We examined the issue of the evolving criminal law – changes to ensure that we, as citizens, are protected from modern day wrongdoing. The chapter highlighted that the law can also protect us from harm and explain why we might act in such a way, as was highlighted in the case of Sally Challen.

Ultimately, we aimed to provide you with a comprehensive and accessible book that explains the synergies between the two parts of your degree programme. The book simply could not cover every single element that you will study at university, but it should provide you with a baseline understanding of some of the issues that will pervade your programme. A lot of this analysis can be applied to differing modules that are not covered in this book.

We hope you enjoyed the book, and that it is of use throughout your degree. Please remember to learn the referencing systems.

As we said at the start, you have a highly enjoyable journey ahead of you and we wish you the very best of luck!

INDEX

Lightning Source UK Ltd.
Milton Keynes UK
UKHW030219130921
390474UK00003B/32